THE WHOLE
Christmas
C·A·T·A·L·O·G·U·E

THE WHOLE Christmas CATALOGUE

The Christmas Tradition *by Meg Crager*
Holiday Entertaining *by Margaret Grace*
Logistics of Giving *by Margaret Grace*
Stories, Poems, and Songs of Christmas Past *compiled by Meg Crager*
Christmas Photographs *by Jack Deutsch*

Revised by Barbara Radcliffe Rogers
Additional Illustrations *by Durell Godfrey*

PRICE STERN SLOAN
Los Angeles

A TERN BOOK

Copyright © 1986, 1988 by Tern Enterprises, Inc.

Published by Price Stern Sloan, Inc.,
360 North La Cienega Boulevard,
Los Angeles, California 90048

ISBN: 0-89586-755-9

Library of Congress Cataloging-in-Publication Data

Rogers, Barbara Radcliffe.
The whole Christmas catalogue.

Bibliography: p. 218
Includes index.
1.   Christmas. 2.   Christmas decorations. I.   Title.
GT4985.R64 1988   394.2'68282   88-1752
ISBN: 0-89586-755-9
ISBN: 0-89586-740-0(pbk.)

THE WHOLE CHRISTMAS CATALOGUE
(Revised and expanded edition)
was prepared and produced by
Tern Enterprises, Inc.
15 West 26th Street
New York, New York 10010

Editor: Naomi Black
Editor (Revised edition): Nancy Kalish
Art Director/Designer: Richard Boddy
Art Director (Revised edition): Rod Gonzalez
Designer (Revised edition): Marcena J. Mulford
Layouts: Thomasina Webb
Photo Researcher: Susan M. Duane
Photo Reserach and Styling (Holiday Entertaining): Margaret Grace
Photo Editor (Revised edition): Christopher Bain
Production Manager (Revised edition): Karen L. Greenberg

Typeset by I, CLAVDIA Phototypesetting & Graphic Design Inc.
Color separations by Hong Kong Scanner Craft Company Ltd.
Printed and bound in Hong Kong by Leefung-Asco Printers Ltd.

C O N T E N T S

CONTENTS

LOGISTICS OF GIVING
PAGE 146

STORIES, POEMS, AND
SONGS OF CHRISTMAS PAST
PAGE 166

CHRISTMAS PHOTOGRAPHS
PAGE 210

CHRISTMAS BOOKS
PAGE 218

INDEX
PAGE 220

Introduction

The Whole Christmas Catalogue is designed to help you and your family experience the holiday at its best. We have included stories and poems that can be read aloud to young children, Christmas carols for the whole family to sing, and crafts and recipes to personalize the festivities. You'll find shopping lists for gifts and stocking stuffers, along with Christmas tips as varied as how to wrap a package to how to return a gift. *The Whole Christmas Catalogue* contains a wealth of ideas, brimming with originality and tradition; the pages are bursting with Christmas spirit.

THE CHRISTMAS TRADITION was put together with the young reader in mind. From the most important story of them all—the joyful tale of the Christ Child's birth in Bethlehem—to a simple story of a nobleman, his three daughters, and their stockings, this collection of Christmas stories goes behind the traditions and offers the tales that explain them. You'll learn why people hang mistletoe, how the bishop Saint Nicholas became our jolly Santa Claus, and why we bring Christmas trees into our homes. Then, as you celebrate your own very special Christmas, you and your children can read how other families celebrate the season—in many regions—all with differing customs.

Whether you celebrate with a traditional English roast turkey or opt for quiche squares provençal with tabouleh, you'll find scrumptious recipes that come from around the world: American cornmeal and sausage stuffing, Mexican chocolate stars, crêpes with lingonberry sauce, German springerle, Norwegian almond crescents, and the list goes on and on into the realm of Guernsey biscuits and gingerbread men.

HOLIDAY ENTERTAINING tantalizes with more than just a good helping of Christmas food; these pages open up to reveal delicate ornaments, country Christmas linens, festive pillows, delightful stockings, and more. The ideas are original and fresh—and they are designed for people who want beautiful results in no time at all.

Once you've made the decorations, trimmed the tree, and dressed the house, you'll be ready to invite friends into your home to share the warmth of the season. For children, there's a special tea with Santa, complete with a Santa's sleigh cake, gingerman circus, and charm necklaces; for the older folks, you'll find a menu for an evening of ornament-making; and for the neighbors—down the road and in the trees—there are tips on preparing a tree for the birds and squirrels.

Christmas is more than just entertaining and sharing the glow of the season. Choosing, making, and giving gifts have become an undeniable part of the holiday. For some this is a task, for others a joy; with this book in hand, you can do your Christmas shopping from an armchair. THE LOGISTICS OF GIVING recommends presents. Hand in hand with this is a list of reliable mail-order houses and suggestions for gift wrapping, sending a present, and returning a package.

The presents and gift-giving, however, are a recent development. Steeped in oral and written traditions, Christmas is a day of song and merriment, storytelling and joy, and sharing of the spirit and soul of years past and to come. STORIES, POEMS, AND SONGS OF CHRISTMAS PAST presents just a selection of the abundant lore associated with Christmas. Read these out loud to the children as well as the adults.

And as you're reading, make sure you have a camera nearby to take festive photographs of family and friends. CHRISTMAS PHOTOGRAPHS is a potpourri of tips for preserving your holiday memories. And to round out this wonderful volume, CHRISTMAS BOOKS lists a treasure trove of reading for the entire family. Enjoy! Merry Christmas! Joyeux Noel! Feliz Navidad! Fröhliche Weihnachten! And a Happy New Year to all!

THE CHRISTMAS TRADITION

The Christmas Story

Long, long ago, when Rome was a great Empire, and Caesar Augustus ruled most of the known world, Israel was governed for Rome by King Herod. Herod was a cruel and power-hungry king who oppressed his subjects, the Jews. All over his kingdom, people prayed for deliverance by the Messiah. Even before the reign of Herod, a prophet had foretold the coming of a Messiah. "A virgin shall be with child," the prophet had said, "and shall bring forth a son, and they shall call his name Emmanuel."

In Galilee, in the village of Nazareth, there lived a newly married couple, named Joseph and Mary. Joseph was a carpenter, a skilled tradesman. His wife, Mary, was a young, gentle woman, a virgin. They lived in a small, clean house that Joseph had built for them.

One night as Mary was standing by the cooking fire, stirring dinner, Joseph looked at Mary more closely than usual.

How beautiful and kind she is, he thought.

After dinner Joseph went outside to enjoy the cool night air. Soon, Mary came out to join him. Joseph could tell by the look on her face that she was happy and excited about something.

"Joseph," she said softly. "I want to tell you about a dream I had." He looked at her in surprise. Mary was a practical woman, and if she had had unusual dreams before she had never mentioned them to him.

"Last night, when I was sleeping, I saw an angel," she said. "This was a real angel, Joseph, not just a figure in my dream." Her eyes sparkled and a joyful smile lit up her face. Joseph stroked his beard with one hand, wondering how his wife could have seen an angel.

Mary closed her eyes and her voice was filled with awe. "This angel, Joseph, was so bright and so beautiful! He was dressed all in white, and on his head he wore a crown of light. When he spoke, his voice was like the music of a harp but even more beautiful. I have never imagined anything like it."

"Well, what did the angel say to you?" Joseph asked. Mary stood up and stretched out her arms to the heavens.

"He told me that I would bear the Son of God, the Savior of Mankind. I didn't understand. I was frightened and I tried to call out to you in my sleep. But the angel told me not to be afraid. He said that I have found favor with God. He said that this child, the Son of God, will be called Jesus, and His Kingdom will last forever."

"I don't understand at all," Joseph said. "How can this be possible?"

"Oh, Joseph," Mary laughed, "I didn't understand either. But the angel told me that for God, everything is possible. And I know now that it's true. I'm so happy!" But Joseph was not smiling. He didn't know what to think. Had God really sent an angel to speak to Mary, or was she just living in an imaginary world of her own? "I must pray to God to help me understand this dream of yours," he said gruffly.

For the next few days, Joseph said little to Mary. Every night when he came home, he prayed for an hour before dinner, and then ate in silence. But Mary didn't mind her husband's silence. She had complete faith in the Lord.

A few days later Joseph's prayers were answered. The angel appeared to him in a dream and told Joseph not to worry. Everything Mary had told him was true. She was bearing the Son of God. The next morning, when Joseph awoke, he told Mary about his own dream, and together they rejoiced.

During her pregnancy, Mary was full of energy. As she went about her chores each day, she sang to herself, remembering the angel's words to her, "Thou hast found favor with God." Everyone she met noticed how well and happy she looked.

When Mary was nearly ready to give birth, the emperor sent out an official notice to all his subjects, decreeing that all citizens must register for a tax. So Joseph had to travel to Bethlehem to follow these orders.

Joseph was worried. He showed Mary the official notice. "I must go to Bethlehem right away," he told her. "We certainly don't want any trouble with the Romans! Perhaps you should stay here. Bethlehem is almost a hundred miles away. I don't know if you should take such a long trip now."

"Dear Joseph," she responded, "don't worry. The Lord will take care of His son. I'll pack a few things and we'll leave in the morning." So Mary packed some food, a cooking pot, some clean clothes, and a special sheet for the Baby because she knew that He would be born in Bethlehem. Very early the next morning, they started out. Mary rode the donkey and Joseph walked beside her. For three long days and nights they traveled, stopping only to sleep under the stars for a few hours at a time.

Joseph and Mary arrived in Bethlehem at night, exhausted and needing a place to sleep. But the town was crowded with people who had come from miles around to register for the tax, and there was only one lodging place in the whole town. Joseph knocked several times on the inn's door. Finally, a short, plump, grizzled man opened the door.

"Would you have a room for us?" Joseph asked.

"A room!" The innkeeper growled. "I've been completely filled up here for three days. I don't even have room for your donkey."

"We have traveled a long way and we are very tired," Joseph said. "We would be grateful if you could find us a small room. As you can see, my wife will soon give birth to a child."

"Had you come alone," the innkeeper said, "you could have found a place to sleep on the floor somewhere. But with your wife in that condition . . . " The innkeeper shook his head in dismay and was about to send them away. As he was shutting the door, though, he caught sight of the joyful light shining out of Mary's eyes. This is a special woman. Perhaps I should try to help her, he thought.

"Wait," he said. "I know of a place where you could stay the night. You see that hill?" Joseph nodded. "There are some small caves over there. They are quite safe and warm. The shepherds often stay there with their cows and sheep when it's cold."

"Thank you," Joseph said. Mary smiled at the man.

So they found a stable room in one of the caves. Joseph cleaned it, swept it, and made two beds out of fresh hay. Along one wall, he found a manger, a feeding trough that the shepherds used for their animals. The manger was long and narrow, just the right size for a crib. Joseph heated some water over the fire and cleaned the manger before he filled it with fresh hay.

The next night, Mary gave birth to the Infant Jesus and a bright star appeared over Bethlehem. The star could be seen for hundreds of miles around. On Christmas night, all of nature celebrated the birth of Christ. The cattle and sheep, the deer and fox all fell on their knees to worship the Lord. The birds sang through the night and even the bees hummed their praises for the Holy Child. Flowers blossomed in the snow and the water in the rivers and streams turned to wine.

Around the town of Bethlehem was a great dry plain where many men eked out a living as shepherds. On the night of Christ's birth, a group of shepherds were sitting around their bonfire, when all of a sudden the sky became as bright as day and an angel appeared to the shepherds, the light from its halo brighter than the light of the fire. One timid shepherd took a look at the angel and ran for shelter. The sheep scattered wildly in all directions, bleating as they went.

"Fear not," said the angel in a voice as clear as a bell. "For I bring you tidings of great joy." He told the shepherds the wonderful news that Christ was born in Bethlehem, and that they could find Him wrapped in swaddling clothes, lying in a manger.

Now one young shepherd was something of a cynic. He whispered to his neighbor, "Is this real? Am I drunk?" The other shepherd didn't answer. He just pointed up at the sky. All the shepherds were staring at the heavens, glowing with hundreds of angels and divine beings singing praises to God and His Son, saying "Glory to God in the highest, and on earth peace, good will toward men." The sound of their singing was so beautiful and melodic that the shepherds fell to their knees and joined the angels in singing God's praises.

After the angels had disappeared, the shepherds stood for a moment, awestruck. Then, they set out for Bethlehem to see the Holy Child. Some gathered fruits and animal skins to bring as gifts to the Infant. Some brought their pipes so they could play music. One shepherd brought four baby lambs. Yet another brought his cow. They found the stable room and saw the Infant wrapped in swaddling clothes. They offered him their gifts while Mary and Joseph looked on, smiling.

Now there were three kings in the East who saw the star of Bethlehem, and they knew the star was a sign. These kings had great wealth in gold and jewels and were very wise, so wise that they could see into the future. They knew that Christ would be the Savior of Mankind. So they gathered beautiful gifts for the Baby Jesus and set out to find the stable where He was born. For several days they traveled on their camels through the mountains and the deserts and plains, following the shining star. Finally they arrived in Bethlehem where they found the Baby Jesus. The three kings fell to their knees and offered Him their precious gifts of gold, frankincense, and myrrh. Although they were kings, they spent the whole night in the stable, rejoicing over the birth of their Savior. The next morning they left Bethlehem and returned to their native lands with the good news.

The Lord was watching over His son; and after many years, Jesus grew to be wise and strong, and filled with the grace of God.

The Story Behind Gift-Giving

Gift-giving is one of the most wonderful aspects of Christmas. Through gifts we can express our love for our family and friends. For some of us, Christmas gifts have an even deeper religious meaning; they can be a reminder of the birth of Christ, God's gift to mankind.

When Christ was born in Bethlehem, the Three Kings came to worship Him in the manger. They brought Him treasured gifts of gold, frankincense, and myrrh. These gifts were special tributes to Him. Gold was a symbol of His Kingdom, frankincense a symbol of His manifestation on earth, and myrrh a symbol of His crucifixion.

The Three Kings had great wealth, but even poor people with few possessions brought whatever they could to honor the Holy Child. The shepherds offered Him fruits and small toys that they had made themselves. One story tells of a little boy who was so poor that he owned nothing at all except a small drum. But so great was his desire to see the Baby Jesus that he went to Bethlehem empty-handed except for his drum. When he saw the Infant and all the light and joy that surrounded Him, the little boy realized that he did have a gift after all. He could play his drum. So he played a gentle tapping rhythm like the sound of the spring rain, and the Baby Jesus turned his tiny head and smiled at him. The little boy's gift, of no material value, was offered in the spirit of love.

Like many of our Christmas customs, gift-giving has its historical origin in ancient pre-Christian traditions. During the ancient Roman celebration of Saturnalia, the harvest festival, small candles and clay figures were given. At Kalends, the Roman New Year, more elaborate gifts were exchanged. The Romans believed that sweet gifts would ensure a good year, so fruits, honey, and cakes were popular gifts. Evergreen branches, called strenae, were given as symbols of continuous health and strength. Wealthy Romans gave each other gold coins for good luck. Everyone gave gifts: children gave to their teachers, slaves gave to their masters, and the people gave to their emperor.

Even though the Three Kings and others gave presents to

the Baby Jesus, gift-giving did not become an established part of the Christmas celebration until several centuries after the birth of Christ. Because the early Christians did not want their religion to be associated with pagan festivals, they shunned gift-giving as a pagan practice.

In the Middle Ages gift-giving began to be part of the Christmas tradition. The kings of England, like the emperors of Rome, demanded gifts from their subjects. The common people also exchanged gifts, but only among the wealthy were elaborate gifts given. The poor exchanged trinkets and entertained each other with songs and parties and plays.

The English Boxing Day, on December 26, originated in medieval times when every priest was supposed to empty the alms box of his church and distribute gifts to the poor. Wealthy people indulged in huge Christmas feasts, and when they were finished they packed up the remains of the feast in boxes and gave them out to their servants. In England, Australia, and Canada today, Boxing Day is still the time to give gifts to tradesmen and servants—and to friends.

On the old plantations of the American South a game called Christmas Gif' developed among the slaves and soon became popular all over the plantation. When two people met up with each other on Christmas day, they both called out "Christmas Gif'!" The first person to say it received a small gift from the other person.

In contemporary North America we usually place our gifts under the tree and open them on Christmas day. Children hang their stockings up over the fireplace to be filled. At Christmas parties we sometimes have a grab bag, a big bag, or basket full of presents. Everyone reaches in and grabs a present, never knowing who it might be from. In other countries around the world, there are similar games for giving gifts in addition to the traditional family exchange.

In northern Germany and the Scandinavian countries, there is an old custom called Julklapp. On Christmas Eve the door of the family room opens a crack, and large wrapped packages are thrown in—one for each member of the family. When the package is opened, it is found to contain another package inside. This second, smaller package is addressed to a different member of the family. The next person opens it, only to find that it is really meant for yet another member of the family. The package gets smaller and smaller, until the true recipient is left with a very small package.

In Sweden the Julklapp is addressed to just one person. It is usually a very tiny but expensive present wrapped in layers and layers of paper, although there are stories of a young woman who received a giant package containing her suitor, all wrapped up like a gift. The Julklapp gift is always a surprise.

The Dutch enjoy various games for giving presents. One example is a hunt: a note is stuck inside a cabbage, and the cabbage is wrapped as a present. The note gives instructions to search for the real present somewhere else in the house, say the

kitchen. In the kitchen another note gives additional instructions that lead to another note, until after several rounds of the house, the searchers finally get their gifts. A favorite Dutch custom is for each family member to receive a chocolate letter of the first initial of his or her name.

Home-baked cookies and cakes are a popular gift wherever Christmas is celebrated. In many countries it is customary to bake a small gift or prize right into the Christmas bread or cake. In Peru, for example, a special cake called Torta de Reyes is baked for Epiphany. Each slice of the cake is supposed to contain a tiny gift. In Greece, a coin is baked into the Christmas bread, and it is said that the person who gets the coin will have good luck throughout the year. An old French Canadian custom was to bake a bean and a pea into the cake. The finders would be the king and queen of the evening's feast.

Christmas cards are a simple but meaningful gift at Christmas time. What could be nicer than a mantelpiece decorated with beautiful cards bearing good wishes from friends and relatives?

The Story Behind Stockings

Long, long ago, in the days when Saint Nicholas was alive, there lived a kindly nobleman. He had a beautiful wife and three pretty, young daughters and all the money his family would ever need. But one day, the mother of the family, who was a sweet, gentle woman with brown eyes, became deathly ill. The nobleman was frantic. He summoned the town's only doctor, a very old, very wise woman who knew everything there was to know about herbs and magic. The old woman tried all the cures, prayers, and incantations she knew, but she could do nothing to save the nobleman's wife. Finally, he called for the priest to come, but by that time, his poor wife had passed away.

The nobleman was in despair. He missed his wife so much that he lost his head. He wasted all his money away on silly projects and useless inventions. He became so poor that he had to move his family out of their castle and into a little peasant's cottage. Meanwhile, his daughters were growing up. Poverty was difficult for them, but they remained cheerful and strong. They soon learned to do their own cooking, sewing, and cleaning and they took good care of each other.

All three girls were very pretty. In time, each of them fell in love and wanted to wed. But they couldn't get married because their father was so poor; they had no dowry—a sum of money or some valuable property to give to her husband's family. The nobleman had absolutely nothing left to give his daughters for their dowries. He felt he had failed his own children, and he became even more sad and gloomy.

Now Saint Nicholas happened to live in the same area as the impoverished nobleman and his three daughters. The kindly saint had devoted his whole life to doing good deeds and was always on the lookout for someone in need.

One night, the saint came riding through the town on his white horse, looking for the house of the nobleman and his three daughters. He rode up to their cottage and peeked in through a chink in the wall. That same night the daughters had washed out their clothes by hand and hung them up in front of the fireplace to dry. There were the stockings, three pairs, hanging right on the chimney. Inspiration struck Saint Nicholas. From his pouch he took out three little bags filled with gold coins. One by one, he threw the bags down the chimney so that they landed in the stockings of the three daughters.

The nobleman, worried about his daughters' futures, had terrible trouble falling asleep at night and was still awake. He heard the clip-clop of the white horse as the saint was leaving and peeked out the door. He called out to Nicholas, but the saint had already disappeared into the dark night.

When the daughters woke in the morning they found their stockings full, with plenty of money for their dowries. When they went to tell their father, they found him sleeping peacefully with a smile on his face. Saint Nicholas had taken care of all his worries. And so, through the goodness of Saint Nicholas, the three daughters were able to marry the men they loved and the nobleman lived on to be a happy grandfather.

Children all over the world hang up their stockings or put out their shoes for Saint Nicholas or another gift-bringer to fill. The stocking tradition is followed in the British Isles, Australia, and New Zealand, as well as the United States. In many European countries, too, children hang their stockings, but they nail them up on the night before Saint Nicholas Day, December 6.

Children in France put their shoes out on the hearth, a tradition that harks back to the days when French children wore wooden peasant shoes called sabots. Although very few people still wear sabots, French candy and pastry shops fashion wooden shoes out of chocolate and fill them with candy.

In Holland children fill their shoes with hay and a carrot for the saint's white horse. In the night Sintirklaas slides down the chimney, gathers the hay for his horse, and puts a present in each child's shoe. Hungarian youngsters carefully shine their shoes before putting them near the door or window sill for the saint to fill. In the morning they find a toy, some candy, and a small bundle of twigs. Even good children get the bundle of twigs as a warning to behave during the coming year.

Other countries follow similar traditions; children put out their shoes on January 5, the night before Epiphany. Italian children set out their shoes for La Befana, the good witch. In Puerto Rico children gather grass and flowers on this day in January. Before they go to bed, they put the greens and blooms into small boxes under their beds so that when the Three Kings come during the night to fill the boxes, the camels will have something to eat. When the children wake up in the morning, the boxes are filled only with gifts.

In whatever guise he comes in, Saint Nicholas brings fruit, candy, and small toys to good children all over the world.

The Story Behind Wreaths and Greens

 When wreaths are hung from the doors of our shops and homes, sprigs of holly grace our walls and windows, and poinsettias brighten our offices, we know that the Christmas season has truly arrived.

Wreaths make wonderful decorations and lovely gifts. They are easy to put together at home, and the materials you can use to make them are limited only by your own imagination (see "Wreath"). Traditional evergreen wreaths may be made of spruce, hemlock, balsam fir, yew, and pine. Some more exotic wreaths can be made of dried red chili peppers, of wheat and wild grass, of natural moss and lichens, of fresh fruits and flowers, of herbs and spices, and even of basic household items like colored paper or scraps of cloth.

Wreaths and greens are an important part of our Christmas festivities. With the wide range of materials available to us, we have created hundreds of modern variations on the evergreen wreath. But even thousands of years ago, wreaths and winter greens had a special significance.

A very special wreath at Christmas time is the

Advent wreath of Northern Europe. Made of evergreen branches, it holds four candles, one for each Sunday in Advent. The evergreen boughs are trimmed with pine cones, ribbons, sprigs of holly and mistletoe, and artificial snow. Many Swedish families have traditional brass Advent candle holders, which they place in the wreath every year. An Advent wreath, with its white candles lit, makes a truly beautiful sight when it's hung over a festive table.

The true origin of the Advent wreath is not known, but some people believe it was inspired by the Swedish Crown of Lights, a candle-bearing crown worn by young Swedish girls on St. Lucia's Day. According to legend, St. Lucia was a young woman, a Christian before Christianity was widely accepted, who gave her entire dowry to the poor. Where there was great poverty in Sweden, she arrived with a shipload of food to feed the hungry. Soon after that, she was martyred for her Christian beliefs. Her halo is symbolized by the crown of lights. Traditionally, the St. Lucia crown is covered in evergreen boughs and holds four candles, just like the Advent wreath.

Christmas Greens

There is something magic about plants that stay lush and green through the cold dark winter. Even today, we decorate our homes with sprigs of holly, ivy, and mistletoe.

Mistletoe was considered sacred by the people of ancient Europe. The Druid priests used it in their sacrifices to the gods. The Celtic people believed it had miraculous healing powers. In fact, the name for mistletoe in Celtic languages is "all-heal." Mistletoe could cure diseases, render poisons harmless, make humans and animals fertile, protect the house from ghosts, and bring good luck.

In eighteenth-century England, mistletoe was credited not with healing power but with a different kind of magic. It was the magic element in the kissing ball, a special decoration used at Christmas parties. The kissing ball had a round frame that was trimmed with evergreens, ribbons, and ornaments. Tiny nativity figures were placed inside it. For the finishing touch, a sprig of mistletoe was tied to the

bottom of the ball. It was then hung from the ceiling and partygoers would play kissing games underneath it. A kiss under the mistletoe could mean deep romance or lasting friendship and goodwill.

The mistletoe's kissing tradition, according to one account, comes from the Norse myths. Frigga, one of the gods, gave her son Balder a charm of mistletoe to protect him from the elements. But because mistletoe grows neither from the water or the earth nor from fire or air—

it grows on trees—it held the power to harm Balder. One of the other god's arrows made of mistletoe struck Balder down, and his mother cried tears of white berries. She brought her son back to life and vowed to kiss anyone who rested beneath the plant. And so the kissing tradition began.

Holly, with its dark green spiky leaves and red berries, was also believed to have magical powers and the abiliy to drive demons away. Germans considered holly to be a good luck

26

charm against the hostile forces of nature. In old England unmarried women were supposed to tie a sprig of holly to their beds to guard them against ghosts and devils.

In medieval times, when people were genuinely afraid of ghosts and demons, supernatural creatures were believed to be especially active at Christmas time. For the northern Europeans, Christmas came in the middle of winter when the nights were very long and dark and cold. The voices of ghosts and demons, witches, goblins, and werewolves could be heard screaming out in the winter winds and storms. So, the magical powers of mistletoe and holly were taken quite seriously.

Ivy was the ancient symbol of Bacchus, the god of wine and revelry. Because of its association with pagan festivals, for a long time ivy was banned from the inside of Christian homes and used only to decorate the outside. Not so anymore. Its green has become part of the traditional Christmas.

Christmas Flowers

Christmas flowers have a unique beauty for people who live in cold climates. A bright flower is a symbol of joy in the middle of a gray winter. Old legends tell of rare plants and flowers that bloom in the snow on Christmas Eve, for just one night in honor of Christ's birth.

In central and northern Europe it is customary to break off a branch of a cherry tree at the beginning of Advent and keep it in water in a warm room; the flowers should burst into bloom at Christmas time. Another treasured European Christmas flower is the Christmas Rose, also called the Snow or Winter Rose. The beautiful pink flower blossoms only in the northern regions of Central Europe.

Poinsettia is the Christmas flower in North America. Native to Mexico, it is called Flower of the Holy Night there. Joel R. Poinsett, who was the United States ambassador to Mexico, first brought it to America in 1828. The bright petals, which look like flowers, are actually the upper leaves of the plant, called bracts. Some say these star-shaped bracts symbolize the Star of Bethlehem.

Christmas Trees

 For families in North America, Germany, and other parts of Europe, the Christmas tree is the symbol of the Christmas season. The sight of Christmas tree lights glowing through a window inspires warm memories.

Long before the tree became part of Christmas, it was a symbol of hope and joy. In ancient pagan religions the tree played an important role. To the Vikings of northern Europe, the evergreen was a reminder that the darkness and cold of winter would end and spring would return. The Druids of England and France decorated oak trees with fruit and candles to honor their gods of harvest and light.

At Saturnalia, the ancient Roman festival, Romans decorated trees with trinkets and candles. In many pagan religions, trees were believed to be the home of gods and spirits.

No one knows exactly how the Christmas tree custom began, but there are several legends surrounding it. One legend tells of Saint Boniface, an English monk who organized the Christian Church in France and Germany. One day, in his travels, he came upon a group of pagan worshipers. They had gathered around a great oak tree to sacrifice a child to the god Thor. To stop the sacrifice and save the child's life, the saint flattened the oak with one blow of his fist. In its place, a small fir tree sprang up. The saint told the pagans that the tiny fir was the Tree of Life and represented the eternal life of Christ.

According to another legend, Martin Luther, a founder of the Protestant faith, was walking through the woods one Christmas Eve. It was clear and cold outside and the light from millions of stars was glimmering through the branches of the evergreen trees. Luther was so awed by the beauty of that sight, he cut down a small tree and brought it home to his family. To recreate the effect of the starlight, he placed candles on its branches.

Yet another Christmas legend tells of a poor woodsman who was returning home on Christmas Eve long ago. He encountered a child who was lost and hungry. Despite his own poverty, the woodsman gave the child food and shelter for the night. When he woke up in the morning, he found a beautiful glittering tree outside his door. The hungry child was really the Christ Child in disguise. He created the tree to reward the good man for his charity.

The actual origin of the Christmas tree may be the "Paradise Play." In medieval times, morality plays were performed all over Europe as a way of teaching the lessons of the bible. The Paradise Play, which showed the creation of man and the fall of Adam and Eve from the Garden of Eden, was performed every year on December 24. An apple tree was a necessary prop, but because the play was performed in winter when all the fruit trees were bare, the actors used evergreens hung with apples.

The Christmas tree tradition first became popular in Germany in the sixteenth century. Devout Christians brought decorated trees into their homes. In areas where trees were scarce, families built Christmas pyramids instead—simple structures built of wood and decorated with evergreens and candles.

Soon the Christmas tree became popular in other European countries. Prince Albert, the husband of Queen Victoria, popularized Christmas trees in England. In 1841 the royal couple decorated the first English Christmas tree at Windsor castle with candles and a variety of sweets, fruits, and gingerbread. As the tree became fashionable in England, wealthy families would use all kinds of extravagant

objects as decorations. In the 1850s Charles Dickens described an English tree that was decorated with dolls, miniature furniture, tiny musical instruments, costume jewelry, toy guns and swords, fruit and candy.

The first record of a Christmas tree on public display in the United States was in the 1830s. Because most Americans considered the tree to be an oddity, the German settlers of Pennsylvania put one on show to raise money for a local church. In 1851 a German minister set up a Christmas tree outside his church. The people in his parish were scandalized and asked him to take it down. They felt it was a return to pagan practices.

By the 1890s, however, American toy importers were bringing in Christmas ornaments from Germany, and the Christmas tree custom was becoming popular around the United States. There was one major difference between the European and American trees: the European tree was small, rarely more than four feet high, while the ideal American tree reached from floor to ceiling.

In the early 1900s Americans decorated their trees primarily with homemade ornaments. Apples, nuts, and almonds were traditional German-American ornaments along with marzipan cookies in a variety of delightful shapes. Popcorn was dyed in bright colors and strung with nuts and berries.

The invention of the electric bulb in the early twentieth century made it possible for Christmas trees to glow with light for days on end. It was then that community Christmas trees began to appear all over North America. Every Christmas, sixteen Irish yew trees sparkle on San Francisco's Union Square. At Rockefeller Center in New York, a giant tree gleams above the outdoor ice skating rink. In Washington, D.C., the President lights a tall spruce on the White House lawn; fifty large colored balls symbolize each state. A tall Norwegian pine graces London's Trafalgar Square, and every year since 1947, the people of Oslo have donated a Norway Spruce to the citizens of London. For people in these and other cities, the tree lighting ceremony marks the beginning of the Christmas holiday.

Scotch Pine

Norway Spruce

Red Pine

Balsam Fir

Umbrella Pine

Douglas Fir

Blue Spruce

White Pine

Choosing and Caring for Your Tree

When choosing a Christmas tree, there are a few factors to consider. Do you want a cut tree or a live tree that you can plant in the spring? If the tree is cut, you want to be sure that it's fresh. Then you'll want to look at its physical features: the length of the needles, the strength of the branches, and the ability of the cut tree to retain its needles. Finally, you may want to consider the tree's aroma.

According to the National Christmas Tree Association, there are two basic tests for freshness. First, bend one needle gently between your thumb and forefinger. The needle should be flexible. If it is brittle and breaks, the tree is probably not fresh. Second, lift the tree a few inches of the ground by its trunk and drop it down again. A fresh tree will not shed its outside needles. It is normal, however, for some of the inside needles of a pine tree to fall off. Another tip: a tree is more likely to be fresh if it is grown nearby.

In North America the most common types of Christmas trees are pines, spruces, and firs. Pine trees have relatively long needles which grow in clusters along the branches.

The *red pine* has long, flexible, dark green needles. It is native to New England, northern Pennsylvania, New York, West Virginia, and southeastern Canada. It retains its needles from four to six weeks.

The *white pine* has soft blue-green needles about three inches long. It grows throughout the northeastern United States, southeastern Canada, and the Pacific coast of North America. However, it does not travel well.

The *Scotch pine* has stiff blue-green needles which usually stay on from four to six weeks. It is grown in the northeastern states and eastern provinces of Canada, and on the Pacific coast. Note that some varieties of Scotch pine have crooked stems.

Unlike other species that must be pruned, spruces grow naturally in the conical shape of a Christmas tree. In colors, they range from dark green to bright blue. Their needles, which occur singly along the branch, are short, stiff, and sharply pointed. Of the three types of trees—pine, spruce, and fir—spruces have the poorest needle retention. They tend to shed their needles very quickly in warm rooms. Spruces can be found in the mountainous regions of North America.

Both the *Norway spruce* and red spruce have a good Christmas tree shape and dark green needles. The *red spruce* is native to the northeastern United States. The *white spruce* has short, blue-green needles that have a strong odor if crushed.

Freshly cut fir trees have excellent needle retention and for that reason they make especially good Christmas trees. However, if they have been cut and then shipped long distances, they will lose their needles in a temperate room. The fragrant needles are blunt-ended, flat, and soft to the touch. The *balsam fir* grows in eastern Canada and northeastern portions of the United States. Its branches are horizontal and rigid, and it has a good pyramidal shape. The *white fir* grows in the western United States.

The *Douglas* is not a true fir tree, despite its name. Its fragrant, blue-green needles are densely set along the branch. It grows in the Rocky Mountains from British Columbia to northern Mexico, and it is a favorite Christmas tree in the Pacific Northwest.

There are a few things you can do to extend the lifetime of a cut tree. Until you're ready to decorate it, store it in a cool place away from wind, sun, and heat. If you plan to keep it for more than a week, make a fresh cut across the trunk, about an inch up from the original cut. Then, immediately plunge the tree stump into a stand full of fresh water. Always make sure the tree has plenty of water. A stand that holds at least a gallon is recommended. Keep an eye on the water level. It should be checked every day and replenished when necessary.

If you purchase a live tree, make sure the root ball is intact and moist when you purchase it. It must then be wrapped in heavy plastic or burlap to hold in the moisture. Once again, keep it in a cool place. Spruce trees are ideal for live Christmas trees. They are quite hearty and are least likely to suffer from the indoor-to-outdoor temperature change. If you plan to plant the tree in the spring, find a sheltered spot where you can store it when the festivities are over. Pack the root ball in straw and plant it when the ground has thawed.

Have a safe tree! Check all your tree lights and connections to make sure that none of the wires are worn or frayed. Do not use lit candles. And make sure to turn the tree off before you go out.

Gathering the Greens

 Those who would gather nature's bounty of Christmas decorating materials must do so early. Often, by mid-November, fallen cones, tiny evergreen groundcovers, and other treasures of the woods are all hidden by the first snow. So, make a late fall walk in the woods a Christmas shopping trip.

A variety of containers makes gathering easier. Paper grocery bags are best for cones, but tiny green plants need to be wrapped in plastic to protect their delicate roots from drying out. Plastic sandwich bags are also good for carrying seedpods which damage easily. Place these in the bag, blow it up like a balloon, and seal it tightly. This air cushion will prevent heavier materials from crushing the seeds as you collect more.

Patridgeberry and checkerberry (also known as teaberry) are the two most popular plants for berry bowls (see page 156). They are easily seen in the late autumn or winter when other plants of the forest floor have died. Their rich green leaves and showy red berries are easily distinguished from the leaf mold on the forest floor.

The very qualities which make these plants winter hardy—their waxy leaves and woody upper stems—give them longevity as decorations. Gather them carefully, taking some moist earth and pine needles to protect their roots, and be sure to leave plenty of plants untouched to regenerate in each area.

Look also for thick clumps of green mosses such as sphagnum, to use as wreath bases and to form the bottom layer of berry bowls.

Cones of all types can be used for wreaths (see page 130) and a variety of other decorations. Large cones can be made into centerpieces by decorating each cone as an individual tree. Tiny hemlock cones fill in spaces in wreaths and are an ingredient of Christmas potpourri. All sizes and shapes in

between are useful as well. Even the coarse cones of the white pine make sturdy wreath bases and are the best choice for firestarters (see page 154).

Store the cones in paper bags until you are ready for them; some people prefer to bake them in a moderate oven to dry them first and to be sure they are uninhabited by bugs.

In addition to the cones of evergreens, there are nuts and seedpods to look for. Beechnuts are lovely and delicate and good for creating miniature ornaments, as are alder catkins which look like tiny, tight pinecones. Hickory nuts, acorns, buckeyes, and the pods from the sweet gum tree are handsome additions to cone wreaths.

The pods of many flowering plants are easy to find at this time of year, and can be used in cone and herb wreaths or even as individual ornaments. Milkweed, iris, Queen Anne's Lace, teasel, bergamot, and many grasses are found in fields and along roadsides as well as in flower gardens.

Note, as you walk, the location of good trees for greens such as the balsam, spruce, and the white pine for cutting live green wreath and roping decorations (see page 105). It is not

Swags of greens make attractive door decorations.

too early to gather berries such as bittersweet since the berries will remain on the vines after they have dried, but leave the holly until closer to Christmas.

Fresh greens, even long-lasting ones like balsam and white pine, should also be picked as close to Christmas as possible. This is especially important for those which will be cut into short sprigs for wreaths and roping, since this causes them to dry out more quickly. Hemlock, which looses its needles within a few days, should be picked at the very last minute, and used only in vase arrangements where it can be replaced or removed easily.

Cut all greens in long branches and place them in a bucket of luke-warm water as soon as possible after cutting. Store them in water in a cool place until they are used. Be careful to cut them neatly from the tree with clippers. Never rip or pull them off, since this damages the tree.

Each part of the country has special things to contribute to the traditional decorations of Christmas. No matter where you live, a walk in the woods or fields will yield a surprising collection of materials for your own Christmas workshop. And be sure to ask friends in other areas to collect different kinds of cones for you — they are light, durable, and easy to ship. Likewise, friends in other places are sure to welcome a box of specialties from your locale.

Santa Claus and the Gift-Bringers

Every Christmas, Santa Claus comes to millions of children around the world. To Americans he comes from the North Pole in a sled pulled by his famous reindeer. To the Dutch he comes by sea in a ship. On his way to visit German children, he rides through the air on a white horse. However he travels, Santa Claus brings gifts and joy everywhere he goes.

The tale of Santa Claus began with a man called Saint Nicholas, Bishop of Myra, who lived during the fourth century. Myra was in Asia Minor, a region that is now in Turkey. Saint Nicholas was known for his wisdom and charity. Legend has it that he came from a wealthy family and gave all his money to the poor. Some claim that the Bishop could even perform miracles. According to one story, three young boys had been murdered by a cruel butcher and stored as meat in a pickle barrel. The saint came to the butcher's house, and with the power of his saintly love and prayer, he restored the three boys to life. He died around A.D. 340 and was buried in Myra.

In the year 1087 some religious sailors from the Italian region of Bari decided to take the remains of the saint out of Asia Minor and bring them to Italy. So they built a church

in their home town to honor him. Bari, a port town in southern Italy, once welcomed ships from all over Europe and the East. Soon, pilgrims from all over Christendom visited the church of Saint Nicholas.

These pilgrims carried the image of Saint Nicholas back home to their native lands. The Russians called him their patron saint. They knew him as a bishop with his bishop's miter and crosier, his red cape, and long white beard. For the Greeks he became the patron saint of sailors, for the French the patron of lawyers, and in Belgium he was believed to be the helper of both travelers and children.

As early as the twelfth century, Saint Nicholas Day became a day for gift-giving and charity; it became an official church holiday and feast day all over Europe. In Germany, France, and Holland, December 6 marked the time when religious people offered presents to children and to the poor. Every year, children would await the arrival of the saint who rewarded them with gifts if they were good and punished them with a rod if they were bad.

The Dutch colonists took Saint Nicholas with them to America, where he was gradually transformed from an austere bishop to a jolly old elf. First, Washington

The poem was eventually published and quickly became popular around the United States. Unlike the European Saint Nicholas who was to be feared by naughty boys and girls, Moore's St. Nick was quite good-natured. His seriousness was gone.

In the 1860s a cartoonist named Thomas Nast drew pictures of Santa Claus for the illustrated *Harper's Weekly*. It was there that his image as a plump and kindly old elf was immortalized.

From the United States this benevolent Santa traveled back to Europe, South America, and even as far away as Japan. The American Santa Claus is now a popular figure around the world, although many countries have their own native gift-bringers as well. In some countries, gifts are still brought by the old, austere Saint Nicholas. In other coun-

Irving, of Sleepy Hollow fame, described the saint as a plump and jolly old Dutchman in his comic *History of New York*. The second step in Saint Nicholas's American transformation was brought about by a professor named Clement Clarke Moore. Moore, the father of several small children, presented his family with a Christmas gift especially for them: the famous poem, "'Twas the Night Before Christmas." This is how he described the bishop:

He had a broad face and a little round belly,
That shook when he laughed, like a bowl full of jelly,
He was chubby and plump, a right jolly old elf,
And I laughed when I saw him, in spite of myself;
A wink of his eye and a twist of his head
Soon gave me to know I had nothing to dread.

bock in the northwestern part of the country, and Hans Muff in the Rhineland. But whatever his name, this assistant, like the Dutch Black Peter, comes with a sack on his back and a rod in his hand.

On Saint Nicholas day German children wait eagerly for the arrival of the saint and his assistant. A member of the family or an adult friend plays the role of Saint Nicholas. He asks the children if they have been obedient to their parents and teachers and if they have said their prayers every day. The Bishop's assistant gives good children a gift, but naughty children are punished with a few hits of the rod and a nasty grimace.

In Italy the good witch La Befana brings gifts to children on Epiphany, January 6. According to legend, La Befana is very, very old and bent, and she dresses all in black. She is

tries, today's gift-bringers were once part of the ancient, pre-Christian folklore.

In Holland the old bishop Sintirklaas arrives every year on December 6. In Amsterdam and other port towns, he sails in on a ship that is said to come from Spain. Sintirklaas wears his red bishop's costume and rides a white horse. Beside him walks his assistant, Black Peter, who is colorfully dressed as a medieval Moor. Sintirklaas carries a big book with him in which he keeps a record of every Dutch child's behavior over the past year. For good children the bishop has a gift, but bad children may be taken away in the sack that Black Peter carries on his back.

In Germany Saint Nicholas also comes with an assistant. This assistant has a lot of different names. He is known as Knecht Ruprecht or Krampus in southern Germany, Pelze-

so old that she was alive on the day that Christ was born, almost two thousand years ago. Even then she was an old woman, widowed and without children. As the story goes, the Three Kings passed by her house on their way to see the Christ Child. They were lost and asked the way to Bethlehem. Rudely, La Befana sent them away. After they left, she realized what a mistake she had made. She should have gone with them! So she left her home to search for the Baby Jesus. But she never could find Him. To this very day she is still searching. At Epiphany she goes from

house to house, looking for Him. For every child she drops off a gift, or if the child is bad, she may leave some coal.

The Three Kings or Wise Men, Caspar, Melchior, and Balthazar bring Christmas gifts to children in Spain, Puerto Rico, Mexico, and South America. Caspar, a young man, is king of Tarsus. Melchior, a long-bearded old man, rules all of Arabia. Balthazar is a middle-aged black king, ruler of Ethiopia.

In France gifts are brought by Father Christmas, Père Noël, or by the Christ Child himself. In Austria and Switzerland the Christkindl or Christ Child bears gifts. In

some towns children await the Holy Child, but in the other towns the Christkindl is a beautiful girl-angel sent down from heaven to give gifts. Father Christmas is the gift-bringer in England. He is thinner and more austere than the American Santa Claus.

The Scandinavian countries celebrate the holidays with an elf, called the julenisse or the juletomte, who brings gifts. He is a small, gray-clad bearded fellow, who predates Saint Nicholas. According to ancient Viking tradition, this elf is the protector of the farm. Farming families must give him a bowl of porridge at Christmas time, or else the harvest will be poor the following year. Swedish legend says the juletomte lives under the floorboards of the house or barn and looks after the family and their livestock. At Christmas he brings gifts in a large sack, which he carries over his shoulder.

There are other gift-bringers, but Santa Claus has become a symbol of Christmas for children everywhere. All around the world, he can be seen in department stores listening to the secret Christmas wishes of children in a multitude of languages.

Ethnic Traditions around the World

England and the Commonwealth

Many of our most hallowed Christmas traditions, including the Christmas card, originated in the British Isles. The merriment of a traditional British Christmas can be easily found in our favorite holiday literature, Yule logs, plum puddings, mince pies, fruit cakes, the wassail bowl, and Christmas goose. Mistletoe, holly, and carol singing are all firmly rooted in British soil. And the Queen's message on Christmas Day is probably second only to the Pope's in the breadth of its broadcast to all parts of the world.

The origins of the Christmas celebration, distinct from earlier pagan winter holidays, date to sixth-century England. By the Middle Ages it was a well established, important holiday, with traditional pageantry, customs, music, and feasting all its own. Customs from pre-Christmas days were incorporated in the celebrations of various areas as well, and many still remain.

The sixteenth century saw England celebrating the Twelve Days of Christmas; Shakespeare's *Twelfth Night* premiered in the first year of the seventeenth century in a performance at the court of Elizabeth I. Later, during Queen Victoria's reign, Christmas became a time of gift-giving and a special season for children. Boxing Day, celebrated on the feast of St. Stephen, December 26, was popularized in Victorian England and is still a public holiday that many British consider quite important.

Christmas songs have their roots in medieval England when minstrels traveled from castle to castle, the forerunners of our modern-day carolers, and some of our favorite carols have rung out in England for centuries. Today in Wales, each village may have several choirs that rehearse well in advance for the holidays. The custom has taken a different twist in Australia, where carols are sung by candlelight throughout the country.

Even though Christmas occurs in the summer in the southern hemisphere, those outposts of the British Empire—Australia, New Zealand and South Africa—still decorate according to the "White Christmas" theme of old England. Snow scenes are popular, although the sleigh has been replaced by the railway in carrying Santa and his sack of gifts to the children of the Outback.

In Ireland, the season is a dual one. Advent is solemn and religious in spirit, while St. Stephen's Day begins the Twelve Days of Christmas, a lighthearted time given over to merrymaking and fun. It is a holiday of homecoming and family gatherings, with candles glowing in the windows as a sign of welcome. There are also glorious and bountiful Christmas feasts attended by family and friends.

North America

All over the United States and Canada, Christmas is a time for gift-giving, celebrating, and feasting. North Americans have developed some of their own traditions, but many maintain the old Christmas customs of their ancestors.

For children in towns and cities around North America, there are Santa Claus parades, Christmas pageants, puppet shows, community Christmas trees, and department store Santas. Schools and churches give out candy canes and wreaths, hold parties, and sponsor caroling events. In the evenings preceding Christmas, children can settle down in front of the family television to watch Christmas specials like *The Nutcracker Suite* or *Amahl and the Night Visitors.*

Although the deep snow, evergreen trees, candlelit villages, and covered bridges of New England make it the home of the stereotypical Christmas, the holiday was not celebrated there until many years after it had gained popularity elsewhere in North America. The residents of Colonial Williamsburg, Pennsylvania's Germans and Moravians, and New York's Dutch were all celebrating Christmas long before similar festivities were allowed in Puritan New England.

Memory quilts mark special occasions and holidays throughout the **United States.**

An American family dances around their candlelit tree following the customs of their Danish ancestors.

Las Posadas is an annual Christmas celebration in San Antonio, Texas.

As a result, many of the historical restorations such as Old Sturbridge Village are restrained in the manner in which they decorate for the season. But many cities and towns throughout New England more than make up for them.

The Boston Common, for example, is ablaze with lights while a giant tree sparkles from the portico of the Prudential Center. Festivities begin late in November with the Bells of Boston, a century-old tradition of English origin. Over thirty choirs of bell ringers participate in the festival, and bell ringers continue to perform in the city during the entire Christmas season.

Another English tradition very much alive in Boston is teatime, and the favorite place to enjoy this afternoon respite from Christmas shopping is at the *grande dame* of Boston hotels, the Copley Plaza. The centerpiece of its marble lobby is a giant tree built entirely of poinsettias, and the famed tea court's marble columns, gleaming crystal, and gilded ceiling are the perfect setting for a Christmas tree.

In the American Southwest, Spanish traditions have shaped Christmas customs. In California, Texas, and New Mexico, Christmas time brings posada processions and Christmas plays.

Missions in Southern California offer pastors that blend scripture with Mexican Indian folklore. The pastors' theme is the conflict between good and evil. The plays' characters include shepherds, the Devil, a hermit, and two angels. The shepherds set out to see the Christ Child. As they travel, they encounter many obstacles that the Devil puts in their way. Eventually, they overcome these obstacles and reach Bethlehem safely. Music and singing are woven through the plays, which can last anywhere from half an hour to half the night.

Around the Southwest, Christmas lanterns glow. These lanterns, called luminarias or farolitos, are simple to make. Set a small candle in a rolled paper bag and weight it with moist sand. The River Walk in San Antonio, Texas, is lit with two thousand luminarias that brighten the way for the annual posada procession.

Yosemite National Park in northern California is the site of a special Christmas celebration. The Ahwahnee Hotel, the oldest hotel in the huge park, holds the annual Bracebridge Dinner. The celebration is designed after the fictional seventeenth-century English Christmas feast in Yorkshire's Bracebridge Hall. Wandering minstrels, costumed Druids, and the music of Bach chorales are all part of the feast. In addition, a medieval pageant is performed. Dinner includes a boar's head, wassail, and Yorkshire pudding. The event has been held every year since 1927.

The American South is noted for its reverence for tradition. Historical tours and festivities are popular Christmas time activities. In some areas people still observe the old tradition of firing guns and setting off firecrackers to welcome in the holiday. In Williamsburg, Virginia, old seventeenth-century customs are revived for Christmas visitors. The townspeople wear colonial costumes, the buildings are decorated with garlands and wreaths, and an annual "Dr. Wythe's Christmas Party" is held. A string ensemble plays in the parlor of the doctor's home and the guests mingle as they drink an old-fashioned fruit punch. Highlights are Christmas concerts, caroling parties, and reenactments of colonial sports events, like footraces, wrestling, and hoop races.

Winterthur Museum, a historic house in Maryland, holds a special Yuletide tour. Twenty-one rooms are decorated for the holiday season in the style of pre-1840 America. The rooms are filled with the smell of ginger and holly. Winterthur's guides prepare special foods for display. Every year, almost 30,000 people come to enjoy the tour. Historic homes throughout North America greet the Christmas season with festivities and unusual activities. From Mystic, Connecticut, to Dearborn, Michigan, to San Francisco, California, houses are prepared for the holidays in the old-fashioned spirit. Check local tourism authorities and keep a careful watch in community calendars, and you should be able to find an interesting Christmas celebration to round out the holidays.

In the Moravian community of Winston-Salem, North Carolina, everyone gathers in church for a special Christmas "Love Feast." As the congregation sings sacred carols, some of the women of the community enter the church, carrying baskets of buns and mugs of steaming hot coffee. Everyone partakes of the refreshments as a symbol of Christian fellowship. Then, each member of the congregation is handed a lighted candle, a symbol of the Light of Christ. During the service the church glows with hundreds of tiny lights.

New York City bustles with shoppers finding gifts for their families and friends. Department store windows are filled with fantastic Christmas scenes. Up and down Fifth Avenue, Christmas music rings out from Salvation Army bands raising money for the poor. Ice skaters spin beneath the huge glowing Christmas tree in Rockefeller Center.

Special Christmas displays and performances abound. New York's enormous Metropolitan museum exhibits a beautiful Christmas tree and a baroque crèche. Radio City Music Hall hosts a *Christmas Spectacular* and the New York City Ballet performs its annual *Nutcracker Suite*. All over the city, churches resound with the joyful music of Christmas.

In the Midwest many families continue to celebrate with European traditions of their ancestors. Many Swedish families in Minnesota make sure to include the traditional lutefisk and white pudding in their Christmas meal. Some farm families of Norwegian descent still follow an Old Norwegian tradition called Yule Nek. The children of the family take the year's largest sheaf of grain and hang it up on a pole or tree as a treat for the birds.

Christmas is an occasion for big family reunions and a huge party, called reveillon, in the province of Quebec. First, French Canadian families attend midnight mass on Christmas Eve. Then, the celebration begins. Family and friends gather together to eat and sing and dance until dawn. The Christmas feast includes all kinds of meat pies, game, and fish. For dessert there is sugar pie, sugar doughnuts, and a maple syrup *tourlouche*. The party continues with live music, dancing, and family games.

In Newfoundland some people still follow the old practice

A giant Christmas tree is the focal point during the holiday season at Rockefeller Center in New York City.

of mumming. Early English settlers brought the custom with them, and it still goes on—raucous plays in which the actors are dressed up in odd disguises. The plays, narrated by Father Christmas, feature a contest between a folk hero and his enemy, as well as a doctor who restores the dead hero to life. Although the actual plays are rarely performed now, many people still dress up in colorful costumes and disguises to pay their Christmas calls on friends.

Toronto, Ontario, has been the scene of a huge annual Santa Claus parade since 1905. Rain or shine, thousands of children come out to watch Santa Claus, the Queen of Hearts, Robin Hood, Goldilocks, and other favorites ride by on their floats.

Canadians of British origin follow the old English customs. Christmas Eve dinner in British Columbia includes beef, fowl, and mince pie. In accordance with British tradition, plum pudding is soaked in brandy and brought to the table aflame, with a sprig of holly on top. Houses are decorated with holly and ivy, wintergreen and cranberry boughs.

The Ukranian communities of Saskatchewan and Alberta maintain many of the traditions of their ancestral homeland. In honor of Christ's birth, some families observe a six week fast. They eat no meat for six weeks before Ukranian Christmas on January 7. On the sixth, Christmas Eve, the children stand outside to wait for the first star of the night. As soon as they see it, they run into their homes, and the Christmas Eve meal begins. Dinner consists of twelve meatless dishes in memory of the twelve apostles of Christ. Everyone must have at least one spoonful of each of the twelve dishes. After supper, the family sings old Ukranian and English Christmas carols until it is time to go to midnight mass.

Christmas in Saskatchewan is observed quietly by the Hutterites, members of a religious German farming community. For three days before Christmas, all work stops and everyone takes time off to pray and contemplate. Church services are held twice a day during this period.

Mexico and South America

When the Spaniards came to South America in the 1500s, they brought many of their traditions with them, including Christmas traditions. In their efforts to spread Christianity, the Catholic priests encouraged people to participate in Christian morality plays, which have now become colorful Christmas processions and pageants.

December 16 marks the beginning of the holiday season in Mexico, Honduras, and El Salvador. This is the first of nine nights of *Las Posadas. Posada* is the Spanish word for lodging. The Christmas time posadas are colorful processions that reenact Joseph and Mary's search for an inn. Families and friends gather together for Las Posadas; at the head of each procession is a child dressed as an angel, followed by two more children dressed as Joseph and

The Christ Child is placed in the Nacimiento on Christmas Eve.

Mary. More angels, shepherds, and the Three Kings follow. Everyone carries a lit candle. As they walk, the posada members sing special carols. Eventually, the procession stops at the house of a friend or family member. Joseph and Mary knock on the door to ask for a room for the night.

"Go away!" the people behind the door say.

"My wife is with child and needs a place to rest," Joseph says.

"Go away!" the people in the house shout. Finally, Joseph reveals the fact that Mary is about to give birth to the Christ Child. The door opens, and the procession goes in. After a prayer is said, the party begins. Piñatas, special candies, sandwiches, fruit punch, singing and games highlight the occasion.

Nacimientos or nativities can be seen all over Mexico and South America at Christmas time. Setting up the nacimiento is a family affair, just as setting up the Christmas tree is in North America. Each year before Christmas, the figures are placed in the manger with great care. The Christ Child is never put in until Christmas Eve.

Christmas Eve, called La Noche Buena, signifies a good night. At midnight, everyone goes to midnight mass. Afterward, families gather together for the Christmas supper.

Celebrations continue until Epiphany, when the children set out their empty shoes to be filled with gifts by the Three Kings. On Three Kings Day, children receive gifts and watch special Christmas plays, called pastores. When all the festivities are over the nacimientos are carefully packed away until the next year.

Germany

In Germany and other European countries, Christians observe Advent, the four weeks before Christmas. The word *advent* means "coming," and it is a time to contemplate the coming of Christ.

The German Christmas season begins on the first Sunday in Advent. Many families have a special Advent wreath—much like those in Scandinavia—which they hang from the ceiling or set in the center of the dining room table. A more recent Advent custom was started by German truck drivers who put a small plastic tree on their dashboards. They connect the colored lights to their truck's battery and at night the little trees glow through the truck windows.

The Advent calendar is still another German custom—one that has carried over to North America. Some calendars are large Christmas pictures with twenty-four small paper windows cut into them. Every day children in the family open a window to find a little picture of a candle, a snowman, or Christmas symbol. Advent calendars also come in star shapes: twenty-four little stars attached to a big star. Every day, a little star is taken off, until only the large star remains on Christmas Eve.

During the weeks before Christmas, German homes are filled with the sweet smell of cakes and cookies baking. There are several special German Christmas treats: the Baumkuchen, or tree cake; the Christollen, which is a sweet bread; and the gingerbread house, to name a few.

Many towns and cities in German also hold Christmas markets. These so-called markets are often more like fairs with music. Christmas plays, and singing, in addition to stalls selling gifts, foods, and crafts. Some of the better-known markets are in Nuremberg, Munich, Berlin, and Hamburg.

In winter the German countryside abounds with "Christmas Card" scenes, such as this one near Schwangau in Bavaria.

Christmas Eve is the climax of German Christmas. At one o'clock in the afternoon the stores and businesses close and everyone goes home from work. The children put on their best clothes in preparation for the moment when the tree is revealed, since most German parents hide the tree in a locked room until then. When everything is ready, a bell rings, and the youngest child in the family opens the door of the Christmas tree room. The room is completely dark except for the glowing lights of the tree. Then the whole family stands around the tree and sings carols. Presents are opened, a big dinner eaten, and then the family attends midnight mass.

After the Second World War, Catholic missionary organizations revived an old custom called Star Singing. On the Sunday closest to Epiphany, young people form troupes of carolers to collect money for missions in Third World countries. Each troupe includes three boys dressed up as the Three Kings. In towns around the country, the troupes compete with each other to see who can collect the most money for the poor.

Italy

At midnight the bells of St. Peter's Basilica, along with those of the hundreds of other churches in Rome, ring out to signal the Midnight Mass. Celebrated in St. Peter's by the Pope, and attended by everyone from scarlet-robed cardinals to the diplomatic community in full evening dress, the mass is broadcast to 41 countries throughout the world.

The Pope also celebrates mass the next morning in St. Peter's, followed by his Christmas Address delivered from the balcony above the main entrance. Crowds fill the great round *piazza* of the Vatican, which is decorated with a life-sized nineteenth century *presepio* (crèche). There is also a Christmas tree decked out in silver garlands and ornaments of white and gold, and ablaze with over 2000 lights.

One of our most treasured traditions, the crèche (or Nativity scene), began in Italy. St. Francis of Assisi, in an effort to help his followers understand the Christmas story, created a living *presepio* of costumed townspeople. The idea spread quickly until churches and entire towns began building Nativity scenes, with carved figures gradually replacing live ones.

Instead of a Christmas tree, Italian homes are decorated with *ceppos*—wooden pyramids on which gifts and ornaments, dried flowers, fruit, and *presepio* figures are placed.

Gifts are exchanged on a variety of holidays in various regions of Italy—St. Lucia's Day, St. Nicholas Eve, Christmas Eve, New Year's Day, and Epiphany are all days of gift-giving in some areas of the country.

The tale of La Befana the gift-giver and Italian folk figure is told to children and adults alike. Legend has it that she rides forever on Epiphany, seeking the Bambino (the Baby Jesus), and leaving gifts for good children as she travels.

France

Gifts are left in children's shoes on St. Nicholas Eve by Père Noël (Father Christmas), according to the French. A traditional supper follows Midnight Mass, and a magnificent cake in the form of a log caps dinner on Christmas Day. In some parts of France, a Yule log is kept burning throughout the Twelve Days of Christmas.

St. Francis's presepios had, by the seventeenth century, spread to other parts of Europe, and in France these créche scenes were made on clay figures called *santons*. Provençe became the center for their manufacture, and each year in Marseilles a Santon Fair heralds the beginning of Advent. These clay figures, dressed in traditional local costumes, are made by the same families that made them in earlier centuries, known as *santonniers*. Each family has its own style. Some glaze the santons, some don't, and still others dress them in clothing.

Above: The Eiffel Tower in Paris, framed by colorful trees.

At left: Christmas fairs and markets, such as this one in Strasbourg, are common in France.

Poland

Christmas is essentially a religious observance in Poland, culminating in the *Wigilia* (vigil) celebrated at home on Christmas Eve. In pre-Christian times, the emphasis was on sharing and the renewal of friendships, so its celebration at the winter solstice coincided with both the spirit and season of Christmas. Hospitality is important, and candles shine in windows to welcome the Christ Child. Christmas trees are decorated with real fruit and cookies as well as ornaments of cut paper and decorated eggs.

Weddings and Christmas in Poland are occasions for traditional clothing and customs.

The Netherlands

Festivities begin in the Netherlands, as they do in other Western European countries, on December 5, St. Nicholas Eve. It is St. Nicholas's legendary gift, dropped down the chimney to three impoverished sisters, upon which the custom of hanging stockings by the chimney is probably based.

Each year the patron Saint of Amsterdam, St. Nicholas, arrives in the city by boat, with his traditional companion in the Netherlands—Zwarte Piet (Black Peter), dressed as a Moor. They are greeted with great pomp; gifts are exchanged, treats consumed, and preparations for the season begin in earnest.

Scandinavia

St. Lucia's Day, December 13, marks the beginning of the holiday celebrations in Sweden, although they officially begin with the observance of the first Sunday in Advent. Early in the morning of December 13, tradition dictates that a family's oldest daughter, wearing a white dress and a crown of candles, brings a breakfast of saffron buns and coffee to her parent's room. For a whole month, Scandinavians celebrate other holidays that mark this festive season ending with children's parties on St. Canute's Day, January 13.

Since Christmas arrives during the long dark days of the northern winter, candlelight and fires on the hearth are strong traditions throughout Scandinavia. Ornaments made of straw abound, from simple stars to fat Yule goats made from bundles, to more elaborate weavings.

The heart is a favorite design, especially in Denmark, but it is not the rounded heart of St. Valentine's Day. It is a straight-sided heart known as the Christmas Heart. These are woven from paper in the form of little baskets, often filled with candy. Myriad special cookies are baked and served, including buttery little spritzes.

Ornaments created of wheat straw are a common sight in Scandinavia.

HOLIDAY ENTERTAINING

Christmas Food

Traditional Christmas Dinner

Our Thanksgiving feasts have ended. Magic lingers. We can honestly say to family and friends who have gathered, "We'll see you again soon." The Christmas season may seem much too long, stretching as it does from Thanksgiving to New Year's Day. But with busy, demanding schedules, there never seems to be enough time to enjoy the beauty and sentiment of the holiday. The Christmas season is our chance to "wear our hearts on our sleeves," to decorate our homes with symbols of warmth, friendship, and nostalgia. 'Tis a season to arouse the sleeping child in us all and to pay respects to the memories of our families' pasts. The lights in our yards, the candles in our windows, reach out to neighbors and passers-by in a spirit of camaraderie and goodwill. Come closer. A beautiful wreath on the door welcomes you, a classic symbol of continuity made of greens, vine, or fabric, decorated to express the character of the household. A kiss under the "mistletoe trap"—as children call it—awaits friends as they enter.

The hall is decked with evergreen roping tied to the banisters with ribbon. Lamps are sashed with brightly striped bows; tiny origami birds perch on top. The mantel over the living room fireplace is decorated with holly and pinecones. Gingerbread sentries, stamped from grandmother's mold, are ribboned and waiting, along with the empty stockings, for Santa's arrival. The tree itself is pure magic, decorated with handmade ornaments, heirlooms, spins of paper and lace, and of course, a very special adornment on top. A favorite quilt is draped around the base of the tree; the children's favorite toys are there, alongside ribboned presents, a train, a childhood rocker. The Advent calendar marks the Great Day's approach. The family brings out its holiday tableware. Cards arrive from friends and are collected in a basket near the door. Children bring home Christmas projects from school that fill every available nook. Neighbors drop in, wassail and cookies are passed, and caroling begins!

Ah! All the ingredients of Christmases past: turkey, sage-scented stuffing, cranberry relish concocted by the children, chestnuts and brussels sprouts, our nanny's red cabbage recipe, and a luscious bûche de Noël. Bring on the family! Toast to the season, to the health of all and peace on earth. Menu serves 8.

CHRISTMAS CONSOMMÉ DOUBLE

ROAST TURKEY

CORNMEAL AND SAUSAGE STUFFING—PORT GRAVY

HEDWIG'S RED CABBAGE—BRUSSELS SPROUTS WITH CHESTNUTS

PURÉE OF TURNIPS AND POTATOES

CRANBERRY-ORANGE RELISH—PEAR CONSERVE WITH CORIANDER

BÛCHE DE NOËL

CHRISTMAS CONSOMMÉ DOUBLE

10 c. beef consommé
1 lb. lean ground beef
1 carrot, diced
1 leek, sliced
1 celery stalk, sliced
1/3 c. finely chopped raw beef
1/3 c. chopped green leek tops
3 T. chopped parsley
1 tsp. dried chervil or tarragon
3 unbeaten egg whites
3/4 c. Madeira
Julienne strips of red pepper,
    green pepper, and turnips (optional)
Juice of 1 lemon (optional)
Salt and pepper

Simmer the beef consommé with the next 4 ingredients for 1 hour. Strain the consommé. Discard all vegetables and meat. Skim fat from broth and set it aside to cool. In a flameproof casserole, combine the raw beef, leek tops, herbs, and egg whites and bring to a low simmer. Pour the consommé, at *room temperature*, into these ingredients, slowly and gently. Simmer on very low heat for 15 minutes, agitating the casserole once or twice. The consommé *must not boil!* Strain the consommé through your finest sieve. It will now be clear and rich. Refrigerate until ready to use.

When you are ready to serve it, gently reheat the consommé without allowing it to boil. Stir in the Madeira, and add lightly steamed strips of peppers and turnips. Just before serving, add the juice of one lemon, and salt and pepper to taste.

CORNMEAL AND SAUSAGE STUFFING

½ lb. sweet Italian sausage,
   crumbled
4 T. butter
1 medium onion, chopped
1 stalk celery, chopped
3 c. roughly crumbled cornbread
2 c. cubed, toasted, crustless bread
1 egg
⅓ c. parsley, chopped
2 tsp. dried sage
½ tsp. dried thyme
Broth (optional)
Salt and pepper

In a frying pan, sauté the sausage until it is cooked and browned. Pour off all but 2 tablespoons of the fat. Melt the butter in the same pan. Add onion and celery and sauté with the sausage until softened. In a large bowl, combine the sausage mixture with the breads. Mix in an egg, a generous handful of parsley, and sage and thyme. Blend well. Add a little broth if the stuffing seems too dry. Salt and pepper to taste. Fill, but don't pack, the turkey with the stuffing.

PORT GRAVY

Prepare a **Roast Turkey** (approximately 15 lb. for 8 adults) using your favorite method.
   1 qt. water or broth
   1 small onion
   2 whole cloves
   1 carrot, peeled and sliced
   1 celery stalk, with leaves
   1 parsley sprig
   1 bay leaf
   Pinch of thyme
   Salt and pepper
   3 T. flour
   3 T. butter
   ¼ c. Madeira or port wine
   Turkey neck and giblets (optional)

While your holiday bird is roasting, have stock simmering on the back burner of the stove. Combine broth or water, onion studded with two cloves, carrot, celery stalk, parsley, bay leaf, thyme, salt, pepper, and the turkey neck and giblets in a large pot. Simmer for at least 2 hours, partially covered. Strain and keep warm while you prepare the gravy thickener. Brown the flour in a heavy skillet over high heat, stirring constantly. Be careful not to burn the flour. Remove from heat when the flour is brown. Allow it to cool slightly, then return to the pan. Over

a low flame, whisk in butter. You may want to add the brown scrapings from the bottom of your roasting pan. Simply lift the bird onto a platter, pour off the fat in the pan, and scrape up the collected drippings. Whisk into the flour and butter. Cook gently for 3 minutes, then add warm stock in a stream, whisking continuously. Taste for salt and pepper. Add wine or madeira to the gravy, and chopped giblets, if desired.

HEDWIG'S RED CABBAGE

½ c. water
½ c. wine vinegar
1 tsp. brown sugar
½ tsp. salt
3 peppercorns
1 bay leaf
1 whole clove
1 apple, cored, peeled,
   and chopped fine
1 large head red cabbage,
   shredded
1 T. butter (optional)

In a large enameled or heavy pan, bring the water and vinegar to a boil with sugar, spices, and herbs. Add the apple and cabbage, and return to a boil. Cover, and reduce the heat. Simmer on low heat, stirring occasionally, until the cabbage is tender but not too soft. Remove bay leaf and clove. (Check for tenderness after 20 minutes.) Stir in a tablespoon of butter just before serving, if desired.

BRUSSELS SPROUTS WITH CHESTNUTS

2 pints fresh brussels sprouts
12 whole fresh chestnuts
¼ c. walnuts or hazelnuts
6 T. sweet butter
3 T. flour
1 c. half-and-half, at room temperature
Salt
White pepper
Freshly grated nutmeg

Trim brussels sprouts of tough stems, bottoms, and outer leaves. Set aside. Make

a small X-shaped incision in the flat side of each chestnut. Roast the chestnuts one by one on an indoor grill or over an open fire, or in an iron pan on a stovetop, turning them frequently until they open and are softened inside. Allow them to cool, then peel. Reserve 8 whole chestnuts. In the container of a food processor, grind the remaining chestnuts, the walnuts, and 3 tablespoons sweet butter together until smooth. Set aside. Steam the brussels sprouts over a small amount of water, beginning with the larger sprouts and adding the smaller ones to the steaming process, until they are tender but not too soft. Keep warm.

In a heavy skillet, cook the flour, stirring, until a light brown color. Be careful not to burn the flour. Allow the pan to cool slightly, then whisk in 3 tablespoons sweet butter and cook, stirring gently, for a minute or two. Whisk in ¼ cup lukewarm half-and-half, followed by the nut-butter. Whisk until smooth and add the remaining ¾ cup half-and-half. When ready to serve,

gently combine the brussels sprouts, the remaining chestnuts, and the cream sauce. Salt to taste, generously add white pepper to taste, and dash on a light grating of nutmeg.

PURÉE OF TURNIPS AND POTATOES

1 large or 2 medium-size turnips, peeled and cut into large chunks
6 large first-quality white potatoes, peeled and cut into large chunks
1 medium onion, grated
Butter
¼ to ½ c. milk
Salt
Pepper
Chopped parsley

Boil the turnips and potatoes in water to cover until very soft. Drain. Keep warm. Sauté the onion in 2 tablespoons butter until softened and very lightly browned. Combine the onion with the turnips, potatoes, and ¼ c. milk and mash until almost smooth, adding more butter, and salt and pepper to taste. Whip until very smooth with an electric mixer, adding more milk if you desire a thinner consistency. Lightly butter the top. Sprinkle with parsley.

For **Cranberry-Orange Relish** and **Pear Conserve with Coriander,** see "Food for Giving," page 82.

BÛCHE DE NOËL (Yule Log Cake Roll)

A very rich, very chocolate version of a Christmas classic.

Cake:
8 oz. semisweet chocolate
4 T. espresso coffee
2 tsp. vanilla extract
8 eggs, separated
¾ c. sugar
Pinch of salt

Filling:
5 T. butter
4 oz. bittersweet chocolate
1 oz. unsweetened chocolate
3 eggs, separated
½ c. sugar
⅓ c. confectioners' sugar

For the cake: Preheat oven to 375°F. Grease the bottom of a jelly-roll pan. Line it with waxed paper. Combine semisweet chocolate and coffee in a small saucepan and melt over very low heat. Add vanilla and remove from the heat. In a large bowl, beat egg yolks with sugar until double in volume. Add the chocolate mixture, folding it in gently. Beat the egg whites with the salt until stiff. Fold them into the chocolate mixture. Bake in the prepared pan for 15 minutes.

When the cake has finished cooking, turn it onto a clean dish towel. Carefully peel off the waxed paper. Cover the cake with another dry towel, and gently roll up the cake in the towels and set it aside to cool.

For the filling: Combine the butter and chocolates and melt over low heat. Cool. Combine the egg yolks and sugar in a bowl, and beat with an electric mixer, slowly at first and then at high speed, until the mixture thickens and ribbons. Reduce speed and add the chocolate mixture, mixing till blended. Beat the egg whites until stiff, and at lowest speed, incorporate them into the chocolate mousse. Cool.

To finish: When the cake is cooled, gently unroll and spread it with two-thirds of the mousse. Roll cake up again, and place it on a serving plate, seam side down. Ice with remaining mousse. Refrigerate, lightly covered, until 15 minutes before serving. Just before serving, decorate with light dustings of confectioners' sugar and holly-shapes either fresh or made of icing (see "Hard Sculpture Icing" page 77).
Note: If your family boasts a jam maker, spread some of his or her best raspberry or black cherry preserves on the cake before adding the mousse. Or give the cake a gentle sprinkling of your favorite fruit or nut liqueur before adding the mousse.

Open House Buffet for Twelve

Tastes from all over the world combine to make this Christmas open house buffet delicious, interesting, and colorful. American ham, Scandinavian sauce, Provençal quiches, Middle Eastern salad, a fruit bowl from Mexico, Chinese-style green beans—this menu is a potpourri of tastes and textures. The dessert, cookies, and sauces can be prepared in advance. The salads are simple combinations. The quiche goes in the oven an hour before serving and may be kept warm on top of the stove. The ham comes out of the oven 20 minutes before serving, as the biscuits go in. Stir-frying is done with presteamed beans just before the buffet is set out.

Ham with Lingonberry Sauce—Sweet Potato Biscuits

Tabouleh—Mexican Christmas Fruit Salad

Quiche Squares Provençal—Sesame Green Beans

Assorted Breads

Figgy Pudding with Cognac Sauce

Christmas Cookies

HAM

Have your butcher help select a ham of an appropriate size.

    1 ham
    Whole cloves
    1 qt. beer
    2/3 c. brown sugar (optional)
    1/3 c. Dijon mustard (optional)
    3 T. cognac (optional)

Preheat oven to 300°F. Score the ham in a diamond fashion; pierce with cloves. Pour the beer over the ham and bake for approximately 15 minutes per pound. Baste occasionally. (If you like a glazed ham, brush the ham with a paste made of the brown sugar, mustard, and cognac.) When ham is warmed through, set the oven to 450°F. and bake for 15 minutes or until browned. Serve accompanied with mustard and with lingonberry sauce.

LINGONBERRY SAUCE

    1 c. light brown sugar, packed
    2/3 c. fruit-flavored vinegar
    4 eggs, beaten
    3 T. dry mustard
    1 T. cornstarch
    5 oz. lingonberries, undrained
    5 oz. currant jelly

Over a very low heat, beat the sugar and vinegar together until sugar is dissolved. Remove from the heat and cool slightly. Add beaten eggs, all at once, continuing to beat vigorously. Make a smooth paste of 1/4 cup egg mixture and the mustard and cornstarch. Whisk the paste into the rest of the egg mixture and beat until smooth. Return this to a low heat, add the lingonberries and jelly, and cook, stirring constantly, until thickened (about 5 minutes). Serve warm.

Note: If it's easier for you to measure in cups, use 1/2 c. plus 2 T. of lingonberries and jelly.

SWEET POTATO BISCUITS

4 c. flour
1 tsp. baking soda
6 tsp. baking powder
½ tsp. cinnamon
1 tsp. salt
½ c. brown sugar, packed
1 c. melted butter
2 c. cooked mashed sweet
   potatoes (about 4 large potatoes)
1¼ c. sour milk or buttermilk

Preheat oven to 450°F. Sift the flour, baking soda, baking powder, cinnamon, and salt together, and set aside. In a large bowl, beat the brown sugar, butter, and potatoes together until very smooth. Gently stir in thirds of the dry mixture, alternating with the milk. (Stir just to blend; don't overwork the dough.) Roll out the dough (it will be sticky) on a floured surface with a floured rolling pin. Cut with a cutter or into rectangles. Bake for about 20 minutes on a lightly greased pan on a rack placed in the middle of the oven.

Note: The addition of a bit of grated orange peel and ½ cup chopped pecans makes these special breakfast biscuits.

TABOULEH
(Bulgur Wheat Salad)

1½ c. fine-grained bulgur wheat
8 c. water
4 small tomatoes, peeled,
   seeded, drained
1 small onion, minced
1 red pepper finely chopped
1 cucumber, peeled, seeded
2 c. chopped parsley
¼ c. chopped fresh mint
   or 1 scant T. dried mint
Juice of 1 lemon
1 tsp. salt
¼ c. olive oil
½ c. cooked stellini (star-shaped)
   pasta (just for Christmas)

Soak the bulgur wheat in the water for 1 hour. Cut cucumber into ¼-inch cubes. Lightly salt the cubes and let drain on a paper towel for 30 minutes. Set aside. Line a colander with a dish towel, and when the wheat soaking is completed, pour wheat into towel and squeeze out as much water as you can. Place wheat in a large serving bowl and gently mix in tomatoes, vegetables, and herbs. Reserve ½ c. chopped parsley. Add lemon juice, salt, and olive oil, and blend. Sprinkle salad with reserved parsley, then with the star pasta.

MEXICAN CHRISTMAS FRUIT SALAD

1 small head firm romaine
   lettuce, shredded
2 beets, cooked and sliced
   in julienne strips
1 c. pineapple cubes
   (fresh or drained)
2 apples, sliced in thin wedges
2 oranges, peeled and sectioned
1 banana, sliced in rounds
1/2 c. unsalted peanuts
1 pomegranate, if available

Gently combine the lettuce, beets, and fruits in a glass bowl—it will create a beautiful confetti effect. Then sprinkle with peanuts and pomegranate seeds.

QUICHE SQUARES PROVENÇAL

This large quiche is cooked in a jelly-roll pan, then cut into 24 squares. (The vegetable filling can be made in advance.)

Pastry:
3 c. flour
1 tsp. salt
1 c. butter (or 1/2 c. butter,
   1/2 c. lard)
1/3 c. ice water
1 egg yolk, beaten

Provençal filling:
1 small eggplant, peeled
1/3 c. olive oil

1 large onion, minced
1 large garlic clove, minced
1 green pepper, peeled,
   seeded, chopped
1 red pepper, peeled,
   seeded, chopped
1 28-oz. can peeled Italian
   tomatoes, drained and chopped
1 tsp. dried oregano
1/2 tsp. dried thyme
Salt and pepper

Egg filling:
6 eggs, at room temperature
1 c. sour cream, at room temperature
1 c. light cream, at room temperature
Salt and pepper

2 c. grated Jarlsburg or Swiss cheese
1/2 c. grated Parmesan cheese
12 black olives, pitted
1 small zucchini, cut into strips
1 roasted pepper, cut into strips

For the pastry: Combine the flour and salt in a large bowl. Cut in the butter with a pastry blender until the flour resembles cornmeal in texture. Make a well in the center of the flour, and pour in the combined water and egg yolk. Blend quickly, then gather into a ball. Roll out the dough on a floured surface with a floured pin to a size large enough to line your jelly-roll pan. Put in the pan. Pinch the edges of the dough for a decorative look.

For the Provençal filling: Cut eggplant into small cubes, salt them, and allow to drain for at least 1 hour. Peel the peppers by grilling them directly on or under an open flame. Turn them once or twice until completely charred. Place peppers in a paper bag immediately, twisting the bag closed to form a seal. Let sit for 5 minutes. Remove. Under cold running water, peel away the skin with your hands and/or a peeler. Pat the eggplant cubes dry with paper towels and sauté in the oil until browned. Toss in the onion, garlic, and peppers and continue sautéing over medium heat until cooked but still crisp and not browned. Stir in the tomatoes and herbs, and salt and pepper to taste, and cook, uncovered, over medium heat for 2 to 3 minutes. Reserve.

For the egg filling: Combine the eggs with the sour cream and light cream, and add salt and pepper to taste. Blend well and set aside.

To finish: Preheat oven to 350°F. Sprinkle the pastry with 2 cups grated Jarlsburg or Swiss cheese. Arrange the vegetable mixture evenly over the cheese. Very lightly dust with flour. Carefully pour the egg filling over the vegetable mixture. Sprinkle top with 1/2 cup grated Parmesan.

Bake for 30 to 40 minutes, until cooked through. As soon as quiche is removed from the oven, arrange vegetable strips and olives decoratively on top, at intervals that will create 24 squares. Cool slightly, then cut and serve.

SESAME GREEN BEANS

4 lb. green beans
3 T. peanut oil
1 clove garlic, crushed
1 small red hot pepper, crushed
2 T. sesame seeds
Pepper

Wash the beans and trim to a uniform length. Steam lightly over a small amount of water until barely cooked and still crisp, then run under cold water to prevent further cooking. Drain. In a heavy skillet, heat the oil, then add the garlic and red pepper. Toss in the drained green beans and stir-fry for 1 minute. Sprinkle with sesame seeds and cook over high heat a few seconds longer. Remove from the heat. Discard the garlic. Add a generous grinding of pepper and toss. Serve warm.

FIGGY PUDDING

"Now bring us some figgy pudding,
now bring us some figgy pudding, now
bring us some figgy pudding, and bring it
here *now!*" Enough said.

2 eggs
½ c. butter, at room temperature
½ c. molasses
½ c. maple syrup
1 c. buttermilk
2 c. chopped figs
½ c. combined raisins and currants
½ orange, ground (with peel)
½ c. chopped walnuts
2⅔ c. flour
½ tsp. baking soda
2 tsp. baking powder
1 tsp. salt
1 tsp. cinnamon
½ tsp. nutmeg
½ tsp. mace

Preheat the oven to 325°F. Beat the eggs

with the butter in a large bowl until light
and fluffy. Beat in molasses and syrup. Add
buttermilk, fruits, and nuts. Mix well. In
another bowl, sift all dry ingredients
together. Stir the dry mixture into the
pudding. Bake in a greased 9-in. tube pan
for 1 hour or until done.

COGNAC SAUCE

⅔ c. butter, at room temperature
2 c. confectioners' sugar
⅓ c. cognac
4 egg yolks
1 c. heavy cream

Beat the butter and sugar together in a
mixing bowl until light and fluffy. Beat in
cognac. Place the bowl over simmering
water or use a double boiler. Beat in the egg
yolks one at a time; then add the cream,
stirring. Stir constantly until thickened.

For **Christmas Cookies,** see pages 71 to
77.

Christmas Eve Supper for Four

By the time Christmas Eve arrives, one looks for a little serenity after all the last-minute shopping. A simple, elegant supper is in order, after the children are tucked into bed and friends have returned from trips to the city. Set the table with candlelight, and try an esoteric approach to the traditional reds and greens of the season—mauve and soft pale green, perhaps. Glassware and napery can provide touches of gold. A centerpiece of fruit, with perhaps gold leaves adorning the pears, would be beautiful.

Zucchini and Potato Soup with Dill

Salmon Steaks with Herb Butter

Mixed Vegetable Sauté

Beet and Endive Salad with Walnuts

Crêpes with Lingonberry Sauce

ZUCCHINI AND POTATO SOUP WITH DILL

1 qt. chicken or
    vegetable broth
2 large potatoes
2 zucchini
½ c. fresh or frozen peas
2 T. chopped fresh dill
Salt and pepper
½ c. sour cream
1 egg yolk
4 thin lemon slices

Scrub the potatoes and cut into ½-in. cubes. Cut the zucchini into half-rounds ¼-in. thick. Bring the broth to a boil in a large pot. Add the potatoes and cook for 10 minutes. Stir in the zucchini and cook another 5 minutes. Add the peas, half of the dill, and salt and pepper to taste, and cook an additional 5 minutes.

In a separate bowl, combine the sour cream and egg yolk. Gradually stir a cupful of hot soup into this mixture, then incorporate the mixture into the rest of the soup. Do not allow the soup to boil. Check the seasoning. Serve the soup in individual bowls, garnished with fresh dill and a thin slice of lemon.

Note: If fresh dill is not available, use 1 T. dried dill.

SALMON STEAKS WITH HERB BUTTER

½ c. butter
1 T. minced parsley
1 T. minced fresh dill
1 small shallot, minced
4 salmon steaks, 1 in. thick
1 lemon, one half sliced thin
Salt and pepper

Combine the butter with the herbs and shallot until well blended and set aside 2 tablespoons. Flatten the remaining herb butter into a ¼-inch-thick slab between two sheets of aluminum foil; refrigerate.

With salmon steaks at room temperature, sprinkle with lemon juice and salt and pepper to taste, lightly spread with half of the reserved herb butter. Grill 3 inches from the flame for about 4 minutes. Turn, brush with remaining butter, and grill 4 minutes more. Cut star shapes from chilled butter. Garnish the salmon with stars and thin slices of lemon.

Note: If fresh dill is not available, use ½ T. dried dill.

For the **Mixed Vegetable Sauté,** use whatever vegetables are available fresh in the market. Try to mix colors and textures. Serve with the salmon.

BEET AND ENDIVE SALAD WITH WALNUTS

3 Belgian endives
2 small cooked beets
¼ c. chopped walnuts
6 T. olive oil
2 T. white wine vinegar
1 T. Dijon mustard
Salt and pepper
2 T. heavy cream
1 T. chopped parsley

Trim the endive of bruised outer leaves and stalks; cut into julienne strips. Cut the beets into matchsticks. Combine the endives, beets, and walnuts and toss lightly. In a large bowl, whisk together the oil, vinegar, mustard, and salt and pepper to taste. Whisk in the cream. Toss the salad ingredients in the vinaigrette, and sprinkle with parsley before serving.

CRÊPES WITH LINGONBERRY SAUCE

Crêpes:
¼ c. butter
½ c. milk
1 T. confectioners' sugar
1½ c. sifted flour
2 tsp. oil
2 eggs
½ c. flat beer

Sauce:
½ c. orange juice
Rind of 1 orange, cut into
   fine julienne strips
2 T. confectioners' sugar
½ c. canned lingonberries
   with sauce

½ c. Grand Marnier

1 pint vanilla ice cream

For the crêpes: Melt the butter in a saucepan, then add milk and sugar and heat but do not boil. Place the flour in a large mixing bowl, and make a well in the center. Pour the oil and eggs into the well and then mix with a whisk until well blended. Whisk in the milk mixture, then the beer. Beat well. Strain the batter through a sieve, and refrigerate for at least 2 hours.

For the sauce: Just before cooking the crêpes, combine the orange juice, orange rind, sugar, and lingonberries in a saucepan, and cook over low heat until the sugar has

melted. Add the Grand Marnier, and heat through. Keep warm.

To finish: Cook the crêpes in a crêpe pan or in a hot, well-oiled skillet. There is enough batter for twelve 8-inch crêpes. Stack them as they are cooked, and keep them in a warm oven, lightly covered with a damp towel, until ready to serve.

For each serving, prepare as follows: Fill each of three crêpes with 2 tablespoons of vanilla ice cream, pour a tablespoon of sauce over the ice cream, and roll up the crêpes, placing them seam side down on a dessert plate. Lightly dust with some extra sifted confectioners' sugar. Any additional sauce may be spooned onto the plate around the crêpes.

Christmas Cookies and Treats

As surely as a wreath on the door says "Welcome," a plate of beautiful, delicious Christmas cookies, served with a heartwarming holiday drink, says, "Stay a while and be of good cheer." Traditional cookie favorites—gingerbread, anise cookies, bourbon balls, and small fruitcakes—will call to mind Christmases gone by. The whole wheat and cornmeal cookies give some old-fashioned tastes a new look and appeal. All of these cookies freeze well in airtight containers. Select one or two recipes to bake each week between Thanksgiving and Christmas. Bake in double batches, and you will have enough to share with drop-in guests and to arrange in marvelous assortments in tins and baskets, to give as gifts.

ROLLED COOKIES

1 c. butter, at room temperature
$2/3$ c. sugar
1 egg
1 tsp. vanilla extract
$2^3/4$ c. flour
$1/2$ tsp. salt
$1/4$ tsp. mace

Cream the butter and sugar together. Beat in the egg and vanilla until smooth. In another bowl, combine the flour, salt, and mace. Add the dry ingredients to the butter mixture. Gather into a ball and chill at least 4 hours in plastic wrap.

When you are ready to bake, preheat oven to 350°F. Leave half of the dough in the refrigerator while you roll and cut out the other half. Roll out approximately $1/4$ inch thick. Make shapes with cookie cutters. Bake 8 to 10 minutes on a lightly oiled cookie sheet. Cool on rack. Repeat with the remaining dough. Makes 48 medium-sized cookies.

BROWN-RIMMED COOKIES

1 c. butter, at room temperature
2 tsp. salt
1 tsp. vanilla extract
$2/3$ c. sugar
1 egg
$2^1/2$ c. sifted flour
$1/4$ c. half-and-half
75 pecan halves

Preheat oven to 375°F. In a large bowl, combine the butter, salt, and vanilla, creaming until light and fluffy. Beat in the sugar, then the egg. Stir in the flour, alternating with half-and-half; beat until smooth after each addition. Drop by teaspoonfuls onto a greased cookie sheet. Let stand 2 minutes. Press flat with the floured bottom of a glass. Press a pecan half into each cookie, and bake for 8 minutes. Makes 75 cookies.

GERMAN SPRINGERLE

2¼ c. flour
1 tsp. baking powder
2 eggs
½ c. confectioners' sugar
2 tsp. grated lemon rind
2 tsp. anise seed

Sift the flour and baking powder together. In another bowl, beat the eggs until light and lemon-colored. Add the sugar and lemon rind and beat again. Stir in the flour mixture and blend well. Form the dough into a ball, cover with plastic wrap, and chill until firm.

Sprinkle the dough with anise seed, then roll it out on a lightly floured board to a thickness of ½ inch. Use a traditional springerle rolling pin or use a regular pin and cookie cutters. Place the cookies on a lightly greased cookie sheet, and leave them exposed to the air for at least 6 hours. Then bake in a preheated 350°F. oven for 30 minutes. Makes 36 cookies.

NORWEGIAN ALMOND CRESCENTS

2 c. butter, at room temperature
2 c. sugar
1 c. ground almonds
4 c. flour

Preheat oven to 350°F. Cream the butter and sugar together in a large bowl until light and fluffy. Blend in the almonds and flour, and shape teaspoons of dough into thin crescents on a greased cookie sheet. These cookies spread while baking, so space generously. Bake until lightly browned, about 10 to 12 minutes. Makes 48 cookies.

KENTUCKY BOURBON BALLS

45 vanilla wafers, crushed
1 c. ground pecans
3 T. light corn syrup
1½ jiggers bourbon
Confectioners' sugar *or*
  ¼ c. semisweet chocolate

Mix the wafers, nuts, syrup, and bourbon until well blended. Form tablespoon-size balls of dough and roll them in powdered sugar. Keep refrigerated.

OR

Mix the wafers, nuts, syrup, and bourbon until well blended. Form 2-inch cylinders of dough and dip one end of each into melted semisweet chocolate. Refrigerate until ready to serve.

Makes approximately 50 cookies.

FUDGE

Christmas cookie gift assortments wouldn't seem complete without a few squares of fudge, decorated with icing or gaily wrapped in foil and ribbon.

As with all things chocolate, the quality of the chocolate used dictates the result. Chocolate chips are widely available and are satisfactory, but try to locate a richer chocolate-by-the-pound for truly luscious candy.

2 c. chopped hazelnuts
  (optional)
12 oz. semisweet chocolate
12 oz. sweet baking chocolate
1 pint marshmallow creme (7 oz.)
1 13-oz. can evaporated milk
3 T. butter
4½ c. brown sugar, packed

Lightly toast hazelnuts in a nonstick pan and set aside. Break up the chocolates into small pieces, combine with the marshmallow, and set aside. Combine remaining ingredients in a saucepan and slowly bring to a low boil, stirring occasionally. Continue cooking and stirring for 6 minutes. Pour this syrup over the chocolate marshmallow mixture, stirring until chocolate melts. Stir in nuts until well blended. Pour into a buttered 9 x 13-inch pan. Cool and cut. Makes 84 1-inch squares.

ELEGANT CHERRY FUDGE

For chocolate-covered-cherry lovers—
  1 c. pitted fresh, frozen,
     or canned bing or black
     cherries (thawed and drained
     where necessary)
  4 T. kirsch
  12 oz. best-quality white
     chocolate (optional)

Marinate the cherries in kirsch for at least 1 hour. Drain thoroughly and chop coarsely. Prepare the fudge recipe above, omitting the nuts—fold in the cherries instead. Chill the fudge. Gently melt the white chocolate in a double boiler. Spread it quickly over the fudge in a thin layer. Allow to harden. Cut into squares, cleaning the knife after each cut.

NUT BRITTLE

Use the nuts you most enjoy, mixing varieties for new tastes—or try adding a tablespoon or two of sesame seeds!
  ¾ c. hot water
  2 c. sugar
  1 c. light corn syrup
  2 c. raw nuts (chopped if
     large nuts are used)
  1 T. butter
  2 tsp. baking soda
  Sesame seeds

Combine the hot water, sugar, and syrup. Cook until the mixture reaches the soft ball stage—238°F. Add nuts, then cook to the hard crack stage—300°F. Remove from heat and add butter. Blend in baking soda, stir, and add sesame seeds. Quickly pour onto a buttered cookie sheet. Set in freezer or in snow to cool for 20 minutes. Break into pieces when cool.

JOHNSON'S RESOLUTION CARROT AND FRUIT CAKES

  1⅓ c. brown sugar, packed
  1 c. raisins or dried currants
  1½ c. orange juice
  1 tsp. butter
  1 tsp. cinnamon
  1 tsp. nutmeg
  1 c. mixed chopped nuts
  2 c. flour
  2 tsp. baking soda
  1 c. chopped dried fruit
     (dates, figs, apricots,
     pineapple, etc.)
  ¼ c. chopped candied ginger

Combine brown sugar, raisins, juice, butter, cinnamon, and nutmeg in a saucepan and simmer for 5 minutes. Cool completely. Blend in the other ingredients. Pour into small greased or paper-lined muffin pans. Bake in a preheated 350°F. oven for 30 minutes. (Or bake in an 8-inch springform pan for 1½ hours at 325°F.) Makes 24 cakes.

MEXICAN CHOCOLATE STARS

1 tablet Mexican chocolate (this is chocolate combined with sugar, almond, and cinnamon and pressed into a tablet shape)
½ c. butter, at room temperature
⅓ c. sugar
½ tsp. vanilla extract
1 egg
2 c. sifted flour
Pinch of salt
1 c. sliced almonds
30 chocolate chips

Place the chocolate in a small bowl and set over hot water to soften. Combine the softened chocolate and the butter in a large bowl. Beat until smooth. Add the sugar; beat until mixture is fluffy. Add the vanilla and egg; blend. Stir in the flour and salt.

Form dough into a ball, cover with plastic wrap, and chill. Refrigerate the dough for 3 to 4 hours.

Preheat oven to 350°F. Roll out the dough ¼-inch thick and cut quickly with a star-shaped cookie cutter. Decorate cookies with slices of almond and chocolate chips. Bake for 12 to 15 minutes. Cool on a rack. Makes 30 2-inch stars.

GUERNSEY BISCUITS

1½ c. whole wheat flour
½ c. white flour
1 T. wheat germ
1 tsp. baking powder
½ c. brown sugar, packed
½ c. sweet butter
3 T. uncooked oatmeal
⅓ c. buttermilk
Red hots and green icing (optional)

Preheat oven to 375°F. Combine the flours and wheat germ with the baking powder and sugar. Cut in the butter with a pastry blender, or combine in a food processor. Stir in the oatmeal, then the buttermilk. Roll out to ¼-inch thickness on a floured surface. Cut out with a cookie cutter, then prick the cookies all over with a fork. Bake

on a greased coookie sheet for 20 minutes or until the edges start to brown. Decorate with icing and red hots, if you like, when cool. Makes 30 cookies.

LINZER-CORN TARTS

½ c. butter, at room temperature
1 c. sugar
1 egg yolk
1 T. water
1 tsp. grated lemon rind
½ c. sifted flour
1 c. yellow cornmeal
Raspberry preserves
Confectioners' sugar

Combine the butter and sugar; blend until smooth. Add the egg yolk and water, then add the lemon rind, flour, and cornmeal. Roll into a ball, cover with plastic wrap, and refrigerate for at least 2 hours.

Preheat oven to 350°F. Roll dough out to ¼-inch thickness on a cold, lightly floured surface. Cut with scalloped cutters. Bake on a greased cookie sheet for 15 minutes. Cool on a rack. Lightly spread one cookie with raspberry preserves, top it with a second cookie, and sprinkle with confectioners' sugar. Repeat with the remaining cookies. Makes ten 3-inch tarts.

GINGER COOKIES

More than any other holiday treat, gingerbread cookies mean Christmas. Ginger people are a charming addition to a Christmas tree. And a little imagination turns Christmas cutouts into wonderful gifts and decorations. If you use an icing that hardens, you can use your fancy in decorating your ginger people. Create a circus like the one shown at the "Children's Tea with Santa" (see page 134). Build a ginger house and give it to a family of children with treats and icing to decorate it—a great holiday gift! Cookies pressed from old Christmas molds are a lovely home decoration—and delicious too. The following is a basic recipe, with variations.

Ginger People, Places, Things

¼ c. sweet butter, at room
    temperature
½ c. light brown sugar, packed
½ c. molasses
3½ c. flour
1 tsp. baking soda
1 tsp. cinnamon
1 tsp. ginger
¼ tsp. nutmeg
½ tsp. salt
⅓ c. water

In a large bowl, blend the butter and brown sugar until creamy. Beat in the molasses. In another bowl, sift all of the dry ingredients together. Add the dry mixture in thirds, alternating with the water. Stir to blend. Knead lightly with floured hands. Form the dough into a ball and cover with plastic wrap. Refrigerate for 3 to 4 hours.

Preheat oven to 350°F. Roll out the dough to ¼-inch thickness and cut cookies into desired shapes. Bake for 12 to 15 minutes. Cool on a rack. Decorate with icing when cool.

Note: For **Dark Ginger Cookies,** substitute dark brown sugar for light, and use blackstrap molasses instead of regular molasses.

Old-Fashioned Molded Gingerbread

Make dough for Dark Ginger Cookies. When you are ready to roll the dough, work in:

4 T. finely chopped
    candied ginger
¼ cup chopped sliced almonds

Icing:
½ c. confectioners' sugar
⅛ c. milk

Preheat oven to 350°F. Lightly oil your molds (spray oil is useful). Roll the dough over the molds, trim off excess dough, and remove from molds. Place the cookies on greased baking sheet. Bake for 12 to 15 minutes for small molds, up to 20 minutes for larger ones. The patterns of an intricate mold usually are more visible when cooled cookies are brushed with a thin coat of confectioners' sugar mixed with milk.

HARD SCULPTURE ICING

3 egg whites
1 lb. confectioners' sugar

Beat the egg whites until stiff but not dry. Sift in the sugar and beat until icing is very stiff. Force a little through a pastry tube. If it holds its shape, then it is ready to use. If not, add a little more sugar. Cover icing with a damp cloth until you are ready to decorate.

Glogg, Nog, and Other

An international collection of holiday drinks: a recipe for wassail bowl from Great Britain, glogg from Sweden, eggnog from the American South, and special hot chocolate from Mexico.

Caution: do not use copper, iron, or brass utensils when making drinks containing wine or beer.

The following recipes will serve 8 to 10 people.

Heartwarming Drinks

WASSAIL BOWL

5 pints beer
2 c. sherry
2½ c. brown sugar, packed
1 lemon, sliced
1 tsp. ginger
3 slices white bread, crusts
   removed, cut into star shapes
   and toasted

In a large saucepan, gently heat the beer with the sherry. Add the remaining ingredients, stirring and cooking over low heat until blended. Float toast stars on the surface just before serving.

GLOGG

Peel (with zest) of ½ orange,
   cut in julienne strips
1 c. raisins
½ c. whole blanched almonds
3 crushed cardamom pods
3 crushed coriander seeds
2 cinnamon sticks
10 whole cloves
2 c. water
1 gal. domestic port wine
1 fifth cognac
1 pint bourbon
½ pint rum
4 T. sugar
½ orange, sliced thin
Whole cloves

Place the first seven ingredients in a large stockpot, add the water, and simmer for 30 minutes. Then add the remaining ingredients, heating until just below the boiling point. Carefully light the surface of the glogg with a match, let it burn a few seconds, then extinguish by placing a lid on the pot. Serve warm in a punch bowl, with a few orange slices studded with one or two cloves floating on top.

HOT MEXICAN CHOCOLATE

2 tablets Mexican chocolate
   (see page 75)
¼ c. water
2 qt. milk
Whipped cream
Cinnamon

Gently melt chocolate tablets in water over very low heat. When chocolate is dissolved, add milk, stirring and heating to just under the boiling point. Remove from heat, and pour into a jug or pitcher. Beat with a whisk until foamy (or use the traditional tool, a *molinillo*). Serve topped with whipped cream and a dash of cinnamon, if you like.

HOT MULLED WINE

1 cinnamon stick
4 whole cloves
½ tsp. grated nutmeg
1 T. sliced lemon peel (zest removed)
½ c. sherry
1 bottle red wine
Sugar to taste

Place the spices and lemon peel in a large saucepan, barely cover with water, and simmer for 30 minutes. Strain, and add the sherry, wine, and sugar. Heat but do not boil.

EGGNOG

6 eggs, separated
½ to ¾ c. sugar
2 c. heavy cream
2 c. milk
2 tsp. vanilla or rum extract
Grated nutmeg

In a large bowl, beat the egg whites until stiff but not dry, gradually adding the sugar. Beat the yolks in another large bowl until they are lemon yellow. Fold in the egg whites. In a third bowl, beat cream until stiff, then add it to the eggs along with the milk and flavoring, stirring. Chill. Sprinkle with grated nutmeg before serving. (The eggnog may need a gentle stirring before serving.)

ROMPOPE de CALABAZA
(Pumpkin Eggnog)

6 eggs, separated
½ c. sugar
½ c. pumpkin purée
2 pints half-and-half
¼ c. Jamaican rum

In a large bowl, beat the egg whites until stiff but not dry, gradually adding sugar. Beat egg yolks in another large bowl until pale lemon yellow. Beat pumpkin into egg yolks, then fold in the egg whites. In a third bowl, beat the half-and-half until frothy. Add it to the mixture, along with rum. Stir to blend. Serve very cold.
Note: For the adults, add 2 c. rum, cognac, or whiskey to the nog.

The following recipes can be prepared and served to your guests, or the dry ingredients can be packaged as a sort of "mix" and given as a gift. That way, all the recipient has to do is add the liquid called for in the recipe to create a spirited, tasty drink. Package these "mixes" simply in plastic bags or more elaborately in decorative jars or clear glass coffee mugs—perfect for serving the finished brew.

Ingredients market with an (*) should be combined to create the mix. Don't forget to include a copy of the recipe as part of your gift.

GLÜHWEIN

1/4 c. whole cloves*
1/4 c. whole allspice*
1/4 c. cinnamon sticks, broken*
1/4 c. dried orange peel in small bits*
1/4 c. whole coriander seed*
1 bottle hearty red wine
1 lemon, sliced thinly

In a large pot, simmer 1/4 cup of the mixed spices in 1 1/2 cups water for 10 minutes. Strain. Add the red wine, and heat the mixture to just below a boil. Float the lemon slices on top and serve immediately.

HOT MULLED CIDER

1/4 c. whole cloves*
1/4 c. broken stick cinnamon*
1/4 c. whole allspice*
1/4 c. dried orange peel in small bits*
6 c. apple cider

Mix the first 4 ingredients in a large jar. Set aside. In a large pot, combine the cider with 6 tablespoons of the mixed spices, cover, and simmer for 10 minutes. Reserve the rest of the spice mix for other batches. Strain and serve hot, garnished with a whole cinnamon stick.

FAMILY GLOGG

1 c. sugar*
1 c. raisins*
8 cardamon seeds*
1/2 lb. whole almonds, blanched*
1 cinnamon stick (3 to 5 inches long)*
1 bottle dry red wine
1 bottle Aquavit
Zest of fresh orange (orange part only)

Place all ingredients except the orange zest in a large pot and heat them slowly until the sugar melts. Do not boil. Serve at once, garnishing each cup with a curl of fresh orange peel.

LEMON TEA BLEND

1 c. loose black tea*
$^1/_4$ c. lemon peel, dried and cut*

Mix ingredients well. Makes 1$^1/_4$ cups blend.

LEMON-MINT TEA BLEND

1 c. loose black tea*
$^1/_4$ c. lemon peel, dried and cut*
$^1/_4$ c. mint leaves*

Mix all ingredients well. Makes 1$^1/_2$ cups blend.

ROSE HIP TEA BLEND

$^1/_4$ c. loose black tea*
$^1/_2$ c. rose hips, dried*
$^1/_4$ c. hibiscus blossoms, dried*
$^1/_4$ c. lemon peel, dried and cut*
1 T. peppermint*

Mix all ingredients well. Makes 1$^1/_4$ cups blend.

For a completely caffeine-free blend, leave out the black tea.

Food for Giving

Special foods from your kitchen make excellent gifts at Christmastime—homemade nut breads, jams, cookies, candies, herb blends and vinegars, relishes and mustards. In addition, foods are versatile gifts that can be presented singly or combined to fit nearly any holiday occasion.

Here are recipes for cranberry-orange relish and hot pepper jelly, two condiments that always seem to make an appearance during the holidays, as well as recipes for a pear conserve and a rich chocolate dessert sauce.

On the savory side, blended herb teas are always a wintertime favorite and are easy to make. Wrap them in small plastic bags, fasten with a twist tie, and cover it with a ribbon and bow. Or purchase some empty decorative spice tins, fill them

with your blended tea, and tie a ribbon around the top.

The same packaging works well for blends of herbs and spices, also easy to make from homegrown or purchased seasonings. If you like, include your own special recipes for using a particular blend, typing or printing the directions on small rectangles of white paper, which then can be folded into tags and tied to the bags or jars of seasonings.

And don't neglect these wonderful recipes for homemade mustards, which can be packed in commercial canning jars or smaller jars that you've saved throughout the year.

Finally, try the recipe for the gorgeous star bread. The decorative egg-rich dough conceals delicious layers of eggs, vegetables, and fish or chicken fillings.

CRANBERRY-ORANGE RELISH

1 12-oz. bag fresh cranberries
¼ c. orange juice
½ to ¾ c. sugar
1 large orange, ground
½ c. chopped walnuts

Combine the cranberries, juice, and sugar in a saucepan and cook over medium heat, stirring, for 10 minutes. Remove from heat. Stir in the ground orange. Chill. Before serving, stir in walnuts. Makes 3 cups.

PEAR CONSERVE WITH CORIANDER

4 c. peeled, seeded,
  and ground pears
1 c. sugar
1 small lemon, ground
6 whole coriander seeds

Combine pears, sugar, and lemon in a saucepan. Slowly bring to a boil, then add coriander and simmer, stirring, for 10 minutes, or until the fruit is translucent. Pack in sterilized jars or freeze until ready to use. Makes 3 cups.

RED PEPPER JELLY

½ c. minced hot red peppers
2 c. minced red bell peppers
1 c. apple cider vinegar
1½ c. sugar
2 oz. liquid pectin (optional)

Combine all ingredients in a heavy saucepan. Bring to a boil, stirring often. Reduce heat and simmer, stirring for 5 minutes. (The addition of pectin assures a thicker result but is not imperative.) Pour into hot sterilized jars and seal. This is wonderful with cream cheese and on cold meats. Makes 2 pints.

CHOCOLATE DESSERT SAUCE

2½ oz. best unsweetened
  chocolate
¼ c. strong coffee
1 c. sugar
1 egg, beaten
¼ c. heavy cream

In the top of a double boiler, over simmering water, melt shaved or broken chocolate with the coffee. Add the remaining ingredients. Bring the water to a boil, stirring the sauce a few times until the boil begins. Then let the sauce cook, without any stirring, until it is thick. Serve hot.

STAR BREAD

A beautiful star-studded bread filled with eggs, vegetables, and cheese. Two variations for this *torte* are given below, one Mediterranean, one mildly curried. Tie the breads with ribbon and offer them as gifts to be warmed, eaten, and enjoyed for breakfast, lunch, or dinner during the holidays.

Dough (2 loaves):
2 pkg. dry yeast
½ c. warm water
2 large cloves garlic
2 c. butter
12 eggs, beaten
8 c. flour
1 tsp. salt

Niçoise Filling (1 loaf):
5 eggs
½ tsp. dried thyme
2 pkg. frozen chopped spinach, thawed
½ c. ricotta cheese
Salt and pepper
2 T. olive oil
1 small onion, sliced
½ red bell pepper, minced
1 small clove garlic, minced
½ small hot red pepper, minced
1 7-oz. can tuna packed in oil
2 tomatoes, peeled, seeded, chopped
10 assorted pitted black and
  green olives, chopped
Chopped parsley
Chopped fresh basil (optional)
1 lb. mozzarella cheese, thinly sliced
Heavy cream

Curry Filling (1 loaf):
5 eggs
1 tsp. chopped parsley
2 pkg. frozen chopped spinach, thawed
½ c. ricotta cheese
½ tsp. grated fresh ginger
  (or ¼ tsp. powdered)
2 T. chopped coriander leaves, if available
¼ tsp. dry mustard
Salt and pepper
1 chicken breast, cooked and
  torn into small pieces
4 scallions, chopped
¼ c. mango chutney
1 tsp. minced hot pepper (optional)
1 c. sour cream
1 tsp. curry powder
Heavy cream

For the dough: Dissolve the yeast in warm water and set aside. Crush the garlic cloves. Melt butter and

allow garlic to "steep" in it for 5 to 10 minutes. Strain the butter; discard garlic. In a large bowl beat the butter and eggs together. Add the yeast, 4 cups flour, and salt. Whisk well. Let dough rest 15 minutes. Stir in remaining flour and blend well. Refrigerate in a covered bowl at least 6 hour.

For Niçoise bread: Beat the eggs with the thyme, and make 3 thin omelets. Set aside.

Drain the spinach and squeeze it dry, then combine it with the ricotta, and salt and pepper to taste. Set aside.

In a frying pan, sauté the onion, bell pepper, and garlic in a small amount of olive oil until tender and lightly browned. Stir in the hot pepper, tuna, tomatoes, and olives and simmer for 5 minutes. Sprinkle with parsley and basil. Set aside.

Lightly oil a 9-in. springform pan. Roll out two-thirds of the dough and line the bottom and sides of the pan with overlap. Fill in this order: 1 omelet, one-third of the spinach mixture, one-third of the tuna mixture, one-third of the mozzarella slices. Continue until all ingredients are used. (Lightly salt and pepper as you go.) Roll out remaining dough and place on top of the torte, trimming off overlap liner (reserve the trimmings). Tuck the top under around the inner edges, pinching lightly to the sides, sealing it as you go. Brush lightly with heavy cream. Cut stars out of the trimming. Brush with cream and decorate top of bread with the shapes. Bake in a preheated 350°F. oven for 45 minutes. Cool on a rack for 15 minutes.

For curry bread: Beat the eggs with the parsley, and make 3 thin omelets. Set aside.

Drain the spinach, squeezing out all moisture, and then combine it with the ricotta, ginger, coriander, mustard, and salt and pepper to taste. Set aside.

Toss the chicken, scallions, chutney, hot pepper, sour cream, and curry powder together. Set aside.

Prepare the dough-lined springform pan as described for Niçoise bread. Fill with 1 omelet, one-third of the spinach mixture, one-third of the chicken mixture. Continue until all ingredients are used. (Lightly salt and pepper as you go.) Place the remaining dough over all, seal, brush with the cream, and add stars as for the Niçoise bread. Bake in a preheated 350°F. oven for 45 minutes, until browned. Cool 15 minutes before unmolding.

Herb Vinegars

The process for making herbal flavored vinegars is quite simple. Fill a jar ¹/₄ full with fresh herbs, then add vinegar to fill the jar. Cover and store for at least 2 weeks in a dark place. The secret is in the choice of vinegars and herbs. The following combinations are favorites:

Lemon balm in white distilled vinegar

Mint in cider vinegar (for salads or with lamb)

Chive blossoms in white distilled vinegar

Tarragon in white wine vinegar (for use in Bernaise sauce or salads)

Purple basil in white distilled vinegar

Salad burnet, basil, oregano, or marjoram in red wine vinegar, with an optional clove of garlic.

GREEK SALAD DRESSING BLEND

¹/₂ c. marjoram
¹/₄ c. oregano
1 T. garlic powder
¹/₄ c. mint leaves

Mix all the ingredients well. Add 1 teaspoon blend to each cup of store-bought oil and vinegar dressing and shake well. Or mix 3 parts olive oil with 1 part red wine vinegar. Add 1 teaspoon seasoning mix and shake well. Makes about 1 cup blend.

ITALIAN SALAD DRESSING BLEND

¹/₂ c. marjoram
¹/₄ c. basil
¹/₄ c. oregano
2 T. garlic powder
2 dried hot red peppers, finely crumbled

Mix all ingredients well. Add 1 teaspoon of the seasoning mix to each cup of store-bought oil and vinegar dressing and shake well. Or mix ³/₄ cup olive oil with ¹/₄ cup red wine vinegar to make your own dressing. Add 1 teaspoon mix and shake well. Serve in a sophisticated cruet. Makes about 1 cup blend.

ITALIAN HERB BLEND FOR TOMATOES

$1/4$ c. oregano
$1/4$ c. basil
$1/4$ c. marjoram
2 T. powdered garlic
2 T. anise or fennel seeds, crushed
4 dried hot red peppers, crumbled
$1/2$ tsp. powdered cloves

Mix all ingredients well. Add to tomato sauce for use on pizza, pasta, or other Italian favorites. Makes about $1^1/2$ cups blend.

RUSSIAN MUSTARD

$1/2$ c. mustard powder
$1/2$ c. sugar
1 tsp. salt
Juice of $1/2$ lemon
Boiling water

Mix dry ingredients with lemon juice and add just enough boiling water to moisten. Blend well, adding water as needed to reach a spreadable consistency. Allow to sit overnight and add more water if needed. The mustard can be stored in the refrigerator until ready to give, or it can be packed in sterilized jars and processed 10 minutes in a boiling water bath and stored at room temperature. Makes about $1^1/2$ cups.

WHOLEGRAIN MUSTARD

3 T. mixed pickling spices
1 c. cider vinegar
$1/4$ c. yellow mustard seed
$1/4$ c. brown mustard seed
$1/2$ c. white wine
1 T. honey

Place pickling spices and vinegar in a small saucepan, and simmer, covered, for 10 minutes. Strain and set aside. Process mustard seeds in blender to crack some of them. Add vinegar mixture and blend until it is just absorbed. Add wine and blend well. Add honey and blend, thinning with a little wine if necessary. Let mustard sit overnight before bottling, since it may continue to thicken and need yet more wine. The mustard can be stored in the refrigerator until ready to give, or it can be packed in sterilized jars, processed for 10 minutes in a boiling water bath, and stored at room temperature. Makes about 2 cups.

HERB BLEND FOR CHEESE

$1/4$ c. dill weed
1 T. onion flakes
3 T. garlic powder
1 tsp. powdered horseradish or dry mustard

Mix all ingredients well. To use, add 2 teaspoons of the blend to 8 ounces cream cheese and 4 ounces softened butter. Blend well. Makes about $1/2$ cup blend.

HERB BLEND FOR POULTRY

$1/2$ c. marjoram
$1/4$ c. celery leaves, dried
2 T. garlic chips or powder
$1/4$ c. summer savory
1 T. curry powder
$1/4$ c. sage (optional)

Mix all ingredients well.

Use one teaspoon of the blend in chicken or turkey soup, or one tablespoon per quart of turkey or chicken stuffing. Makes about $1^1/4$ cups blend.

SEASONED CROUTONS

2 c. day-old premium or home-baked bread, cubed
2 T. basil, finely crumbled
2 T. marjoram, finely crumbled
2 T. garlic powder
$1/2$ c. olive oil

Spread bread on a baking sheet and sprinkle with seasonings. Drizzle with oil and place under broiler for 30 seconds. Stir well and continue broiling, stirring at 30 second intervals, until lightly brown. They burn very easily, so watch them constantly! Allow to cool and package.

SEASONED BREAD CRUMBS FOR TOPPING

1 c. dry, coarse, white breadcrumbs
$1/4$ c. grated Parmesan cheese
1 T. basil
1 T. garlic powder
$1/2$ tsp. black pepper, coarsely ground

Mix well and package in plastic bags or jars tied with decorative bows.

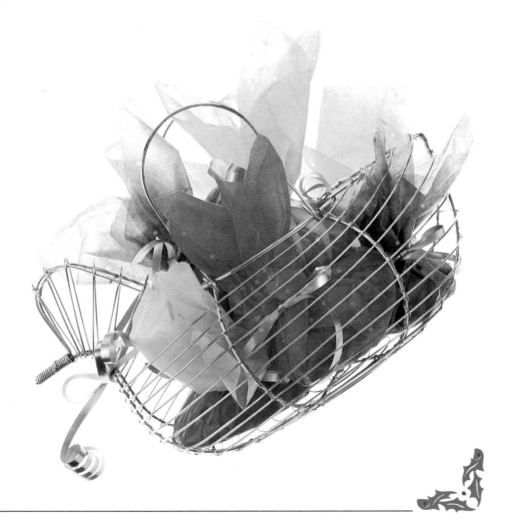

Gourmet Baskets and Collections

Italian Pantry: Gather together the ingredients below to create a unique and tasty gift. Pack wooden pasta fork, Italian herb blend for tomato sauce, seasoned breadcrumbs or croutons, Parmesan cheese, 2 heads of garlic, a jar of pesto sauce, and a package of premium pasta in a glossy red shopping bag with green and white tissue and ribbon. Add a red plaid dish towel, rolled and tied, and a bottle of Italian wine to make this an even more elegant gift; or add jars of commercial antipasto ingredients such as roasted peppers or olives.

Tea for Two: Place several tea blends, a tea infuser, a loaf of tea bread (or a recipe for one), 2 small cloth napkins, and individually packaged Scottish shortbreads in a basket.

Hostess Set: Place herbs for cheese spreads, mulling spices, breadsticks, and an olive-wood cheese spreader (and a package of cream cheese if the gift is to be delivered in person) on an olive-wood cheese board. Wrap it all up in cellophane, tying ribbons around each end to keep the ingredients in place. For a larger gift, add a bottle of red wine for mulling. Or simply attach a package of mulling spices to a bottle of hearty red wine.

Breakfast Set: Place several tea blends, an infuser, English muffins and preserves in a napkin-lined basket.

HOLIDAY ENTERTAINING

Decorations and Crafts

Christmas Decorations and Crafts

The following collection of craft ideas for the Christmas season—pillows, stockings, and table decor—you will be proud to give and delighted to receive. The projects require only basic skills: machine sewing and simple embroidery stitches. These are ideas for the artist in us all—who is willing, but perhaps not able to create the gorgeous but time-consuming and complex projects that fill crafts journals and magazines in the months before Christmas. For those with beginner's craft skills, here are ideas with results that are both beautiful and achievable. The decorations and gifts are simple, elegant, witty. The appliquéd pictures have clear, strong designs. Sew them as illustrated, or use the ideas as a foundation for your own Christmas visions. If there are children in the household, by all means let them participate! A child's drawn and cut version of "A Christmas Tree Tale," sewn by an adult, would be a treasured gift. Provide liners for small stockings and pillows to be filled with this year's tree needles when the holiday ends—a charming Christmas memory! Enjoy!

A Basket of Christmas Supplies

Use these supplies as you would your pantry staples in a kitchen. Collect them all, put them in a basket, and place it in its own corner where you can find it easily and quickly.

1. Florist's wire: fine and heavy (available at florist's shops, hardware and garden stores)—useful year-round.

2. Adhesives: white glue, rubber cement, transparent tape (all available at stationers).

3. Ribbon: You will save time and money if you purchase 25- to 50-yard rolls of good quality ribbon from your florist—1½-inch print ribbon, 2½-inch plaid ribbon, ½-inch gold ribbon. (Wonderful ¼-inch ribbon collections are available through the Lillian Vernon mail-order catalogue.)

4. Liquid starch: This may seem like an odd addition, but as you will see, it is of great use—as a stiffener of bows and as a colorless fabric glue. It is also very messy, since it is best applied with one's hands.

Christmas Stockings

Won't your child love to see one of these stockings hanging over the fireplace this Christmas? Easy to make and wonderful to look at, the stockings shown above (from left to right) are the Crazy-Quilt Stocking, Dancer's Stocking, Christmas Window Stocking, Child's Pine Needle Stocking, Sport Sock, and the Red Chintz Stocking.

One of the most charming traditions of the season is hanging a stocking on the mantel (or front door) in expectation of Santa's arrival on Christmas Eve. Six stocking ideas are pictured here; four are variations on a basic pattern. The tiny stocking is for a very small child, to be filled later with aromatic needles from the Christmas tree. Finally, there is a Sport Sock, using two basic needlework stitches on a purchased sock.

The instructions for the stockings—and for all of the crafts in THE WHOLE CHRISTMAS CATALOGUE—are basic. For more details, see "Tips on Machine Applique," page 100, or consult a beginning needlework book.

Sport Socks

This is a great gift idea for friends and family members. Wool socks are always welcome, and the needlework detail gives them charm.

Materials needed: a pair of purchased gray wool socks (the heel and toe detail is optional), red and green yarn, bells, pompoms

Using a feather stitch, as illustrated on page 92, create a vine along the heel and up the center back of the sock. Detail the vine with French-knot fruit, using the stitching instructions provided. Pull a couple of strands of yarn through the sock top and tie bells or pompoms on the ends for a whimsical touch.

Crazy-Quilt Stocking

Materials needed: one 10×14-in. piece of crazy-quilt fabric (see "Crazy Quilt Pillows," page 99, for crazy-quilt instructions), a 10×14-in. piece of fabric for the back, scraps of red fabric for patches, 16 in. of green rickrack

Cut out sock pattern for front and fabric back. Cut out patch heel and toe pieces. Using a straight stitch, border the patches with rickrack placed under the edges of the patches. Machine-appliqué patches to the sock along the edge of the red patch. Add an appliquéd heart at the top on a random square. Sew stocking front to stocking back, right sides together. Trim close to curves. Turn and press. Make a ½-in. hem at stocking top.

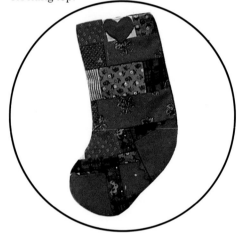

Christmas Window Stocking

This stocking is made entirely of old pieces of fabric and trim. There are new fabrics that approximate the look, but try to collect special trims and flower prints for this effect.

Materials needed: one 14×20-in. piece of quilted fabric, one 14-in. piece of "roof" trim, a scrap of green for tree inside window, 1 ft. rickrack for the tree

Cut stocking front and back using the pattern provided. On the wrong side of stocking back, machine-appliqué the Christmas tree. Hand-sew the rickrack detail to tree. On stocking front, following the pattern, outline the window with a close machine-appliqué stitch. Cut out window panes. Sew stocking front to stocking back, right sides together. Trim curves, turn, and press. Sew a ½-in. hem in top of stocking. Straight-stitch a piece of trim to stocking top, following the hem stitch line.

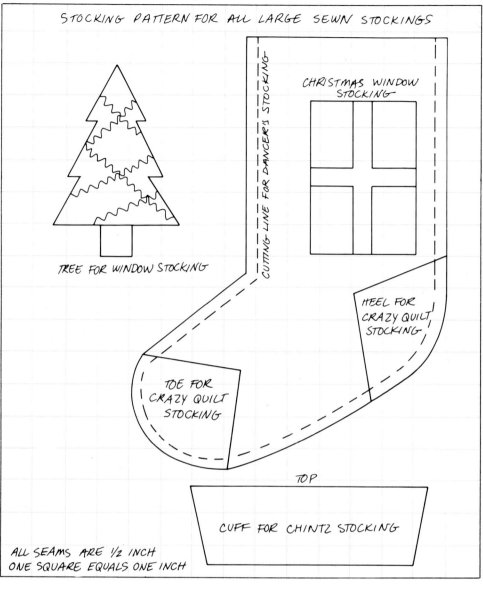

STOCKING PATTERN FOR ALL LARGE SEWN STOCKINGS

TREE FOR WINDOW STOCKING

CUTTING LINE FOR DANCER'S STOCKING

CHRISTMAS WINDOW STOCKING

HEEL FOR CRAZY QUILT STOCKING

TOE FOR CRAZY QUILT STOCKING

TOP

CUFF FOR CHINTZ STOCKING

ALL SEAMS ARE ½ INCH
ONE SQUARE EQUALS ONE INCH

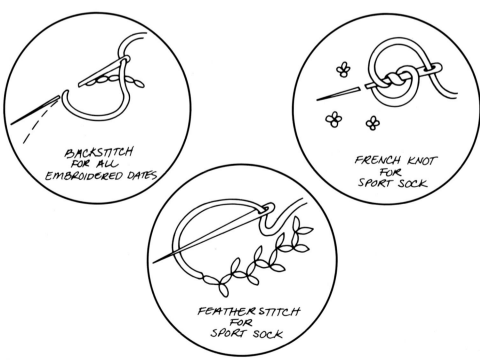

BACKSTITCH FOR ALL EMBROIDERED DATES

FRENCH KNOT FOR SPORT SOCK

FEATHER STITCH FOR SPORT SOCK

Child's Pine Needle Stocking

Materials needed: 1 sq. ft. print fabric, a small piece of red corduroy or felt, a small piece of green cloth, 1 ft. polkadot trim

Using the pattern provided, cut out 2 stocking shapes and 1 set of detail shapes. Machine-appliqué the red cliffs and tree to the sock front. Stitch snowflakes in place using dots cut from the trim. Stitch red band to sock top. Turn under upper edge and sew on the dot trim. Stitch stocking front to stocking back, right sides together. Trim close to curves, turn right side out, and press. Make a cotton liner the same size as the stocking. Fill liner with tree needles and sew top seams closed. Insert in stocking, and sew top seam closed.

Red Chintz Stocking

Materials needed: one 14×20-in. piece of red chintz, one 10×14-in. piece of quilted red chintz, gold ribbon

Cut the stocking front and back using the pattern provided. Cut the cuff using pattern provided. Sew cuff side seams together. Hem cuff ¼ in. at bottom. Sew stocking front to stocking back, right sides together. Trim curves, turn, and press. Fold the cuff top under ½ in. Hand-sew cuff to stocking top. Add a gold ribbon bow.

Dancer's Stocking

Materials needed: one 14×20-in. piece of pink mohair cloth, 2 ft. of 1½-in.-wide black ribbon, 1 yd. of ½-in.-wide black ribbon

Cut out the stocking front and back using the pattern provided. On the right side of the fabric, pin the wide ribbon along the slipper lines. Straight-stitch along the bottom of the "shoe." Straight-stitch along the top of the "shoe," easing and gathering the ribbon as it turns along the foot line. Leave ½-in. open 1 in. from the heel, to insert narrow ribbon. Trim off excess wide ribbon. Insert ½ yd. of narrow ribbon in "shoe" opening. Stitch closed. Repeat process for other side of stocking. Sew stocking front to back, right sides together. Trim curves. Turn and press. Make a ½-in. hem in stocking top. Lace ribbons around dancer's ankles.

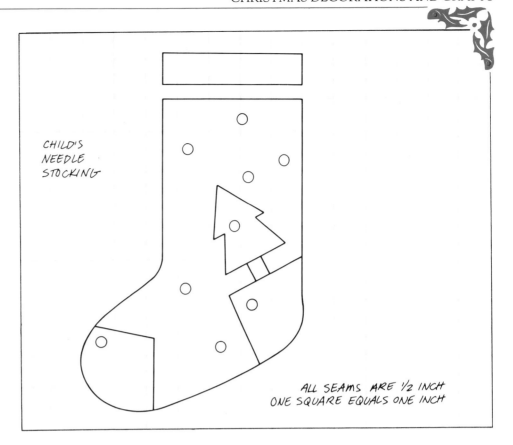

CHILD'S NEEDLE STOCKING

ALL SEAMS ARE ½ INCH
ONE SQUARE EQUALS ONE INCH

Hungarian Embroidered Christmas Stocking and Heart Ornament

Hungarian folk embroidery combines floral motifs with colors as vibrant as the music of gypsy violins. Yet, you need to know only the satin, chain, and outline stitches to create the lovely Christmas stockings and tree ornaments traditional in Hungary.

Embroidered Stocking

Materials needed: two 12-by-7-in. pieces of heavy, closewoven wool fabric, preferably with a felted finish (Melton cloth is perfect) in red, green, or another bright color, a piece of white felt the same size, $1^{1}/_{4}$ y. thin gold cord, 8 in. wide gold braid or grosgrain ribbon in the same color as the wool fabric, embroidery floss (thread) in an assortment of bright colors, pinking scissors. Note: If the stockings are to be used as decoration only, they can be made of felt instead of wool, but keep in mind that felt is not sturdy enough to stuff with presents and hang.

Cut two stockings from wool (see diagram) using the pinking scissors. Then cut another one, 1 in. smaller on all sides, from the white felt, again using the pinking scis-

SCALE: 1 SQUARE = 1 INCH

sors. Transfer the designs (see box) to the white felt stocking, and embroider, using a double strand of floss and the outline and satin stitches. Assemble the stocking by placing the two fabric sides together, and centering the embroidered felt stocking on top. Stitch through all layers $1/4$ in. inside each edge except the top one. Leave the top edge unstitched. Stitch a hanging loop into the top of the seam on the heel side. Cover stitching with gold cord or a row of embroidery in the chain stitch.

Embroidered Tree Ornament

Materials needed: two 4 in. squares red felt, one 3½ in. square white felt, embroidery floss (thread) in bright colors, 4 in. narrow red ribbon, a small amount of stuffing materials such as cotton balls or puffs, pinking scissors

Using the pinking scissors, cut two hearts of the same size from the red felt. Then, again using the pinking scissors, cut another heart from the white felt, about ½ in. smaller on all sides. Transfer the design (see box below) at the right or another design of your choice to the white felt heart and embroider it in bright colors, using a double strand of floss and the outline and satin stitches.

Place a small amount of stuffing between the two red hearts and pin a loop of ribbon between the red layers at the notch in the top. Center the white heart on top of the red hearts, and stitch through all the layers about ¼ in. from the edges on all sides. Cover your stitches with a single row of red chain embroidery.

FULL SCALE

SATIN STITCH

CHAIN STITCH

OUTLINE STITCH

To Transfer Patterns to Paper or Fabric

There are three different methods that can be used to transfer any of the patterns in this book to paper or fabric. But before you transfer it, you may need to enlarge it.

To enlarge a pattern shown on a grid, draw a grid with the square the size indicated on the pattern (usually 1 square = 1 in.) then copy the pattern free-hand, one square at a time. This allows you to maintain the correct scale. The first method is to trace the pattern onto tracing paper or tissue paper. Then, if you wish to cut out the design, simply pin the tracing to the fabric and cut along the outline.

If you wish to transfer the design to the paper or fabric without cutting it out (for embroidery, for example), first trace the pattern in the book. Then, turn it over, and go over the outline with a soft lead pencil on the back.

Finally, turn the tracing back over to the right side, place it face up on the fabric, and go over the outline with a pencil again. This method works like carbon paper to transfer the design to the fabric.

Or, after tracing the pattern onto a piece of tissue or tracing paper, place a piece of tailor's carbon (available at fabric stores) between the tracing and the fabric, and go over the outline with a pencil to transfer the design.

A Wooden Shoe Alternative

Pictured are three boots set out on Christmas Eve, waiting to be filled by St. Nick. Wooden shoes are not plentiful in the U.S., and the family inside, lacking a fireplace, found a very American alternative: three pairs of Sears' best foul-weather boots, ribboned and waiting. (The boots are available in children's and adult sizes through the Sears catalogue—a wonderful gift idea—filled by Santa, of course!)

Christmas Pillows

Decorative pillows are a wonderful, welcome gift. Add an embroidered date and they will call to mind a particular holiday season. Fill small pillows with needles from this year's tree to use as sachets year-round. Start a tradition—give a new needle pillow each year! The needles stay fragrant for a couple of years, and the scent can be freshened by dabbing a few drops of pine bath oil on the pillow liner. Your friends will love having the pillows at future Christmastimes.

Since children will insist on keeping them to enjoy all year, there is one design with detachable trees, for a less seasonal gift.

The techniques used in making these pillow gifts are basic ones, employing machine stitching, straight and zigzag, and backstitch embroidery. The sewing is within the ability of the basic home machine operator. Young sewers may need help mastering the feel of using a zigzag stitch. Very young children can help with cutting

out, slip-stitching the liners closed, and gathering the pine needles. (Consider letting them draw the Christmas tree story to use as a pattern instead of using the one provided.) The appliqué pillows could be felt pictures simply glued to a square, then sewn into a pillow by mother or father.

Note: For all pillows, an embroidered date should be stitched before the pillow front and back are sewn together.

A Christmas Tree Tale

This makes a great family gift. The large version stays at the family house, and each family member is given a "memory" needle pillow to take with them as they scatter after the holidays.

Materials needed: for large pillow, approximately 1 sq. ft. each of red, green, blue, and black pinwale corduroy, 1 yd. of heavy white cotton, 1 ft. narrow gold ribbon, polyester fiberfill. For 4 small pillows you will need the same amounts of fabric, plus 1½ yd. muslin, and pine needles saved from the Christmas tree

For the large pillow, cut fabric pictures using the illustration as a guide. Pin the pictures to the blue background. Machine-zigzag the details to the background. Cut four 1-yd. strips of white fabric 2 in. wide. Following the illustration and the instructions in "Fabric Borders," join the four pictures to the white, cross-shaped center border as follows. Start on the right side of the upper left picture square. Then move to the left side of the upper right picture square. Repeat for the bottom two pictures. To join top pictures with bottom, cut a fabric strip as long as the joined top section. Sew the top of this strip to the bottom of the top section. Then, sew the bottom of the strip to the top of the bottom section. The interior edges of the four individual pictures will now be bordered. Border the outside of this central design as indicated in "Fabric Borders." Cut a piece of fabric the size of the bordered picture for the pillow back. Sew front to back, right sides together, leaving an opening at the bottom large enough to insert fiberfill or pine needle liner. Turn inside out and stuff. Hand-sew pillows closed. For small pillows, make liners, ½ in. smaller on each side than the finished pillowcase.

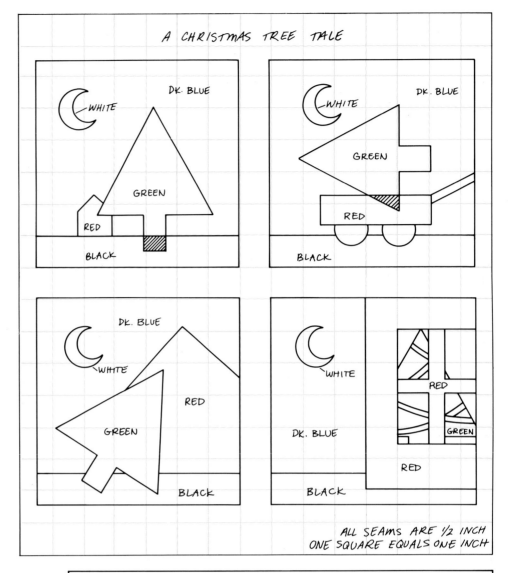

A CHRISTMAS TREE TALE

ALL SEAMS ARE ½ INCH
ONE SQUARE EQUALS ONE INCH

Fabric Borders

Borders of fabric—solid colors and prints—enhance any appliqué or patchwork design beautifully. All of the pillows illustrated have fabric borders. The fabric strips used should be 2½-in. wide and will become 1½-in. wide finished borders when sewn in ½-in. seams. To assemble, cut four 2½-in.-wide strips the length of the appliqué or picture square you are bordering, plus 2½ in. Begin by sewing one strip along the lefthand side of the square, right sides together, with the extra 2½ in. of strip extending from the bottom; turn and press flat. Next, take the second strip and sew the narrow end, right sides together, to the inside edge of the 2½-in. extension; turn and press flat. Then, turning the strip up, with right sides together, sew it along the bottom of the square; turn and press flat. Repeat with the last two strips until the whole square is bordered. If you wish to enlarge any one of the designs, simply add extra border strips in the same way, using the now-bordered picture as the center square.

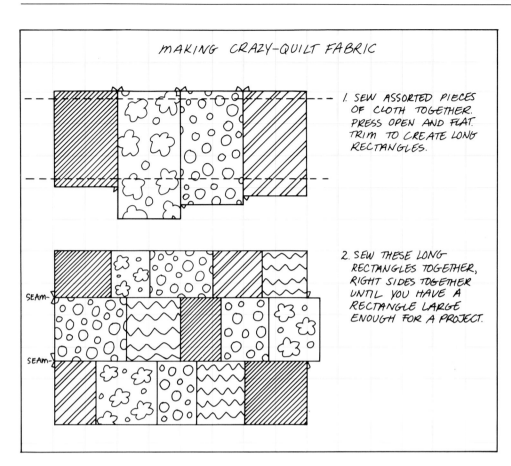

MAKING CRAZY-QUILT FABRIC

1. SEW ASSORTED PIECES OF CLOTH TOGETHER. PRESS OPEN AND FLAT. TRIM TO CREATE LONG RECTANGLES.

2. SEW THESE LONG RECTANGLES TOGETHER, RIGHT SIDES TOGETHER UNTIL YOU HAVE A RECTANGLE LARGE ENOUGH FOR A PROJECT.

SEAM

SEAM

Crazy-Quilt Pillows

These are very easy to make—they can be as large as your ambition. Young sewers will have greater success if their collection of scraps is enlarged with some bold black and white pieces. The simple, clear border helps the centerpiece stand out at its hodgepodge best.

Materials needed: fabric scraps, polyester filling

Look at illustration for a guide to making crazy-quilt strips or come up with your own pattern. Sew the strips, right sides together, to create as large a surface as you'd like. Carefully trim your finished quilt piece to the size rectangle or square you've chosen. Make sure the corners make accurate, neat right angles. Border with fabric strips. Cut a piece of backing from a fabric piece as large as the total crazy quilt with border. Sew front to back, right sides together. Leave an opening to insert fiberfill. Turn inside out. Stuff. Stitch pillow closed.

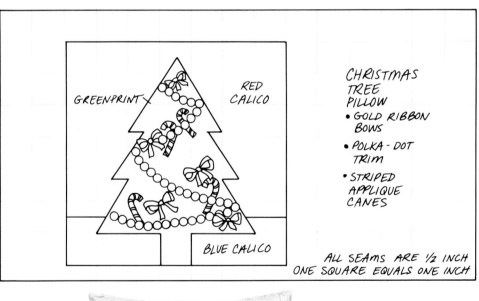

GREENPRINT

RED CALICO

BLUE CALICO

CHRISTMAS TREE PILLOW
• GOLD RIBBON BOWS
• POLKA-DOT TRIM
• STRIPED APPLIQUE CANES

ALL SEAMS ARE 1/2 INCH
ONE SQUARE EQUALS ONE INCH

Christmas Tree Pillow

This pillow is especially appropriate as a gift to a person with a "filled-to-overflowing" Christmas tree. Try approximating the look of your friend's tree with trim or special appliqués.

Materials needed: 12-in. square of fabric for pillow back, 7-in. square of cloth for picture background, bright pieces of cloth, trim, tiny gold ribbon bows, star, polyester filling

Cut out the fabric picture as illustrated. Pin the tree to the 7-in. background, pinning trim in place. Machine-appliqué picture using a narrow-width zigzag for the tiny details. Sew on bows by hand. Border the picture with fabric strips, as in "A Christmas Tree Tale" instructions. Cut a fabric back 9 in. square, as large as the bordered picture. Sew seams together on all sides, right sides facing, leaving an opening at the bottom large enough to insert fiberfill or a pine needle liner cut 1/2 in. smaller than the outer pillow size.

Country House with Detachable Trees

Materials needed: two 1-ft. square pieces of cloth, country print fabric pieces, gold rickrack, polyester filling

Cut out the house picture as in the illustration *(right).* Pin pieces in place on one of the square pieces of cloth, then machine-appliqué. This is your picture base. Cut out 4 Christmas tree shapes. Pin rickrack to 2 of them. Tack in place. With right sides together, sew a plain and decorated tree together with a ¼-in. seam, leaving the base of the tree open for filling. Turn right side out, fill, and stitch closed. Border the picture with country print strips. Use the second square for the pillow back; make sure it is the same size as the bordered picture. Sew front to back, right sides together, leaving an opening to insert fill. Turn inside out. Fill and stitch closed. Pin the trees to the finished pillow with tiny safety pins.

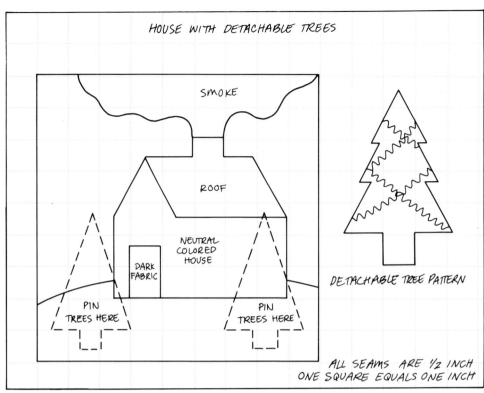

HOUSE WITH DETACHABLE TREES

SMOKE

ROOF

NEUTRAL COLORED HOUSE

DARK FABRIC

PIN TREES HERE

PIN TREES HERE

DETACHABLE TREE PATTERN

ALL SEAMS ARE ½ INCH
ONE SQUARE EQUALS ONE INCH

Tips on Machine Appliqué

Number one rule: Practice before you begin a project! If you are using lightweight fabrics, cut a piece of slightly heavier cloth to back the entire picture surface, pin it in place, and sew as one with the picture. This will give a smoother, more uniform look to the stitching. Assemble all of your appliqué projects, cut and ready to sew, before you begin. Complete all of the sewing with a particular color of thread before changing threads. Use sharp needles. Center the zigzag stitch on the edge of the picture piece, half on the background, half on the appliqué.

Country Kitchen Tableware

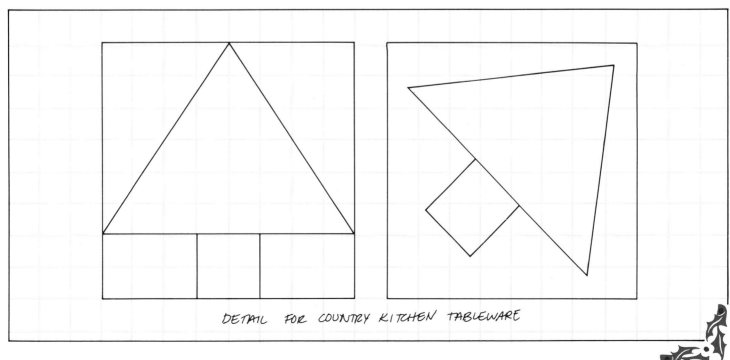

DETAIL FOR COUNTRY KITCHEN TABLEWARE

Pictured on page 101 are a table runner, placemat, and napkins—all made from checkered dish toweling. The woven stripes and checks are reminiscent of Amish rug runners. The fabric is widely available in finished 18-in. widths. The pine tree design will be useful year-round. The runner will be especially appreciated by friends with modern "island" kitchens, for their holiday buffets.

Materials needed: *For runner:* one length of 18-in.-wide red dishcloth material, long enough to drape across your counter or table (usually 7 ft. will do), plus 2 ft. of additional red fabric to use as a border, 1 ft. contrasting checks for corners, 1 ft. green checks for pine trees

For 4 placemats: 2 yd. blue 18-in. dishcloth fabric, 1 ft. each of green and red checked fabric

For 4 napkins: 2¼ yd. of 18-in. red fabric, 1 ft. each of blue and green checkered fabric

For runner: trim a 2 ft. length of cloth from the piece of fabric. Trim it on the raw edge to within ½ in. of the red stripe. Sew this stripe to the end of the runner. Do the same with other stripe from the 2-ft. length. Hem the raw edges. Cut four 4-in. squares of blue cloth and machine-appliqué them to the corner of the borders. Cut 4 green checked Christmas trees from four 4-in. squares of green fabric and appliqué those to the blue square.

For placemats: cut blue fabric into four 14×18-in. rectangles. The 14-in. edge will be hemmed. Turn and press the raw edges of each mat twice, ¼ in. at each turn. Sew with a straight stitch. Appliqué a 4-in. square of red cloth to the lower right corner of each mat, then a pine tree on top of the red square. The finished mat will be 18×12 in.

For napkins: cut the red checked fabric into four 19×18-in. rectangles. The 19-in. side is unfinished and will have to be hemmed on the raw edge. Appliqué a 4-in. blue rectangle to each of the napkins. Appliqué a green pine tree cut from a 4-in. square to each blue square. The finished napkin will be 18×18 in.

White-on-White Napkins

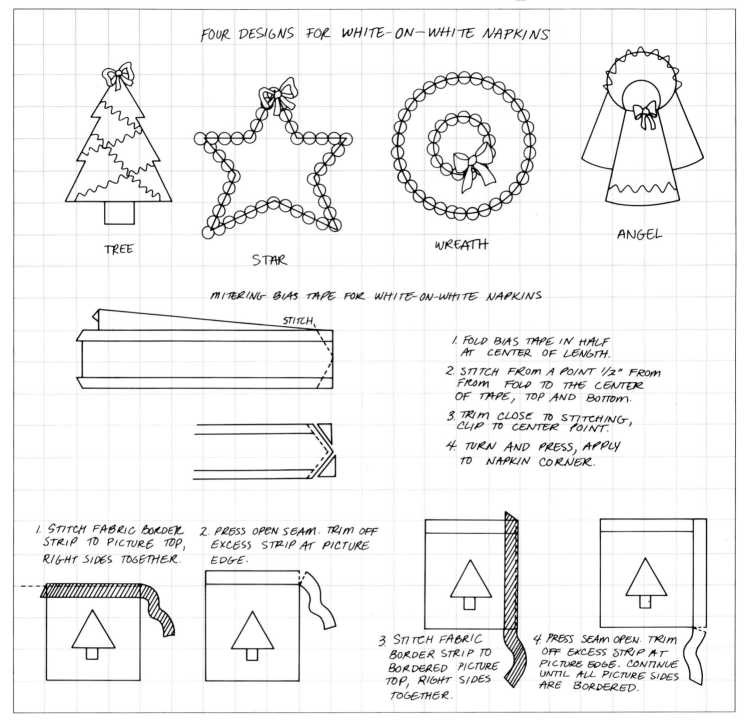

FOUR DESIGNS FOR WHITE-ON-WHITE NAPKINS

TREE

STAR

WREATH

ANGEL

MITERING BIAS TAPE FOR WHITE-ON-WHITE NAPKINS

STITCH

1. FOLD BIAS TAPE IN HALF AT CENTER OF LENGTH.

2. STITCH FROM A POINT 1/2" FROM FROM FOLD TO THE CENTER OF TAPE, TOP AND BOTTOM.

3. TRIM CLOSE TO STITCHING, CLIP TO CENTER POINT.

4. TURN AND PRESS, APPLY TO NAPKIN CORNER.

1. STITCH FABRIC BORDER STRIP TO PICTURE TOP, RIGHT SIDES TOGETHER.

2. PRESS OPEN SEAM. TRIM OFF EXCESS STRIP AT PICTURE EDGE.

3. STITCH FABRIC BORDER STRIP TO BORDERED PICTURE TOP, RIGHT SIDES TOGETHER.

4. PRESS SEAM OPEN. TRIM OFF EXCESS STRIP AT PICTURE EDGE. CONTINUE UNTIL ALL PICTURE SIDES ARE BORDERED.

These are an elegant addition to the Christmas table—the perfect napkin to accompany champagne and sugarplums!

Materials needed: 4 purchased white dinner napkins (not damask), 1 pkg. of 7/8-in.-wide single-fold bias tape, 1 sq. ft. of white fabric, white rickrack, white polkadot trim, 1/8-in. ribbon, embroidery floss Using the patterns for Christmas details—tree, wreath, star, angel—that are provided, make a tracing of each; use these as your master patterns. Cut one design from each on the small piece of fabric called for. For each napkin cut a 10-in. strip of bias tape. Miter each strip as shown in the illustration. Press the tape in half lengthwise. Press under 1/4 in. at each end. Fit and pin the tape around the corner of the napkin. Sew in place with a straight stitch very close to the tape edge. Pin cut designs to the corners of the napkins and machine-appliqué to the napkin cloth. Add trim or embroidered detail by hand.

Swags and Chains

Swags of greens and vines have such a graceful appeal. They can transform a stair, a mantel, a doorway, more surely than any other decorative touch. Soft ribboned pine roping lends a traditional air to the most modern decor. Rows of paper and popcorn swags add whimsy to a Christmas tree—whether decorated with balls and tinsel or gingerbread men and cloth bows.

Wild Vine Swags

Materials needed: vines, thin florist's wire, dried flowers, ribbon

Collect or buy wild vines (honeysuckle, Virginia creeper, etc.) in lengths of at least 10 ft. Lay 3 or 4 vines in a straight line on the floor, wrapping them with 3 or 4 other vines. Repeat this process until you have the desired density for your swag. (You may need to wire them together to hold their shape.) These natural, rangy swags are easily bent into graceful bough shapes and are beautiful when decorated with dried flowers, pine cones, and bows.

Natural Evergreen

Materials needed: evergreen roping, artificial fruit, ribbons, pine cones, etc.

It is easiest to attach roping to a door or window frame by stapling the center of a strand of wire to the frame, then wrapping that along the roping in several places around its length. On staircases, it is easiest to tie the roping onto the rails with ribbon.

Chains

Materials needed: construction paper or ribbon in 2 or 3 different colors, double-sided gift-wrap paper, paperclips

The endless chains we all made of construction paper as children also can be made using many other materials to create charming decorations. Along with the numerous designs available in double-sided gift-wrap paper, stiff calico ribbons are perfect—and precisely the right width. To make a paper chain, cut strips about 3/4-in. wide and 5-in. long. A paper cutter makes this a lot easier.

Bend a strip into a circle, fasten

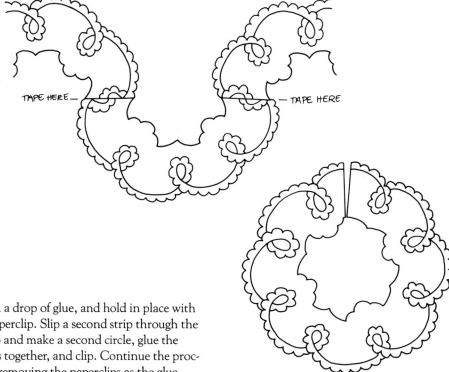

with a drop of glue, and hold in place with a paperclip. Slip a second strip through the loop and make a second circle, glue the ends together, and clip. Continue the process, removing the paperclips as the glue dries (after about 5 loops), and reusing the clips as you go. If you are using double-sided paper, alternate the outer sides of the paper to add interest.

Ribbon chains are made in the same way, and although they cost more, they last for years if stored in a box.

Chains are festive on the Christmas tree, or used as swags around windows and doorways, where they can hang alone or be combined with greens.

Paper Lace

Materials needed: 3 to 5 pkg. of 8-in. paper doilies, transparent tape

Trim the solid patterned center from each of the doilies, clipping through the circle once as shown above. Join doilies end to end, taping them together right side up, upside down, etc., as in the illustration.

Roping

Fresh evergreen boughs are everyone's favorite Christmas decorating material; they are symbolic of the season and they smell so good! There are many different natural materials that make good roping. Balsam is a favorite for its rich fragrance. White pine is soft, easy to use, and drapes well. The material doesn't have to have needles—boxwood and other plants with small leaves work just as well, and cedar makes a lovely, fragrant garland.

Materials needed: cotton clothesline rope, evergreen boughs, fine florist's wire

To keep the rope in place as you work, tie it between two firm objects, such as a table leg and a door knob, and work along it.

Cut greens in 4- to 5-in. lengths and bundle 3 or 4 of them together into a little bouquet. Wrap the stems together twice with fine wire. Make a whole bag of these little bundles (a job that you don't have to do in one sitting, so it is less tedious than it sounds).

Wire these bundles to the stretched rope so that each bundle covers the stems of the preceding one. Use fine wire, wrapping it around the rope as you go. You can make the roping fuller by using more bundles per foot, thinner by using fewer. (Tip: if you get pitch on your hands, rub well with shortening and wash with soap.)

These ropes are perfect for spiraling around banisters or newel or lampposts, or draping around a window frame. The easiest way to hang roping is to put a thin nail into the back of the window frame where it joins the wall (so the hole won't show later), and hang the swag over it. Wide windows and arched doors will need a center nail as well. Place a bow or a bundle of pinecones or dried flowers at the corners if you like.

Roping can be decorated with bunches of pinecones or entwined with strung popcorn for accent. Short pieces can be laid around a punch bowl to form a wreath. Be careful when you use roping on a mantel, however, if you plan to light a fire. Real evergreens should never be near an open fire or woodstove, since they become very flammable as they dry.

Christmas Paper Work

Do you remember making strings of paper dolls as a child?

Look what has evolved from that childhood paper-and-scissors art: beautiful end-to-end holiday cutouts to decorate gifts, windows, and trees. The shapes are simple, highlighted by details of sequins, foil, cut paper, or paint. Use good-quality paper (avoid construction paper)—the cutouts pictured here are made from flint paper, available at art supply stores. Wrapping paper in solid colors also works well.

Another wonderful paper craft ideally suited for holiday decorating is the Japanese art of origami. Charming on a Christmas tree, origami creations are also fun to perch throughout the house, and they are a delightful addition to place cards. See page 112 for instructions for making a wonderful origami penguin ornament.

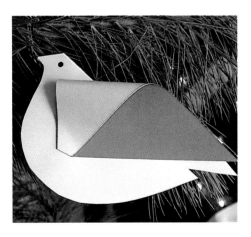

Papercutting

Papercutting is an ancient folk art found in cultures as diverse as those of China, Mexico, Switzerland, and the Orient. Today, in Mexico, certain Indians cut crop idols from folded paper and plant them with seeds in hopes of an abundant harvest. In the Germanic countries papercutting is called Scherenschnitten, and it is from examples made by early German immigrants to Pennsylvania that we take our inspiration. A common German papercut was a repeating motif cut to lay along the edge of a cupboard shelf. Mantel decorations can be made in the same way.

Papercut Angel Ornament

Materials needed: sturdy white and yellow paper (construction paper will not work), gold paper, white thread, red and black fine-line marking pens, small scissors, white glue

Trace or transfer the body of the angel pattern on this page onto white paper (see page 95). Trace the wings on the yellow paper and the halo on the gold. Cut out the shapes and carefully clip the slit in the body. Draw the face on the angel.

Make a loop of thread and secure the knot at the dot on the angel's head. Put additional drops of glue on each side of the head and press the halo in place. Let the glue dry. Fold wings in half and push them through the slit from the back of the body. Bend wings outward to desired position. When the angel hangs on the tree, the slightest movement of the air will cause it to flutter.

SLIP FOLD THROUGH SLIT
IN CENTER OF ANGEL

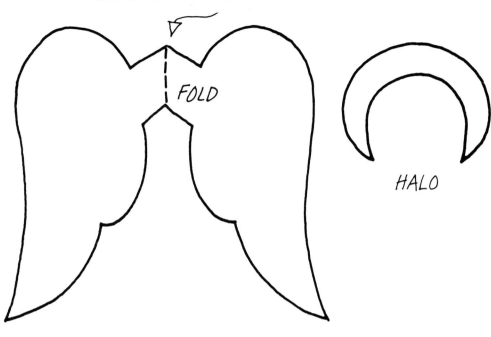
FOLD

HALO

GLUE THREAD LOOP HERE
FOR HANGING

GLUE GOLD HALO HERE

SLIT

WINGS WILL STAND OUT IN BACK
OF ANGEL, HANDS IN FRONT

Chains of Angels

Materials needed: a roll of fairly thin white shelf paper or other thin rolled paper and small, sharp, pointed scissors

Measure the length of the mantel and cut a strip of paper the same length and 2¹/₂ in. wide. Fold the paper in half, then fold back and forth like an accordion, making each fold 4 in. wide. If there is not enough paper at the end to make a complete fold, leave the last pieces longer than the rest.

Trace or lightly sketch the angel design from this page onto one side of the folded stack, making sure that the trumpet faces toward the end that has all the folds, and the skirt toward the end with the two cut edges. Cut through all layers, following the traced outline. If the paper is too heavy, work with one half at a time, tracing the motif on each side. You may find a sharp paper knife easier to use on the area between the arm and chin.

If there is extra paper left at the ends, fold the leftover flap in half and cut a heart shape into it. If the piece is over 2¹/₂ in., fold it in fourths and make two hearts to fill out the edges. When the strip is completed, unfold and tape it to the edge of the mantel.

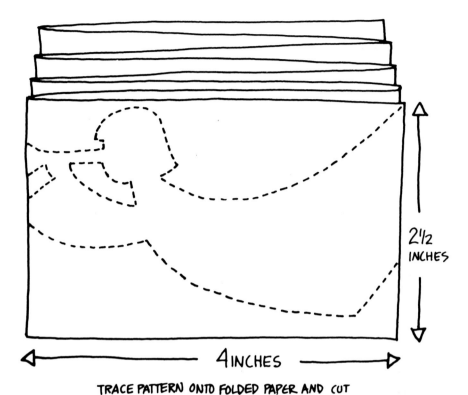

2¹/₂ INCHES

4 INCHES

TRACE PATTERN ONTO FOLDED PAPER AND CUT

PLACE ON FOLD

PLACE ON EDGE

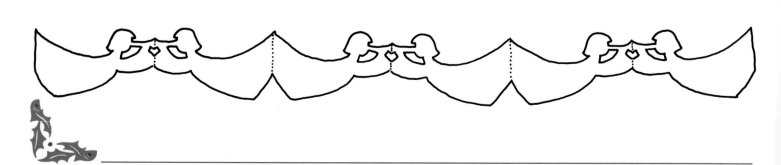

Papercut Christmas Cards

Materials needed: lightweight, good-quality colored papers (Japanese origami paper is the best and readily available at craft and hobby supply stores), sharply pointed scissors, plain greeting cards (either store-bought or homemade), spray adhesive

Before you begin, keep in mind that your papercut should be in proportion with the size of your greeting card. Your papercut design should be small enough so that it is surrounded and set off by some white space at the edges of your card.

The paper for these designs must be folded before being cut. This can be done in two ways for different results.

Fold the paper accordion style to create a chain or repeating design; this method works best with rectangular cards. Or fold the paper in quarters, and cut along the two folded edges to create a "snowflake" design, which unfolds to reveal one larger design. This method works best with square cards. Feel free to experiment.

After the paper is folded, lightly sketch a simple design on the back of one side. Be sure the design reaches all the way to both edges on an accordion fold and to the center or both sides of a circular fold so that the final piece will hold together. Keep designs simple—a row of teddy bears, gingerbread figures, or houses in brown, angels with candles, Christmas trees in green, sleighs, or birds. Nearly any simple motif can be adapted to the paper-doll chain style of cutting. Details can be snipped with fingernail scissors. Most can be used in a circle as well.

After you have cut the design, spray the back with adhesive and place it on the card, centering carefully. Or, make larger designs and mount them on richly colored matte board to frame for holiday pictures.

Origami Penguin Ornament

The Japanese have perfected paper folding (origami) to such a fine art that they can create nearly any animal or bird with amazing accuracy. This penguin is simple enough for even the beginning paper folder, but makes a perfect tree ornament, package decoration, or gift tag.

Materials needed: 6-in. square of black origami paper that is black on one side and white on the other (available at crafts, hobby, and art supply stores). Paper that is black on both sides (such as construction paper) will not work.

With the black side down, fold the paper diagonally to mark the center and unfold. Then fold the upper left and lower right corners to the center line to make a kite shape (A).

Fold the sides back along the center fold so that the black sides are on the inside (B). Next, fold the top right corner up and at a right angle to the body to form the head (C). Then, unfold this last fold, and repeat on back side. Unfold again.

Using the crease lines formed by the last step, fold the head the opposite way along the creases, so that it encloses the body on both sides. This is called an outside reverse fold (see the diagram). Then, make one short zigzag fold about halfway up the head to form the beak and to hold the head folds together (D).

Fold the wing flaps under to expose more of the white side, keeping this fold parallel to the back fold (E).

Then, fold the bottom point up inside the body (F).

Fold the two bottom points formed by the last step up inside the body, taking care to make them even (G).

Either stand the penguin up by reaching between the two halves and pushing down the bottom fold to form a flat base, or glue a loop of black thread at the top of the head between the two halves in order to hang it.

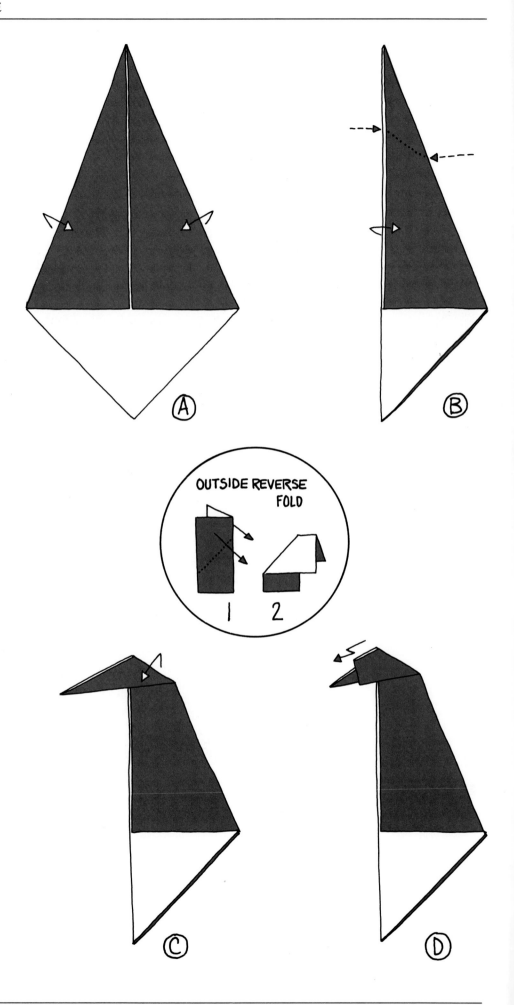

OUTSIDE REVERSE FOLD

1   2

E

F

G

Ornaments

Glass Balls

The centerpiece of holiday decorating is the Christmas tree. Ideas for ornaments fill the pages that follow, and added to your own collections, they will create a tree that is a treasure to behold. A wonderful idea for the arrangement of the tree itself is the use of a basket, instead of a stand, to hold the tree. It is very simple to set up: You will need a basket large enough to hold a bucket, and of a size and shape that suits your tree (a laundry or toy basket might do nicely). Just trim off the lowest branches so that the trunk can rest in the bucket. Surround the trunk with large stones to anchor it, and fill the bucket with water. Wrap a thin wire around the treetop and secure it to the nearest wall for firmer support.

But the tree needs decorations to be the bounteous Christmas green that most people expect. The first three decorations use common Christmas tree ornaments as their foundation: a glass ball, a silver ball, and a feather bird. It is especially nice to start off an evening of ornament making with family and friends with these classic bases. It allows the "designers" to begin well, to have some

success early on (especially important for children), contributing to the enthusiasm and creativity of the holiday artists.

Paper flags: Just curl the paper flags around their wooden "pole," then insert by lifting up the metal cap of the ornament.

Trimmed sheet music: Cut a 3-in. length of music so it measures approximately ½ in. narrower than the diameter of the ball. Place it inside the ornament.

Dried flowers: This decoration requires so little work and becomes almost magically transformed when it's finished. Drop dried flowers one by one into the ball, then replace the cap and tie a ribbon around the top.

Curled paper ribbon: This festive ornament can be kept out until New Year's Day. First, cut 4 or 5 pieces of paper ribbon into 6-in. pieces. Curl at both ends. Place the ribbons in the glass ball so that ⅔ of the ribbon is inside. Drape the other ⅓ over the lip of the ball and secure the top.

Special messages: Write whatever Christmas greeting or message you want on a strip of paper approximately 6 in. long. Color it if you wish to add an extra festive touch. Curl the paper and insert.

Silver Balls

Stickers: Use the self-adhesive kind.

Silver bells: Search through your collection of Christmas treasures for an appropriate addition to a silver ball. The bells shown in the photograph are part of an old decoration. Glue the treasure onto the neck of the ball with white glue.

Gold animals: Another small treasure can be a plastic animal from the dime store. Here it is painted gold and attached with white glue.

Fruit: A bunch of papier-mâché or plastic fruit can add color to a tree. Glued to the neck of the ball, the fruits' leaves hold the fruit and wires in place. The bows are also glued on.

"Earth": Children can transform a silver ball into a very special ornament using paint pens made especially for glass.

Ribbon balls: Thoroughly saturate a length of ribbon with liquid starch. Wrap it around the ball and tie a bow. Wipe off any excess starch on the ball with a damp sponge. Allow to dry.

Lace appliqué: Cut designs from pieces of lace fabric or trim. Saturate the lace with liquid starch. Apply the lace to the ball, wiping off excess starch with a damp sponge. Allow to dry.

Feather Doves

Ribbon: Simply tie a ribbon loosely around the bird's neck.

Fig branch: Trim a few artificial leaves for effect and glue them under the bird's beak.

Carrying bells: Buy a set of small bells and silver trim. Tie the trim to the bells in a bow. Glue to the bird's feet.

Music: Cut a line of sheet music, roll it, fold it, then glue it to the bird's beak.

Child on wings: The seat is made from a piece of ribbon; the child, a small doll from the dime store. Glue the ribbon into place first. Then glue the child to the ribbon.

Working with Burlap

For the burlap ideas in this book, there are a few time-saving tricks that will greatly simplify your efforts. First, always begin with unwashed burlap. Second, cut accurately. This is the key to bringing out the beauty of this rough, natural material. When cutting lengths of burlap, begin at the selvage edge of the cloth. Then carefully trim the piece of all selvage edges. Measure the width of the strips from this trimmed edge. An easy way to mark the necessary width is to clip a burlap "length" thread, pull it out, and use the empty space in the weave as a guide for cutting. When fraying a very long strip of burlap, try clipping the fabric thread from the edge of the length to the unfrayed edge of the center of the length. The strands of burlap are then easier to pull out.

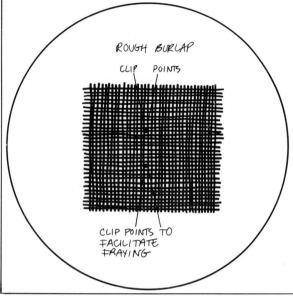

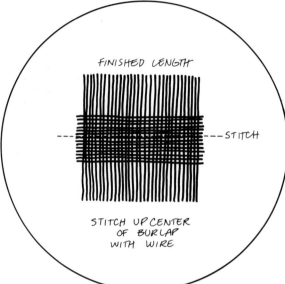

Burlap Wreaths

These tiny wreaths are lovely on the tree, on doll's houses, or used as napkin rings.

Materials needed: 8-ft. length of burlap, heavy florist's wire

Fray the lengths of burlap $^3/_4$-in. on each side of the length, leaving intact a $^3/_4$-in. strip down the center of the length. Using the wire as your thread, sew down the center of the length with $^1/_4$-inch running stitches, gathering the burlap as you sew. Trim the wire to 12 in. Tie the ends together. Decorate with ribbon, flowers, or ornaments wired onto the base wire.

Burlap Bird's Nests

Materials needed: burlap threads (left over from wreath making), liquid starch, white glue, 1 ft. gold $^1/_2$-in. ribbon, candy eggs or feather birds

Gather eight to ten 2-ft. strands of burlap thread in your hand. Coat the strands with liquid starch. Using the round end of a light bulb or soup ladle as a form, wrap and shape a nest by pressing the threads against the bulb. Repeat the process once more, wiping the excess starch off with a damp sponge. Remove the nest from the mold before it is completely dry. When the starch is dry, glue the ribbon to the underside of the nest with white starch, tying it in a bow on top. Add candy eggs, a feathered bird, or tiny glass balls to the nest.

Children's Blocks

These ornaments are simply two elements glued together. Inexpensive, widely available wooden toy ornaments are greatly improved when combined with blocks. Match up the alphabet blocks with objects that begin with the block's letter; it makes a fun project for preschoolers and young readers (see "Alphabet Blocks," page 141).

Materials needed: small wooden blocks, assorted small treasures (see page 127) and inexpensive wooden toy ornaments, white glue, gold thread, gold spray paint

Simply glue the objects to appropriate alphabet blocks. Add a gold thread for hanging, if needed. For a more elegant effect, spray gold when the glue is dry.

Fabric Fans

While these fans can also be made of paper, fabric gives them a quality look. When you use scraps of fabric reminiscent of your childhood (a piece of lace, upholstery fabric, a scrap from a favorite dress), the fans become keepsakes, reviving memories year after year.

Materials needed: liquid starch, rectangles of fabric or lace 10 to 12 × 4 to 5 in., trim, tassels, gold thread

Saturate your choice of fabric or lace rectangles with liquid starch. Lay out strips of saturated ribbon or fabric to form borders on the edges of the wet rectangles for interesting detail. The starch will act as glue to hold it together. Fan-fold the wet rectangles, making 7 to 10 vertical folds. Place the wet fans on a hard surface and weight them with a book until set and dry. (Line the cover of the book with foil to protect it.) Carefully open the folds, tying the ends with ribbon and decorating by tying on tassels. Add a gold thread for hanging on the tree.

Clothespin Dolls

Materials needed: round-headed wooden clothespins, medium-weight florist's wire, narrow beige bias tape, fine-line marking pens in red and black, black wide marker, Aileen's Tacky Glue or other thick, quick-holding white glue, small pieces of fabric, lace, trims, ribbon, and needle and thread.

Wrap the center of a 12 in. length of florist's wire around the "shoulders" of a clothespin to form arms. Then fold back the extra wire to make the arms the right length. Secure with glue, and wrap the clothespin with a criss-cross of bias tape over the wire. Hold the tape in place with another spot of glue. While this is drying, draw a face on the clothespin with fine markers and paint hair and shoes on with the wide black marker. Wrap the wire arms with bias tape, folding the tape neatly at the ends to form hands. Secure tape with a few stitches. Cut blouse from fabric folded at shoulders (see diagram), stitch lace to cuffs. With right sides of fabric facing, sew side seams from waist to cuff. Turn right side out and run gathering stitches around neck opening. Put blouse on doll and pull neck gathering tight. Cover neck with a lace ruffle and stitch or glue in place.

Cut a rectangle of matching fabric to make the skirt. Hem the bottom or cover the edge with lace. Then, with right sides of fabric facing, sew side seam. Put the skirt on the doll and tie a ribbon around its waist to cover gathering. For the pantalets traditional to these dolls, cut 2 sections of wide lace or eyelet and glue each around a leg so the fancy edge shows below the skirt. Costumes can be varied by using wide embroidered trims or ribbons for the skirts and lace or eyelet for the aprons. More hair can be added by glueing on some black yarn or a topknot can be made from a small button glued to the top of the head. A cap can be made from a small circle of lace gathered around the edge or a sunbonnet folded from ribbon. A cord or ribbon loop will turn the doll into a tree ornament.

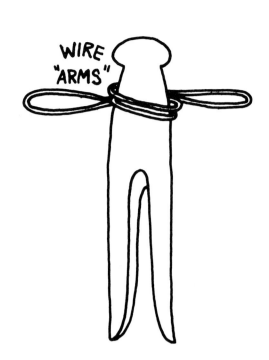

WIRE "ARMS"

BIAS TAPE

DOLL'S ROBE

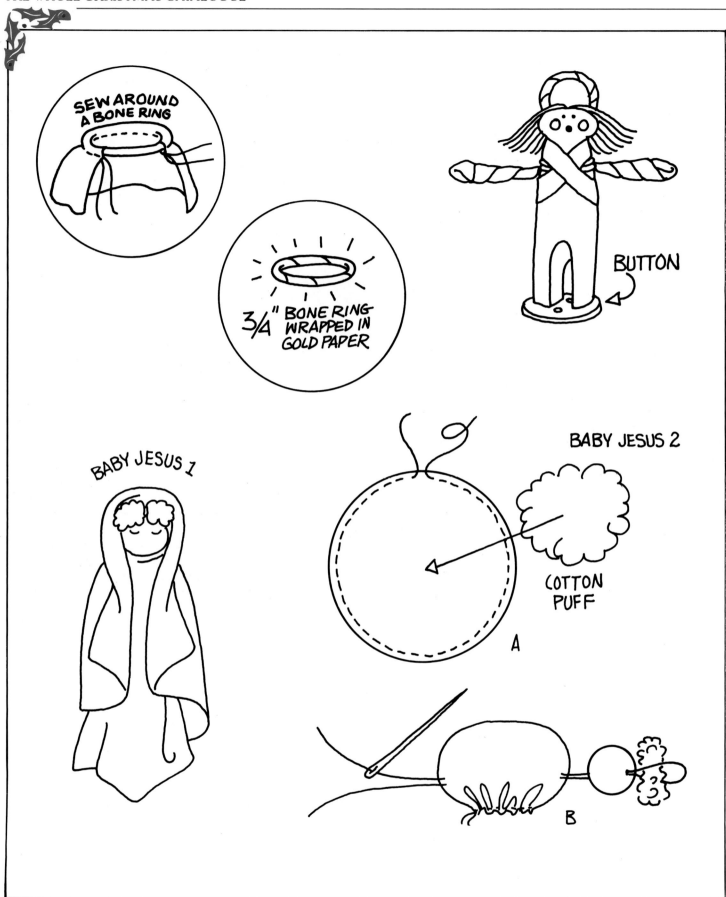

SEW AROUND A BONE RING

3/4" BONE RING WRAPPED IN GOLD PAPER

BUTTON

BABY JESUS 1

BABY JESUS 2

COTTON PUFF

A

B

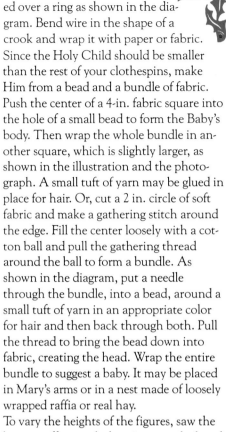

Clothespin Crèche

Materials needed: in addition to the materials listed for clothespin dolls, you will need ³/₄ in. bone rings, large flat buttons, gold paper, a small round wooden bead, and silk, velvet, and other fabric scraps in solid colors

Make basic dolls as directed in instructions for clothespin dolls, but dress them in flowing robes—velvet for the kings and simpler fabrics for the Holy Family and shepherds. Thin fabrics or lace are good for angels. Make halos for the angels from bone rings wrapped with narrow strips of gold paper. The shepherds' headgear can be stitched over a ring as shown in the diagram. Bend wire in the shape of a crook and wrap it with paper or fabric. Since the Holy Child should be smaller than the rest of your clothespins, make Him from a bead and a bundle of fabric. Push the center of a 4-in. fabric square into the hole of a small bead to form the Baby's body. Then wrap the whole bundle in another square, which is slightly larger, as shown in the illustration and the photograph. A small tuft of yarn may be glued in place for hair. Or, cut a 2 in. circle of soft fabric and make a gathering stitch around the edge. Fill the center loosely with a cotton ball and pull the gathering thread around the ball to form a bundle. As shown in the diagram, put a needle through the bundle, into a bead, around a small tuft of yarn in an appropriate color for hair and then back through both. Pull the thread to bring the bead down into fabric, creating the head. Wrap the entire bundle to suggest a baby. It may be placed in Mary's arms or in a nest made of loosely wrapped raffia or real hay.

To vary the heights of the figures, saw the bottom off some clothespins to make kneeling figures and fold their robes under them. Glue large buttons to the bases of all the figures to give them stability. The buttons can be covered by the robes.

Accessories such as wings, crowns, and the gifts of the Kings can be made from gold paper, or the crowns can be made of gold trim glued into circles around the heads of the dolls.

Wreaths

Holiday decorating begins at the door with a beautiful wreath. Here is a potpourri of ideas to choose from. Create a wreath for your family or friends that reflects the household it is given to. A second wreath will be beautiful over a mantel, a sideboard, near the children's table. A dried wreath is a fragrant addition to a powder room. A wreath made of everlasting materials—vines, wood, fabric—will be a treasured gift that will be used year after year.

Green Wreaths

Materials needed: crimped wire single-wreath frame, fine florist's wire, evergreen boughs

The best greens are those with short needles and long staying power; balsam and the firs are the best, but spruce and even white pine will do nicely, as will cedar and juniper. Hemlock drops its needles too quickly and Scotch pine will leave you looking as though you have been in a cat fight!

Cut the boughs into short pieces, 6 to 8 in. long. Attach the wire to the frame by twisting it a few times. Place 2 to 3 sprigs of greens parallel with the frame, not at right angles to it. Wrap once or twice with wire to secure. Place another bundle of greens against the wire frame, stems in the same direction as the first, but so the needles cover the stems of the previous bundle. Wire in place and continue to work around the frame in this manner. Keep the wire tight; if it seems to loosen easily, tie it around the frame after every few bundles. Leave enough wire at the end to make a hanging loop.

Pine Needle Village

Materials needed: one 8-in. straw wreath base, long pine needles, a toy village made of wood, baby's breath, white glue, tape, brown thread, 2½ yd. of 1½-in. ribbon, cardboard

Gather the needles. (Red, Scotch, and white pine are recommended.) Carefully lay the needles against the straw base, wrapping with thread as you go, to secure them. Pay attention to one area at a time and continue around the entire wreath. Cut out pieces of cardboard the size of the village pieces. Glue the cardboard in place where you are going to position the village. Arrange village and people on the wreath, gluing them to the cardboard. Use tape to secure them until the glue dries. Fill in spaces with baby's breath, tucking them under the cardboard or, if necessary, gluing them in and around the village. Wrap the ribbon around the wreath, tying it in a bow at the base of the village (see photograph).

Wild Vine Wreath

Materials needed: freshly cut vines (honeysuckle, Virginia creeper, etc.) in 4- to 6-ft. lengths, wire, a bird's nest (found or homemade—see "Burlap Bird's Nests," page 117), a feather bird, dried hydrangea flowers, baby's breath

Trim fresh vines of their leaves. Tie 4 lengths together at one end with wire. Simply bend and shape them into a heart. Lay flat on a table. Allow the shaped vines to dry out overnight under the weight of one or two heavy books. Make a second bunch of 4 vines. Tie these together at one end and lightly wire this bunch to the shaped vines at the base of the heart. Twist the unshaped length of vines around the first bunch, bending them as you go around the heart. Trim off excess and secure with wire. Insert branches of hydrangea. Lightly glue the nest to the hydrangea; place bird in nest. You may want to secure the bird with glue as well.

Packing Straw Wreath

Materials needed: one 8-in. straw wreath base, packing straw (saved from shipments), candy canes, 2 yd. of 1½-in. ribbon, thread or string

Gently pull the packing straw apart so that it's loosely meshed together and not in tight bunches. Wrap it around the straw base until the entire wreath is lightly covered. With the ribbon, tie a bow around each of the candy canes. Tie these canes onto the wreath with string or thread. This will hold both the straw and the candy in place.

Mexican Spice Wreath

Materials needed: one 8- to 12-in. grapevine wreath. (See "Simple Grapevine Wreath," page 129), fine florist's wire, needle and thread, several types of whole dried peppers, stick cinnamon, bay leaves, ¼-in. gold fabric ribbon

With a needle and thread, sew together bunches of 3 or 4 small dried red peppers, running the needle through the stems. Tie these to the vine wreath. Secure the larger peppers between vines. Tie bunches of cinnamon sticks to the wreath as shown. Wrap the gold ribbon around the wreath as in the photograph; tie the ends together in a bow. Insert bay leaves under ribbon and between vines for color and fragrance.

Streamers

Materials needed: 3 to 4 pkg. multicolored paper streamers, four 1-yd. strands bright paper ribbon, one 8- or 10-in. wire wreath frame, white glue

Spread glue lightly over all sides of wire frame. Beginning at the inside of each streamer tube, unravel a 2-streamer width of streamers, taking care not to separate into individual curls. Loosely wrap this length around the wire frame and wet with glue. Build up the density of the wreath using this technique. No more glue is necessary, as the streamers hold each other in place. Take care to alternate colors of streamers. In 4 places on the wreath, loosely tie the streamers with curled paper ribbon.

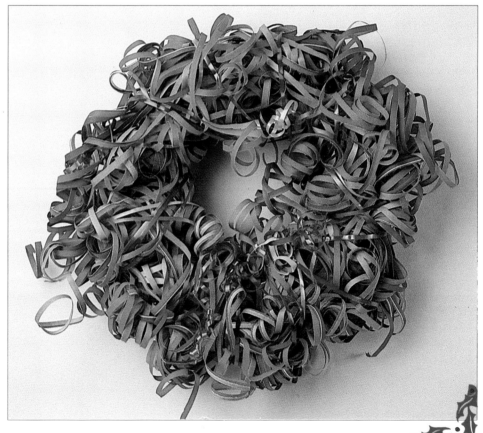

Fresh Everlasting Wreath

Materials needed: one 10- or 12-in. evergreen wreath, assorted dry flowers: statice, roses, baby's breath, yarrow, wheat, strawflowers

Insert the stems of the everlastings into the green wreath. The branches will hold them securely.

Raffia Wreaths

Materials needed: 2-in. wide bundle of raffia strands at least 1 yd. long, wide calico ribbon for bow, optional dried grasses or flowers for decoration

Without tangling the rest of the raffia, carefully pull out 2 or 3 strands. Using one of these strands, firmly tie the entire bundle together at one end. Divide the bundle into three bunches and braid firmly. As you braid, always pull the bunch at the left a little tighter than the one on the right. This will cause the braid to curve slightly and eventually form a circle. When the wreath is the proper size, or when you've almost reached the end of your raffia, cross the ends, leaving a few inches of raffia on each end. Tie the two ends together with a strand of raffia, crossing them so that the tails hang evenly. Wrap the tie over and over to secure it and to keep the wreath in an even circle. Untie the first end and shake loose its strands. Trim ends to match. The wreath may be decorated with dried herbs, flowers, grasses, or a calico bow. Tiny raffia wreaths for the tree are made in the same way from just a few strands of raffia. Narrow red or green satin ribbon makes attractive bows for these.

Small Treasures

Collect a box of found objects to inspire you when you get the creative urge at Christmas time. Included could be small toys, party favors, artificial fruit, parts of jewelry and old ornaments, fabrics and trim, dried flowers. The simplest, most ordinary trinkets become charming and whimsical when taken out of context, painted, combined, and ribboned. And, of course, the addition of personal mementos transforms these ornaments into extra-special treasures.

Golden Toy Wreath

Materials needed: one 8- or 10-in. wire frame, white glue, gold spray paint, transparent tape, ¼-in. gold cloth ribbon, assorted "small treasures"

This wreath is built up in three steps. First, glue an assortment of unpainted, flat-sided objects to the wire frame. Second, spray paint the rest of the "small treasures" *lightly*. (You will have to rotate them to completely cover them with paint, so you will be applying more than one coat of paint in some places.) Glue the dried odd-shaped objects to the flat-sided objects already on the frame. Allow the glue to set. Spray a light top coat of gold paint to the entire wreath. Finally, tie small golden bows to the finished wreath, securing them to any exposed section of the frame. **Note:** This is a very fragile wreath. It is wonderfully fascinating for children. Take care to place it in a high, stationary place.

Green Burlap Wreath

Materials needed: 8 yd. of 6-in.-wide green burlap strips (this yardage can be assembled from different lengths of burlap), 30 in. heavy wire (a straightened coat hanger will do)

See "Working with Burlap," page 116. Fray the lengths of burlap 2 in. on each side, leaving the center 2 in. intact. Gather these lengths on the wire by "sewing" up the center of each strip with the wire, making the "stitches" 1/4 to 1/3 in. apart. Bend the wire into a circle, crimping the ends to close the wreath. Add a bow, tied on with a piece of the burlap thread.

"Natural" Burlap Wreath

Materials needed: 8 yd. of 4-in. burlap strips, 28 in. heavy wire

Follow directions for the Green Burlap Wreath. (The natural burlap gives this wreath a drier look, and the narrower strips used in its creation make it less plush than the preceding wreath.)

Simple Grapevine Wreath

Materials needed: grapevine branches, wire

It is best for grape plants if you harvest the vines once the weather has become cold and the vines are dormant. Cut vines in 3- to 6-ft. lengths. If you are buying the vines from a florist, you may want to ask them to cut the lengths for you. Long vines are easier to work with. If the vines don't bend easily, soak them in hot water. To make a circle, simply hold one end of the vine in one hand and bend the other end into a circle, tucking one end behind the other and securing it with wire. If your vines are short, make several discrete circles, wiring each, and then tie them together by wrapping them with a single long vine. If the vines are long, make your first circle and continue wrapping around the circle for the length of the vine. Tuck and wrap the other individual vines onto the circle and secure each with wire.

This beautiful array of wreaths shows just a few variations of a simple theme. The instructions at left give you the basics; you improvise from that!

Cone Wreaths

Materials needed: Double-wire wreath frame, fine florist wire, white glue, long flexible pinecones, such as white pine or blue spruce, an assortment of other cones and seed pods

Soak the long pinecones in water until they close. Push the wet cones into the space between the two layers of wire on the frame, keeping them close together and making sure they are held securely between the wires. Allow the wreath to dry thoroughly, a process which can be hastened in a very slow oven.

Cut florist's wire into 8- or 9-in. lengths and attach to the stems of the remaining cones, wrapping them with the centers of the wire pieces and leaving both ends free. Place these cones in a second layer on top of the cones in the wire frame. Move them about until you are pleased with the arrangement and balance, then secure by pushing the wires through to the back of the wreath and twisting to hold.

Fill in the spaces and any spots where the frame shows using smaller cones and seed-pods. It may be easier to glue some of these smaller ones in place with white glue. These wreaths may be left in their natural state, or sprayed with clear shellac to give them a shiny finish. They are not usually decorated with bows.

Cornhusk Wreaths

Materials needed: 8 oz. dried inner cornhusks (available at craft supply shops or Mexican grocery stores), several strands of heavy raffia, an 8 in. crinkle-wire wreath frame (from florist or craft supply shops), a large bowl of warm water

Soak husks in water for about 10 minutes. When they soften, work with one at a time, leaving the rest in water. Add more husks to the bottom of the bowl, as you use the softened husks at the top.

Tie one end of the raffia to the wire frame. Take a husk from the water. If it is more than 5 in. wide, tear it in half lengthwise (it will rip like paper). Fold it in half crosswise and gather the ends into a bundle. Be sure to leave the fold round and puffy. Lay this along the wreath frame (NOT at right angles to it)

with one end near the place where the raffia is tied to the frame, and wrap the husk twice with raffia to secure. Repeat with another husk, laying it along the frame just below the first so that it covers the base of the first. Repeat, working along the frame so that the ties are all covered, the wreath is full, and the husks are evenly distributed between the inner and outer

edges. The back of the wreath should be fairly flat.

Continue until the wreath is full of husks. If there are bare spots when you are finished, simply tie additional husks into the spaces to fill it out. Dry wreath thoroughly before storing. Although cornhusk wreaths traditionally do not have bows, feel free to add one. A red calico bow would be attractive.

Cornhusk Stars

Based on the traditional Scandinavian straw stars, these are made of more available cornhusks. They are attractive hanging in windows or on the Christmas tree.

Materials needed: 2 or 3 flat, dry inner cornhusks (available from craft supply shops or Mexican markets), beige sewing thread, 6 in. red gingham cotton ribbon, white glue

Cut cornhusks into 4 strips, about 5 in. long and 1/2 in. wide. The strips can be shorter and narrower as long as they are all the same size.

Form the 4 strips from each cornhusk into two crosses and lay one cross on top of the other. Keep the ends even. Weave thread around the arms of the star, leaving a tail of thread for tying. The thread should go over the top husks and under the bottom ones as shown in the diagram. Wrap the thread around the star twice. The thread will show only on the top four arms. Tie firmly and cut off the excess thread. Clip ends of husks at angles (as shown in the diagram) so they all point the same way.

Cut the ribbon lengthwise to make a narrow strip. Fold in thirds and tie in center with thread, pulling tightly to gather the ribbon into a bow shape. Tie and clip the thread. Attach the bow to the center of the star with a drop of glue. Make a loop of thread, secure it with a knot, and glue it to back of top point of the star. Allow to dry thoroughly before hanging.

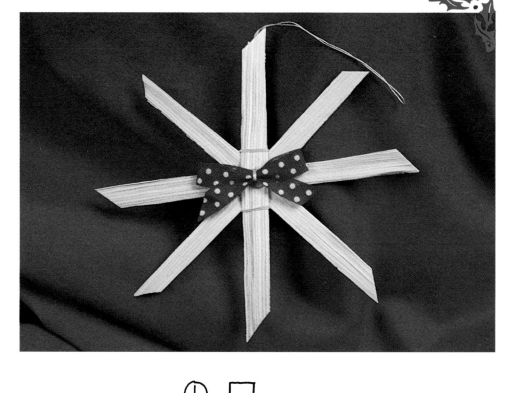

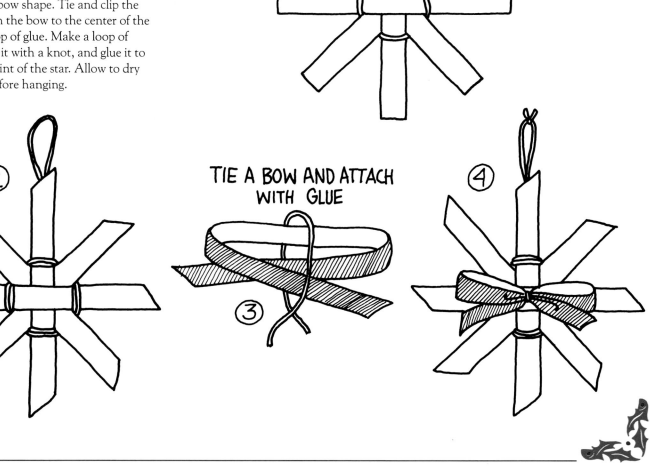

TIE A BOW AND ATTACH WITH GLUE

HOLIDAY ENTERTAINING

Merry Christmas
Parties

Children's Tea with Santa

What better way to begin the Christmas season than with a party for neighborhood children and an appreciative Santa! Parents will be delighted with this charming alternative to visiting Santa Claus at a crowded store. Santa will be most helpful judging the "Pin the Red Nose on Rudolph" contest (who would know better about such matters?). The children will have fun playing the "Mystery Gifts" game. "Charm Necklaces" will be given as party favors—to wear, to eat, or to hang on the tree. Of course

the highlight of the afternoon will be each child's chance to sit on Santa's lap and divulge fondest Christmas wishes. A festive children's tea will be shared with Mr. Claus, featuring a "Gingerman Circus" centerpiece and a special dessert cake decorated in his honor!

This menu, which serves 8 to 10 children, can easily be prepared by youngsters with the help of an adult. The cake should be made the night before the party, but all of the other foods can be prepared a few hours before the tea.

FRUIT—NUTS

CHEESE STARS

TEA SANDWICHES

WARM CINNAMON CIDER

SANTA'S SLEIGH CAKE

GINGERMAN CIRCUS

CHARM NECKLACES

CHEESE STARS

Four ½-in.-thick slices of firm cheese
(such as mild cheddar or Muenster)

Cut cheese in star shapes with a cookie cutter, reserving scraps for a later use.

HAM AND PARSLEY SANDWICHES

1 loaf each thin-sliced wheat and
    thin-sliced white bread,
    crusts removed (save them for the birds)
1 c. butter at room temperature
¼ c. minced parsley
½ c. finely minced red bell pepper
1 lb. ground cooked ham
½ c. mayonnaise
Mustard

Combine ¼ lb. of the butter, the parsley, bell pepper, ham, mayonnaise, and mustard to taste. Lightly spread the tops of all of the bread slices with the remaining butter, then spread two thirds of the slices with the ham mixture. Make 3-layer sandwiches alternating wheat and white bread, topping with a buttered slice. Cut each sandwich twice, into 4 triangles.

OPEN CHRISTMAS SANDWICHES

1 loaf heavy thin-sliced pumpernickel
   bread
1 lb. cream cheese at room temperature
Walnuts
Hard-boiled eggs
Vegetables
Watercress or parsley

Remove the crusts from the bread, and cut
the slices in half. Spread them with cream
cheese and decorate as illustrated with nuts
and vegetables in holiday motifs.

WARM CINNAMON CIDER

1 gal. apple cider
2 cinnamon sticks
2 to 3 whole allspice

Warm (but don't boil) the cider with
cinnamon and allspice. Serve warm.

SANTA'S SLEIGH CAKE

1 batch brownies
½ gal. vanilla ice cream,
   slightly softened
2 candy canes (optional)
1 pint heavy cream

Coconut
Holly leaves
Purchased Santa-and-Sleigh decoration

Using your favorite recipe or a mix, prepare
brownies and cook in a well-greased 8-in.
round pan. Remove from pan in one piece.
Cool.

Spoon ice cream (if you have a larger bowl,
use more ice cream) sprinkled with crushed
peppermint stick into an aluminum or glass
bowl that has a diameter of 8 in. at the top.
Pack the ice cream into this mold and freeze
until hard. Unmold the ice cream by
wrapping a warm towel around the bowl,
and invert it onto the circular brownie. Frost
this "mountain" with heavy cream, whipped
until stiff. Refreeze the cake. When the cream
is frozen hard, loosely cover the cake with foil
and return to the freezer for at least 6 hours.
Fifteen minutes before serving, remove the
cake from the freezer. Transfer it to a serving
plate, sprinkle it lightly with coconut, and
decorate it with holly and the Santa.
Note: The cake base and ice cream can be
any flavors you wish. The cake can also be
served with a dessert chocolate or fruit sauce,
but for children the cake is sweet and rich
enough without the sauce.

GINGERMAN CIRCUS

This assembly is tricky and should be
done in stages for best results.

2 recipes "Ginger People, Places,
   Things" (page 76)
2 recipes "Hard Sculpture Icing" (page
   77)
Pastry tube
8 x 12-in. piece of cardboard covered
   with paper
1 doily

Prepare the gingerbread dough and roll it
out, one batch at a time, into one large
¼-in.-thick rectangle. Using the pattern
provided, cut out heads and bodies from the
dough rectangles. Cut two 4-inch diameter
gingerbread bases for side men.

To assemble your gingermen, plan on
placing the men close together. Using a wide
decorative tip on an icing bag, and using the
icing as glue, glue 3 pairs of arms and thighs
to the base board. Ice the tops of the arms
and thighs and carefully lay bodies on top of
them. Attach forelegs and hands at joints
with icing. When this is set and hard, ice
decorative collars on the bodies. Insert
decorated heads into the icing collars, as in

PYRAMID MEN

CUT SIX PAIRS OF HANDS, ARMS, LOWER LEGS AND UPPER LEGS.

CUT SIX HEADS-

LOWER LEGS

HANDS

CUT SIX BODIES-

ARMS

UPPER LEGS

CUT ONE TOP MAN

CUT TWO ATTENDANTS
ONE SQUARE EQUALS ONE INCH

the illustration. When the heads are set, begin the next layer of men, and so on. Decoratively ice the 3 whole gingermen. Tie candy canes to their arms with ribbon. Secure the 2 side men to their cookie bases with icing. Support them until they are dry. Hold the bases in place with a little icing underneath. Secure the top man with icing at his foot. He will need support until his icing is set also.

Note: It is the 3 whole men that will be most troublesome. If they start to tip, you can add a wood skewer brace behind them, or even a small cardboard prop.

CHARM NECKLACES

These are easy-to-make edible jewelry.

1 recipe each of "Ginger People,
   Places, Things" dough (page 76)
"Rolled Cookies" dough (page 71)

Tinted "Hard Sculpture Icing"
   (page 77)
Sprinkles
1/4-in. paper ribbon

Prepare and roll out the cookie doughs. Using small and large cutters, bake a selection of cookie sizes and shapes. As soon as they come out of the oven, make holes with a toothpick for stringing the cookies. Ice when cool. String on paper ribbon.

Holiday Games

A Christmas version of Pin the Tail on the Donkey, "Pin the Red Nose on Rudolph," will be as popular as the eponymic song. If you have the record, play it to enliven the game. Be creative and have fun making the noses. They can be as big and as crazily colored as you want. The sillier they are, the more fun it will be when they are pinned on Rudolph's toes, antlers, etc.

The little ones will enjoy "Pin the Red Nose on Rudolph" and the "Alphabet Blocks"; children of all ages will have fun with "Mystery Gifts" and "Christmas Verses vs. Verses."

Alphabet blocks, shown below, can be used for a learning game and then as Christmas-tree ornaments. By introducing new blocks and objects, the game can be continued and the children will have more than one ornament to take home.

Pin the Red Nose on Rudolph

Materials needed: 1 large sheet of white poster or mat board, poster paints and brushes, double-stick tape, a blindfold

Using the illustration provided, pencil the drawing onto the board. Color in everything but the snowflakes with poster paint, leaving a small, rough white border all around the painting. When the picture is dry, paint white snowflakes across the entire surface. Paint the noses and cut out as many noses as there are players, attaching double-stick tape to the back of each nose.

Pin the painting to a wall, low enough for children to reach it easily. One at a time, at a point 5 to 10 feet from the painting, blindfold the children and turn them around in place 3 times. Point them in the direction of the reindeer and let them try to attach the nose to the end of Rudolph's face. The winner is the child who comes closest to the mark. After the game, have the children sign the picture around the border as a keepsake of the occasion.

Alphabet Blocks

This is an ornament assembly game that is especially fun for young readers.

Materials needed: see "Children's Blocks," (page 117)

Select as many alphabet blocks as there are children. Gather enough small objects to match the lettered blocks (apple for "A" block, car for "C" block, etc.). Seat children around a small table. Pile the children's blocks and objects in the center of the table. Instruct each child to match an object to a block letter until all the blocks and objects are used up. Help the children glue the toys to the block bases. Tie strings on to hang the decorations from a Christmas tree. Give one to each child as a party favor.

Mystery Gifts

Materials needed: wrapped and ribboned boxes containing 1 gift each. The boxes shouldn't be larger than 1 ft. square, the contents loose within (no packing material, please). Contents are up to your imagination, but should be simple and identifiable if children are playing. A piece of paper with 2 clues to the contents should accompany each box. Each box is given a number. For adults, provide a pencil and paper for each player

Select a "leader" who will be the holder of the lists of clues to the contents of the boxes. First, the leader holds up the box and tells the number of the box to the group. He then passes the box from player to player so that each can "hear" and "feel" its contents. Children guess out loud, adults write down their hunches. The leader reads out the clues. If the object is a watch, a child's clue would perhaps be, "Begins with the letter *W.*" The second could be, "It tells you something." For adults, provide a more puzzling clue: "Available through Tiffany or your pharmacist." The winner is the person who guesses the most box contents. Adults will have a great time preparing intriguing clues!

Christmas Verses vs. Verses

What fun this will be when you've assembled a group that loves to sing—especially if it's a gathering peppered with Mitch Millers, carol aficionados, children, and a piano player!

Materials needed: people who love to sing, a collection of Christmas music, a piano (optional)

The object is to discover who can outsing whom *correctly* in an evening of caroling. It's a fairly noncompetitive project until you reach second and third choruses! Begin by assembling the group in a room. Appoint a "choirmaster" who will hold on to the written verses. Each carol begins with everyone singing, but people have to stop if they forget the verses or melody as the song continues. You will be surprised to discover who outlasts whom. A nice party gift for this crowd would be copies of Christmas sheet music with verses!

Christmas for the Birds

Have you ever thought of including the wildlife of your neighborhood in all the feasting and merriment of the season? Begin a tradition that will charm the children and your gathered friends. Prepare a special treat tree for the birds and squirrels of your neighborhood. Plan a party to decorate it with small squares of suet tied in ribbon, strings of cranberries and popcorn, small net sachets filled with fat or butter, and roping of tiny pretzels strung on paper ribbon. Decorative crackers placed among the pine branches also make endearing ornaments. Use paper ribbon to attach the decorations; make the colors festive. Make sure, too, that it is easy for the birds and squirrels to loosen and remove food gifts tied with the ribbon. You won't have to worry about food—serve the snacks that you'll be using to decorate the tree: popcorn, pretzels, crackers, and cranberries. Add some steaming hot chocolate as the finale and you should have a satisfied crew.

An Ornamental Evening

Plan a party close to Christmas for an evening of making ornaments. Gather your friends and neighbors and add the basic elements of a simple, satisfying supper and shared conversation.

Refer to the "Ornaments" section, page 114, for helpful hints. You'll probably want to make less complicated decorations: The ornaments based on the silver balls, the glass balls, and the feather birds are recommended. Set out the supplies for the tree decorations and add cooked gingermen that haven't been iced, cranberries and popcorn to be strung, and holiday music for a festive evening.

The menu below serves 8 people. It's a simple supper that will complement the evening's activities. For the eggnog recipe, see page 79.

MINESTRONE SOUP

SIMPLY DRESSED GREEN SALAD

SESAME TOAST

CHEESE—FRUIT

FLORENTINE CORNMEAL CAKE

EGGNOG

MINESTRONE SOUP

3 T. diced salt pork
4 T. olive oil
1 large onion, grated
2 small zucchini, sliced in thin
  circles
1/2 green cabbage, shredded
1 carrot, sliced thin
2 leeks, white part only, sliced thin
1/4 lb. string beans, chopped
2 small beets, peeled and cubed
1 clove garlic, minced
10 c. beef stock or bouillon
1 28-oz. can peeled Italian tomatoes
Salt and pepper
1 14-oz. can kidney beans, drained
Bouquet garni
1/2 c. peas
2 c. cooked rigatoni
1/2 c. grated Parmesan cheese
Chopped fresh basil or parsley

In a large stockpot, sauté the salt pork in the olive oil with the onion for about 5 minutes. Add the vegetables and garlic and continue to sauté until wilted. Pour in stock or bouillon and tomatoes. Season with salt and pepper to taste. Bring to a

boil and simmer uncovered for 30 minutes. Add kidney beans and bouquet garni and cook slowly for 1 hour. Add peas and cook an additional 5 minutes. Serve cooked pasta and cheese on the side, to be added by guests. Sprinkle with Parmesan cheese and chopped basil or parsley.

SESAME TOAST

2 loaves Italian bread
1/2 cup butter
2 cloves garlic, crushed
1 tsp. thyme
1/4 c. sesame seeds

Preheat oven to 450°F. Cut the bread into slices 1-in. thick. Melt the butter in a saucepan. Add garlic and thyme and cook gently 3 to 5 minutes (don't burn). Stir in the seeds. Spread both sides of bread slices with butter-seed mixture, using a pastry brush. Heat in the oven for 5 to 8 minutes, until crisp and bubbling. Turn over once halfway through, if desired.

FLORENTINE CORNMEAL CAKE

2/3 c. butter, at room
  temperature

2 2/3 c. sifted confectioners' sugar
1 tsp. vanilla extract
2 eggs
1 egg yolk
1 1/4 c. sifted cake flour
  (not self-rising)
1/3 c. yellow cornmeal
rind of 1/2 orange cut in julienne strips
  1/2-in. long
2 T. confectioners' sugar

In a large bowl, beat butter and sugar with an electric mixer until creamy. Beat in vanilla. Then add eggs, one at a time, and the yolk, beating well after each addition. In a separate bowl, blend flour and cornmeal. Add the flour mixture, a portion at a time, to the batter, mixing well after each addition. Blend in orange rind.

Preheat oven to 325°F. Generously grease and flour a 10-in. deerback pan, an 8 1/2 x 4 1/2-in. loaf pan, or a 3 1/4- to 4-c. tube pan. Spoon batter into pan and spread evenly. Bake for about 1 hour and 15 minutes, or until a wooden pick tests clean and cake springs back when lightly touched in the center.

Cool cake in pan 3 minutes, then turn it out onto a wire rack. Sift confectioners' sugar over warm cake.

THE
LOGISTICS
OF
GIVING

Logistics of Giving

Christmas is the quintessential time of sharing. Homes and shops share visual good cheer as they display wreaths, trees, and Christmas lights. Holiday parties—from eggnog gatherings to full-scale feasts—spread festive tidings. Whether it's good feelings or wished-for objects, presents are a long-established part of the holiday season, and the presentation of gifts is an ancient and honored custom. And well it should be. The creative energy and thoughtfulness that go into selection will be as appreciated as the gift itself. With advance planning, a workable budget, and a combined sense of adventure and humor, gift-giving will be a pleasure—as rewarding to yourself as to your recipient.

Advance Planning

Advance planning is really the key to an easy shopping season. All year long, keep notes of what you wish for and what you think your loved ones will want. Keep it in a safe place—perhaps the back of an address book or engagement calendar. (Where appropriate jot down sizes now.)

Order and purchase sure-fire gifts *early*. This won't dampen your Christmas spirit if you wait to wrap the gift until just before giving; and add an extra small touch—an ornament, a special card, or a handmade tag at the last minute. Large department stores publish catalogues that arrive shortly after Thanksgiving. These highlight their collections of fail-safe gifts and most popular items (see "Reliable Mail-Order Houses," page 158). For the disinterested shopper, these selections are useful eye openers for what's on the market. If you are buying for a friend in a rural area, what may seem obvious to you could be a delight to them!

Shopping for gifts can be a happy adventure. Treat yourself to a spree on behalf of those on your gift list. Visit that interesting cookware boutique, sporting-supply shop, or bookstore that you haven't yet found time to visit.

Fine Arts and Crafts

Friends often share comparable views on life and art. With that in mind, you may want to choose a more extravagant gift—a painting, a ceramic sculpture, a photograph! The best guideline in general is to buy with a conservative eye. Remember that a small print or photograph can be framed very inexpensively to produce a beautiful effect. For the best buys in art, seek out cooperative artist-owned galleries. As a rule, you will choose from art by lesser-known artists. The price will be much reduced because gallery overhead costs are lower. Photographs by wonderful artists are becoming more widely available, and the prices still compare favorably with small paintings, drawings, and prints. Check the "Arts" section of your paper for gallery hours. Ceramics and crafts make wonderful gifts. Craft fairs abound in this country year-round. Generally, ce-

ramics and crafts carry a higher price in a gallery than at a fair, but galleries weed out less desirable items. One rule for ceramics and crafts gift-giving: steer clear of the watchama-callit handmade item. Some of the more useful—and treasured—items include ceramic bowls, teapots, mugs; wooden breadboards, bowls, boxes; and handloomed throwrugs. Fine art and crafts are often overlooked as good Christmas presents; they are a true reflection of both the giver's and the recipient's aesthetic sensibilities.

Handmade Touches

Gifts from your home are gifts from the heart. Homemade breads, cookies, ornaments, cards, and family photographs are always cherished presents. A well-thought-out store purchase will be enhanced by the addition of a beautiful handmade ornament tied to its box or a special photograph tucked into the gift card. For ideas of handmade presents, see "Wreaths," "Ornaments," "Cookies and Treats," "Food for Giving," "Christmas Pillows," and "Country Kitchen Tableware."

Last-Minute Notes

If you're really pressed for time during the holiday season, there are many alternatives to shopping trips to the store or mall. A few long-standing favorites are tickets to the theater, ballet, or ball game; memberships to a museum or hobby club; and dinner at a special restaurant. With magazines becoming increasingly expensive, send a subscription to a friend to extend the selections they already have! For the cook, try *Gourmet, Bon Appetit*, or *The Cook's Magazine*; for the decorator, *House and Garden, Architectural Digest*, or *Abitare*. Outdoorsmen will like *Outside, Natural History*, and *Field and Stream*; and travelers can take a copy of *Travel and Leisure, National Geographic's World*, or *Signature* on the plane with them. There are many others in all categories. Browse through a good magazine store to see what the possibilities are; it's a pleasant surprise.

Although there are no hard and fast rules, a few basic hints can make the logistics of giving seem simple and less taxing. Don't forget the spirit of the gift or the personality of the recipient, and you'll do well.

Basic Hints

1. Write down gift ideas year-round.
2. Use the telephone for inquiries.
3. Don't hesitate to purchase sure-fire gifts well in advance.
4. Allow three to four weeks for delivery of catalogue items.
5. Purchase several small last-minute gifts.
6. Keep your receipts.
7. Mail early.

Kids' Gifts to Give

The children in the household will want to participate in the excitement of giving gifts. They will be bringing projects home from school to give as gifts to parents and other family members. Invariably, though, children will want to add to their gift list and plan some home projects. During the weeks before Christmas help the kids create presents for those special people. Set aside a few of their best "I decorated it myself" gingermen at cookie time. If your child is a budding writer, publish his or her illustrated story by binding it in a piece of folded construction paper or a paper folder, sewing the pages and cover together with an open zig-zag machine stitch at the fold on the outside of the book. Have your child autograph it, of course. Wonderful calendars can be created by simply attaching (with rubber ce-ment) your child's drawing over the existing monthly pictures of an inexpensive purchased calendar. The pictures will be nicely accented if "framed" on a piece of construction paper before gluing. Or have your child draw on a piece of heavy cardboard and staple a calendar "pad" directly onto the board. With a little help and encouragement your child can create a piece of little folks art. Let your young artist draw his favorite motif (dinosaur, spaceship, animal) on a piece of muslin with waterproof markers. Cut out the object 1/2 inch from the outside of the motif. Cut another shape of identical size from another piece of muslin, and sew the front to the back, right sides together, leaving 4 inches open at the bottom. Turn the pillow right side out, press, fill with polyester filling, and slip stitch closed. Voila!

Christmas Stocking Stuffers

Christmas stockings are the surest test of Santa's ingenuity. He's given a small space to fill with every sort of sugarplum, gift, and gadget in a selection to express the humor and imagination of the giver—and the inclinations of the receiver. Santa can begin with a wonderful handmade stocking (see "Christmas Stockings," page 91) or a great, useful sock, such as Early Winters' Afghan socks. Or get really silly—and extravagant—with a pair of L.L. Bean's double layer long johns!

Fruits and whole nuts are wonderful stocking stuffers, and one beautiful piece of candy and a ribboned candy cane at the top will complete the stocking. But that's working from the top down . . . stocking fillers include those free, small calendars and date books given as gifts by banks, dry cleaners, and stationers; pens; perfume samples from department stores; and gift certificates for everything from fast food to a mink coat. And more food: the stocking will be stuffed in no time if you drop in a large salami or pepperoni. If you're near a specialty food store, you might pop in to get a collection of Japanese cookies, fortune cookies, packets of herbs, a jar of jam, fancy tea bags, hot peppers, small liquors, and packets of medicine for indigestion.

Look to catalogues for dozens of great ideas . . . tiny compasses and thermometers for jacket zippers (from Early Winters); a snakebit kit, waterproof matches, "survival candy," and a smoke signal (from Campor); personalized pencils, pop-up washcloths and boo-boo strips (from Lillian Vernon); a constable's whistle, sonic ear "plugs," and a rain gauge (from Brookstone); Almond Cold Cream Soap and quill toothpicks (from Caswell Massey). And the list goes on . . . cotton sleeping gloves, bag balm, balsam incense, a wooden ladle, thick cut Seville oranges (from the Vermont Country Store, Inc.); a mushroom brush, pop-up sponges, tomato paste in tubes, and crystallized ginger from Williams-Sonoma. Round out your stocking stuffers' collection with small tools from your local hardware store; a beautiful, esoteric magazine; a farmer's almanac; and a special ornament for the Christmas tree!

Gifts from Nature

Mistletoe Balls

Materials needed: one set embroidery hoops* (about 6 in. in diameter) dark green floral tape, fine florist's wire, mistletoe (and small sprigs of other greens if desired), 1 yd. narrow red or white satin ribbon

Place smaller hoop inside larger, at right angles to each other, so they cross and form a three-dimensional ball. Wire firmly together, criss-crossing the wire around the two places where the hoops meet. Wrap each hoop with floral tape, pulling slightly as you wrap to activate the tape's adhesive. Attach one end of a piece of 2-ft.-long wire to the top of the ball and, holding the mistletoe against each ring as you work, wrap the wire around the rings in a spiral to secure the mistletoe to the hoops. Cover as much of the hoops as possible with the greens. Other plants may be mixed in, but the mistletoe should predominate. When the rings are covered, make a bundle of mistletoe and tie a bow made of 1/3 of the ribbon around it. Tie it to the underside of the top cross, so it is suspended inside the center of the ball. Make a wire hoop for hanging, and attach it to the top of the ball. Use the remaining ribbon to tie a bow at the bottom of the ball, and let the ends dangle like streamers.

* Note: some crafts stores carry pairs of small brass hoops that are already attached at right angles.

SUSPEND TINY SPRIG IN CENTER

WIRE RINGS TOGETHER FIRMLY

SECURE MISTLETOE SPRIGS BY WRAPPING WITH WIRE

HANG MISTLETOE BALL IN A DOORWAY OR FROM A CHANDELIER

Topiary Tree

An elegant ersatz topiary tree makes a centerpiece which can be created in a short time.

Materials needed: firm round potato, nail, 12-in. dowel, flowerpot full of sand, boxwood or germander sprigs

With the nail, poke one small hole for each plant stem in the top and sides of the potato. Make the holes at a slight angle. Insert the stems and make sure the leaves are turned upward. The foliage should be quite thick. Prune the tips if necessary to keep an even, round shape.

Sharpen the dowel with a pencil sharpener and impale the potato on it. Stand the "tree" up in the sand in the flowerpot. Cover the base with moss or extra sprigs of boxwood. The moisture in the potato will keep the greens fresh for several weeks.

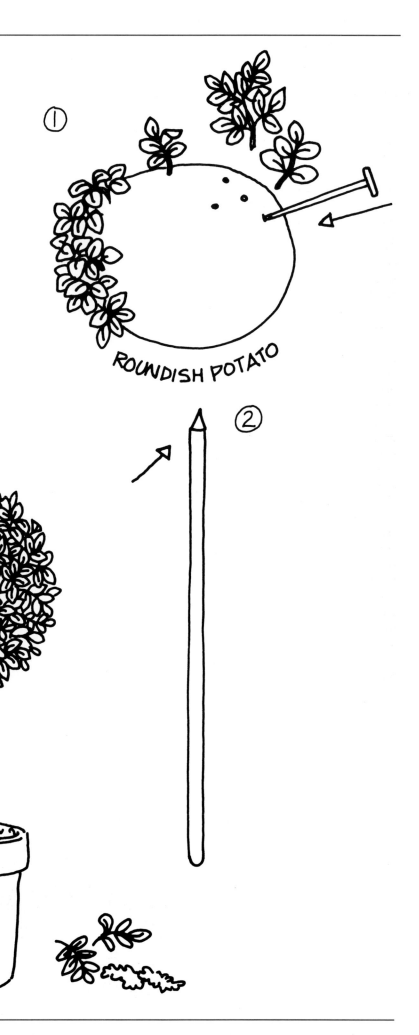

ROUNDISH POTATO

Pomanders

Apples studded all over with whole cloves and allowed to dry slowly on the shelf of a woodstove or another warm, dry place, create a fragrant favorite whose origins date far back into history. Hang them as fragrant decorations or pile several in a basket for a centerpiece. In addition to apples, try making pomanders from crabapples, seckel pears, bosc pears, or even kumquats.

Materials needed: firm apples, whole cloves, a hairpin or short length of florist's wire, 12 in. narrow ribbon, a terry towel to cover your work place

Beginning at the stem end, push the points of the cloves into the apple so only the heads remain. Work in small patches and avoid making rows of cloves which will make the skin tear in a line. There should be a little space (1/16 in.) between clove heads to allow for shrinkage as the apple dries. Leave a small open space around the stem. Finish covering the apple in one sitting or it will begin to soften and break apart when you resume work. Some of the clove heads will break as you work; others will have no heads. Mix those with and those without heads as you work.

Allow the apple to dry, rolling it gently in your hands each day to press cloves in and to help create a nice round shape. When it has dried somewhat, but is still pliable, push the hairpin or bent florist's wire into the stem end to make a hanger. When the apple is completely dry, after about a week, run a ribbon through the loop and tie a bow at the top.

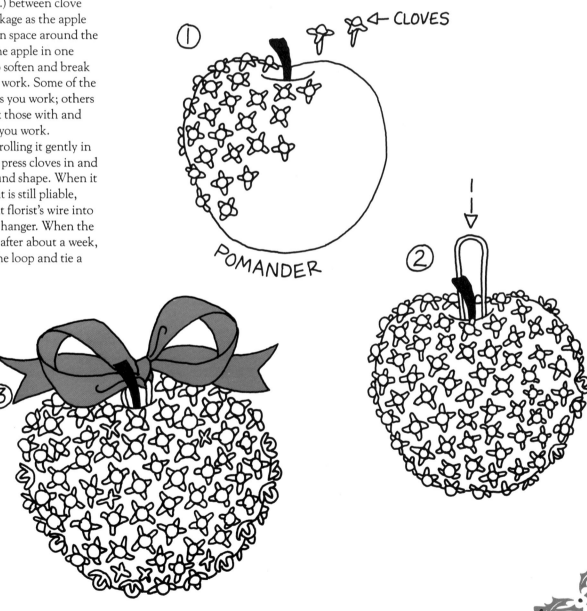

Firestarters

Materials needed: long, narrow pinecones such as white pine or blue spruce, old candle stubs or candle wax and wicking, miniature muffin tins, a pan for melting wax, wax paper

Melt the candle stubs by placing them in the top of a double boiler over boiling water (wax ignites easily, so it should not be melted over direct heat or near an open flame). Remove the pieces of wick with a fork and set aside to let them cool. Trim the dark ends from the wicks and cut into 2 in. lengths.

Quickly and carefully dip pinecones into hot wax and lay them out on their side on the wax paper. Half fill muffin tins with hot wax and quickly press wick into the edge of each one. Stand wax-coated cones in muffin tins, holding wicks to one side so that the ends will be free to light.

Allow the pinecones to cool. To unmold, place the muffin tin in the freezer for 5 to 10 minutes. Remove, turn the muffin tin upside down, and the cones will fall out easily. To use firestarters, place under wood in fireplace and light wick. As the cone burns, it deposits pitch and wax on the wood above it, making it ignite quickly. To package firestarters as gifts, stand them in a basket or round Shaker-style box.

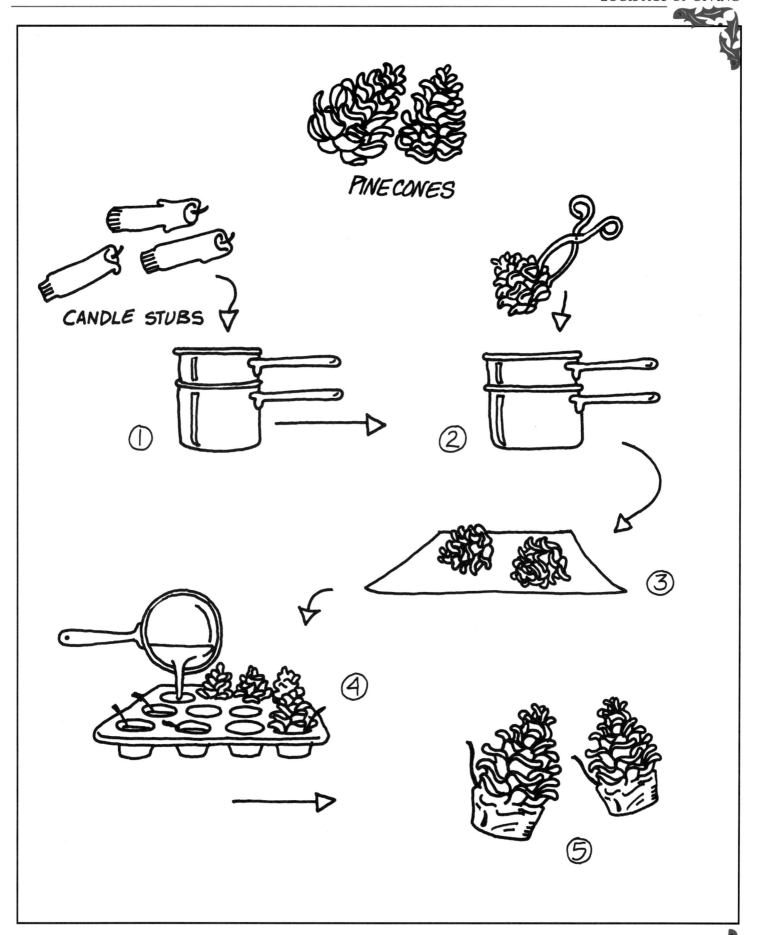

PINE CONES

CANDLE STUBS

①

②

③

④

⑤

Berry Bowls

Materials needed: a rose bowl (available from florists), live small forest evergreens with roots, such as partridge berry and checkerberry, green moss with roots and soil attached

Place moss, root and soil side up, in the bottom of the bowl. Arrange the greens so that they encircle the inside of the bowl with as many berries showing as possible. Gently press the tiny roots into the soil, if possible. The bowl should be between 1/2 and 3/4 full. If the soil or plants seem dry, sprinkle with a little water. Cover the bowl with clinging plastic wrap to seal in the moisture.

Leave the bowl in a shady place for a few days. If moisture condenses on the inside, loosen the cover for a few hours to let some moisture escape. If the top of the bowl has a lip or rim, you can tie a narrow red ribbon around it to decorate it and hold the covering in place.

Berry bowls keep well if they are not left in the sun or allowed to dry out completely.

TINY VINES
WRAPAROUND
INSIDE
LIKE A NEST
(6"-8" LONG)

USE
TINY PLANTS
WITH ROOTS

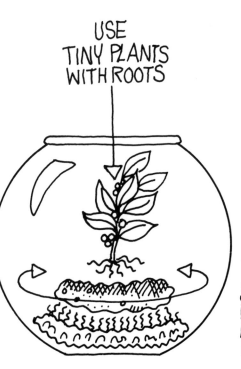

SOIL AND
ROOTS AND
MOSS IN THE
BOTTOM

(CUT AWAY VIEW)

5" BERRY BOWL
(FINISHED)

Christmas Potpourri

A bowl or basket of fragrant potpourri in bright Christmas colors adds grace to any room, and is easy to assemble. Along with the dried flowers and kitchen spices you may have on hand, you can purchase many of the ingredients in health food stores or from florists and craft supply stores.
The amounts are not important; the following list is simply a guideline. If you wish to add more or less of anything, feel free. This is what makes each potpourri an individual work of scented art. But you should have several of the highly scented ingredients as well as the evergreens. If you have to substitute other varieties of evergreen tips, you may need to add a few more drops of balsam oil.

    1 c. balsam tips and needles
    1 c. cedar tips
    1 c. hemlock cones (or other tiny cones)
    1 c. red rose petals
    1 c. cedar shavings (available at pet stores)
    1/2 c. dried rosemary
    1/2 c. cut orange peel
    1/2 c. broken cinnamon sticks
    1/2 c. bay leaves
    1/4 c. whole cloves
    1/4 c. whole allspice
    1/4 c. chipped orris root
    10 drops balsam oil
    10 drops rose oil

Mix all ingredients in a large jar or plastic bag and seal tightly. Shake or stir daily for two weeks. This potpourri is fragrant enough to be displayed in an open container without having to be closed at night to recover, as most potpourri does. This recipe will fill several bowls, but you can make less or package the extra in bags for your friends.

Reliable Mail-Order Houses

The following is a list of reliable mail-order businesses from throughout the country. It is by no means complete. There are hundreds of wonderful mail-order merchants to choose from. If you feel you are dealing with a less than established merchant, simply contact the Better Business Bureau to check a company's reputation before you send off your order. The Federal Trade Commission has nationwide jurisdiction over operations of these business. Mail-order catalogues are a wonderful, traditional part of the national marketplace. As the audience and appeal of these catalogues grow, so does the fun and convenience and luxury of using them.

CHILDREN'S GIFTS

BUTTERCUP & FRIEND
535 Piermont Ave.
Piermont, NY 10968
(914) 359-7408

CHILDCRAFT
20 Kilmer Rd.
Edison, NJ 08818
(800) 631-5652

THE ENCHANTED DOLL HOUSE
Manchester Center, VT 05255
(802) 362-3030

JUST FOR KIDS
Winterbrook Way
Meredith, NH 03253
(603) 279-7031

MY CHILD'S DESTINY
Dept. 1313 P.O. Box 7337
San Francisco, CA 94120

CLOTHING

BROWNSTONE STUDIO
P.O. Box 770
Old Chelsea Sta.
New York, NY 10014
(800) 221-2468

FRENCH CREEK SHEEP AND WOOL CO.
Elverson, PA 19520
(800) 345-4091

HONEY BEE
2745 Philmont Ave.
Huntington Valley, PA 19006
(800) 523-6534

JAMES RIVER TRADERS
James River Landing
Hampton, VA 23631
(804) 827-6000

LAND'S END
Land's End Lane
Dageville, WI 53595
(800) 356-4444

THE PERUVIAN CONNECTION
Canaan Farm
Toganoxic, KS 66086
(800) 255-6429

THE TALBOTS
164 North Street
Hingham, MA 02043
(800) 225-8200

WINTER SILKS
2700 Laura Lane
Middleton, WI 53562
(608) 836-4600

DEPARTMENT STORES

J.C. PENNEY CO., INC.
1301 Avenue of the Americas
New York, NY 10019

MONTGOMERY WARD
1000 S. Monroe
Baltimore, MD 21232
(800) 428-2800

SEARS ROEBUCK AND CO.
4640 Roosevelt Blvd.
Philadelphia, PA 19132

SPIEGEL
1040 W. 35th St.
Chicago, IL 60609
(800) 345-4500

GADGETS AND TOOLS

BROOKSTONE COMPANY
127 Vase Farm Rd.
Peterborough, NH 03460
(603) 924-9511

EDMUND SCIENTIFIC
101 E. Gloucester Pike
Barrington, NJ 08007
(800) 257-6173

GARRET WADE
161 Avenue of the Americas
New York, NY 10013
(800) 807-1757

HAMMACHER SCHLEMMER
Southeast Operations Center
115 Brand Rd.
Salem, VA 24156
(800) 368-3584

HERRINGTON
10535 Chillicothe Rd.
Kirtland, OH 44094
(216) 256-1446

HOFFRITZ
515 W. 24th St.
New York, NY 10011
(212) 924-7300

INNOVATION
110 Painters Mill Rd.
Owings Mills, MD 21117
(800) 638-6170

LEICHTUNG
4944 Commerce Parkway
Cleveland, OH 44128
(800) 321-6840

MARKLINE
P.O. Box C-5 Dept. F
Belmont, MD 02178
(800) 225-8493

ROBERT EDMUNDS
101 E. Gloucester Pike
Barrington, NJ 08007
(800) 257-6173

RUSSELL'S
450 Sutter St.
P.O. Box 77904
San Francisco, CA 94607
(415) 543-6620

THE SHARPER IMAGE
680 Davis St. Dept.
San Francisco, CA 94111
(800) 344-4444

SPORTY'S TOOL SHOP
Clermont County Airport
Batavia, OH 45103
(800) 543-8633

GARDEN SUPPLIES

GARDENER'S EDEN
P.O. Box 7307
San Francisco, CA 94120-7307
(415) 428-9292

PARK SEED
Cokesbury Rd.
P.O. Box 46
Greenwood, SC 29648-0046
(803) 374-3341

W. ALTEE BURPEE CO.
2075 Burpee Building
Warminster, PA 18974
(215) 674-4900

WHITE FLOWER FARM
Litchfield, CT 06759
(203) 567-0801

KITCHEN GIFTS

ACE PECAN
P.O. Box 65
Ninth and Harris
Cordele, GA 31015
(800) 323-0891

COMMUNITY KITCHENS
P.O. Box 3778 Dept. AH
Baton Rouge, LA 70821-3778
(800) 535-9901

HARRY AND DAVID
Medford, OR
(503) 776-2400

WILLIAMS-SONOMA
P.O. Box 7456
San Francisco, CA 94120
(415) 652-9007

THE WOODEN SPOON
Rte. 6
Mahopac, NY 10541
(800) 431-2207

ZABAR'S
2245 Broadway
New York, NY 10024
(800) 221-3347

MISCELLANEOUS GIFTS

CHRIS CRAFT
7822 S. 46 St.
Phoenix, AZ 00000
(800) 338-3080

COMFORTABLY YOURS
52 W. Hunter Ave.
Maywood, NJ 07607
(201) 368-0400

THE HORCHOW COLLECTION
P.O. Box 819066
Dallas, TX 75381-9066
(800) 527-0303

JOAN COOK
3200 S.E. 14 Ave.
Ft. Lauderdale, FL 33316
(800) 327-1611

LILLIAN VERNON
510 S. Fulton Ave.
Mount Vernon, NY 10650
(914) 633-6300

METROPOLITAN MUSEUM OF ART
CATALOGUE
Madden Village, NY 11381
(718) 326-7050

PARAGON
Tom Harvey Rd.
Westerly, RI 02891
(401) 596-0134

THE STITCHERY
Dept. 161
204 Worcester St.
Wellesley, MA 02181
(800) 225-4127

UNICORN GALLERY
P.O. Box 4405
Colesville, MD 20904
(800) 638-2616

THE VERMONT COUNTRY STORE
Weston, VT 05161
(800) 824-6932

WILLOUGHBY AND TAYLOR LTD.
8909 Ambassador Row
Dallas, TX 75247
(800) 972-1000

SPORTING GOODS

CAMPMOR
P.O. Box 999
Paramus, NJ 07653
(800) 526-4784

EARLY WINTERS
110 Prefontain Place S.
Seattle, WA. 98104
(206) 624-5599

EDDIE BAUER
P.O. Box 3700
Seattle, WA 98124
(800) 426-8020

L.L. BEAN, INC.
Freeport, ME 04033
(207) 865-3111

MOSS BROWN
5210 Eisenhower Ave.
Alexandria, VA 22304
(800) 424-2774

NORM THOMPSON
P.O. Box 3999
Portland, OR 97208
(800) 547-1160

RAMSEY OUTDOOR
226 Rte. 17 N.
Paramus, NJ 07652
(201) 261-5000

Gifts That Give Twice

Finding interesting and unusual gifts is a challenge to even the most creative shopper. Catalogues featuring merchandise from non-profit organizations and museum shops can help meet that challenge and allow you to contribute to a worthwhile cause.

Profits go to maintain the museums' collections, support educational programs, protect rare species, purchase and restore historic properties, carry on research, or preserve a dying art. Gifts come in all price ranges and for all interests and ages.

Historical restorations everywhere, large and small, have shops or sales desks featuring unique gifts relating to their era. Check your own local museums and historic homes, or add museum shops to your list if you travel to a city to shop.

MUSEUMS

Several non-profit organizations publish merchandise catalogues in addition to maintaining extensive gift shops. If you cannot visit the following shops, you can view a sample of their offerings in their catalogues.

BROOKLYN BOTANIC GARDEN
1000 Washington Avenue
Brooklyn, NY 11225
(718) 622-4433

METROPOLITAN MUSEUM OF ART
Fifth Avenue at 82 Street
New York, NY 10028
(212) 535-7710

THE METROPOLITAN OPERA GUILD
1865 Broadway
New York, NY 10023
(212) 582-7500

MUSEUM OF FINE ARTS
465 Huntington Avenue
Boston, MA 02115
(617) 267-9300

MUSEUM OF MODERN ART
11 W. 53 Street
New York, NY 10019
(212) 708-9480

MUSEUM OF NATURAL HISTORY
Central Park West at 79 Street
New York, NY 10024
(212) 769-5100

MUSEUM SHOPS OF HARTFORD
SCIENCE MUSEUM OF
CONNECTICUT
950 Troutbrook Drive
W. Hartford, CT 06119
(203) 236-2961

OLD STURBRIDGE VILLAGE
1 Old Sturbridge Village Road
Sturbridge, MA 01566
(617) 347-3362

The following is a listing of a few museums which do not offer merchandise catalogues, but which do maintain wonderul gift shops:

ALABAMA
MONTGOMERY MUSEUM OF FINE
ARTS
440 South MacDonald
Montgomery, AL 36119
(205) 244-5700
Crafts, books, and jewelry

ALASKA
ANCHORAGE HISTORICAL AND
FINE ARTS MUSEUM
121 W. 7 Street
Anchorage, AK 99501
(907) 343-4326
Excellent Eskimo art, sculpture, and crafts

CALIFORNIA
SAN DIEGO MUSEUM OF MAN
1350 El Prado
San Diego, CA 92101
(619) 239-2001
Crafts from other cultures

LAWRENCE HALL OF SCIENCE AT
BERKELEY
Centennial Drive
Berkeley, CA
(415) 642-5132
Gifts relating to science

COLORADO
DENVER ART MUSEUM
100 W. 14 Avenue Parkway
Denver, CO 80204
(303) 575-2295
American Indian Publications

ILLINOIS
MUSEUM OF CONTEMPORARY ART
237 E. Ontario Street
Chicago, IL 60611
(312) 280-2660
Contemporary jewelry, crafts, and clothing

LOUISIANA
THE HISTORIC NEW ORLEANS
COLLECTION
Royal Street
New Orleans, LA
(504) 523-4662
Local crafts and unusual gifts

MASSACHUSETTS
BOSTON CHILDREN'S MUSEUM
Museum's Wharf
300 Congress Street
Boston, MA 02210
(617) 426-6500
Craft kits, books, science gifts, and stocking
stuffers

MUSEUM OF FINE ARTS
49 Chestnut Street
Springfield, MA 01103
(413) 732-6092
Oriental accessories, fine art prints, and
jewelry

THE PEABODY MUSEUM
East India Square
Salem, MA 01970
(617) 745-1876
Maritime and Oriental gifts and books

PLIMOTH PLANTATION
P.O. Box 1620
Plymouth, MA 02360
(617) 746-1622
New England Indian and Pilgrim era items

THE QUADRANGLE MUSEUMS
236 State Street
Springfield, MA 01103
(413) 733-1194
Inexpensive mineral specimens, African art

MICHIGAN
HENRY FORD MUSEUM AND
VILLAGE
P.O. Box 1970
Dearborn, MI 48121
(313) 271-1620
Americana and folk craft kits

NEW HAMPSHIRE
STRAWBERRY BANKE
P.O. Box 300
Portsmouth, NH 03801
(603) 433-1100
Two shops—one a general store, the other
specializing in China Trade reproductions
and needlework kits

NEW MEXICO
MUSEUM OF ALBUQUERQUE
2000 Mountain Road
Albuquerque, NM
(505) 243-7255
Traditional and contemporary crafts

NEW YORK
BROOKLYN MUSEUM
200 Eastern Parkway
Brooklyn, NY 11238
(718) 638-5000
Inexpensive handmade goods from around
the world

N.Y. HORTICULTURAL SOCIETY
128 W. 58 Street
New York, NY 10019
(212) 757-0915
Annual holiday plant sale

OKLAHOMA
GILCREASE MUSEUM
1400 Gilcrease Museum Road
Tulsa, OK 74127
(918) 582-3122
American Indian items

PENNSYLVANIA
UNIVERSITY OF PENNSYLVANIA
MUSEUM OF ARCHAEOLOGY
33rd and Spruce
Philadelphia, PA 19104
(215) 898-8304
Crafts from primitive cultures and books

TEXAS
SAN ANTONIO MUSEUM OF ART
P.O. Box 2601
San Antonio, TX 78299-2601
(512) 226-5544
Locally discovered artifacts and crafts

WASHINGTON
SEATTLE ART MUSEUM
14th and E. Prospect
Seattle, WA 98109
(206) 625-8901
Crafts of the northwest

Along with gift shops, most museums and
some other non-profit organizations offer
memberships, which also make thoughtful
gifts. Benefits include free admission,
discounts on merchandise, admittance to
special events, trips, and classes. Several
museums also publish outstanding
magazines for their members.

Animal lovers would appreciate
membership at a local zoo or at one offering
the elegant magazine "Animal Kingdom",
published at Bronx Zoo for its own
members and those of affiliated zoos.

The National Wildlife Federation
membership includes one of its excellent
magazines including "Ranger Rick" for
younger naturalists. Its catalogue offers nature
and science gifts and books (1412 16th Street,
Washington, DC 20036).

A more expensive but memorable gift
for the animal lover who has everything is
the adoption of a resident of the London
Zoo in his name. While an elephant at
around $10,000 a year may be a bit
ostentatious, a pair of crocodiles costs only
about $1,000, and a modest, but lovable
doormouse less than $100. A picture of the
animal, a certificate, and periodic reports
give the adoptive "parent" a sense of
involvement.

Gift Wrapping

Wrapping gifts is one of the most creative tasks of the holiday season. Gorgeous papers and boxes are widely available; now it's easier than ever to express your individuality and thoughtfulness. Pieces of cloth, fabric, paper, and ribbon combined in new ways turn a simple gift into a special one.

Pictured at right are several ideas for incorporating available materials into your decorative ideas.

Inside-Outside

Why restrict the use of packing straw to the inside of a box? The color and texture are wonderful—and it's a treat to watch everyone's faces as you bring forth a "hairy" gift!

When you need to protect a gift against breakage, consider popcorn! Simply line your box with heavy paper, pop a *lot* of popcorn (use little or no oil please) and enclose a note to assure that yes, it is edible. Here, too, the color, texture, *and* taste are wonderful. Children especially will love the surprise of it!

Paper and Fabric

Pictured is a book wrapped in a small piece of wallpaper, ribboned and tied with a folk art piece of wooden fruit. Wallpaper scraps can double the available patterns and colors in any household's gift wrap selection.

Gift paper cut with pinking shears is a simple, interesting touch. First cut ¼-inch strips of cloth, wetting them thoroughly with liquid starch and allowing them to dry flat on a hard surface. Trim the strips to the desired

widths with pinking shears. Then, tie the package with your new fabric ribbon.

Brown paper is a good, informal wrapping selection. The variation shown here is brown paper with fabric hearts sewn directly onto the paper with a wide zig-zag stitch. The possibilities for special touches are endless when you use machine stitching—monograms, thread stitch plaids, appliqué.

Cut Paper

Sheets of music, pieced and taped to a package look especially festive when they are ribboned in red. Use simple colored paper as a perfect background for paperdoll cutouts that can be transformed into Christmas shapes (see "Christmas Paper Work," page 107). Make gift tags with a personal touch by using extra cutout shapes.

Store-bought Ideas

In addition to the gift wrapping ideas that you create yourself, you can find beautiful wrappings from stores and from mail-order houses. Boxes and colored bags are plentiful; most card stores carry a wide selection and many boutiques are now beginning to carry Victorian Christmas stickers and furbelows. Brand-name wrappings range from simple to ostentatious; depending on your tastes, you may fall absolutely in love with a selection or you may just want to draw on a brand-name wrapping for an idea that you carry out on your own. Whatever you choose, don't overlook the store wrappings. You may be surprised by what you find.

Sending Your Package

The United States Postal Service recommends that all parcel post packages be in the mail by the first week of December. If you are shipping at the last minute, the Postal Service has Express Mail Service for guaranteed next-day delivery to certain locations. Your local post office sells padded mailing envelopes, for under $1.00, which are handy for small mailings (the largest will hold an unboxed sweater). To protect the gift and its wrapping, it's wise to place the gift first in a manila envelope, then in the shipping envelope.

Couriers like Federal Express and Emery Air Freight can be of invaluable assistance to the last-minute shipper, with their guaranteed next-day delivery policies. They will provide door-to-door service, although there is a savings if you are able to drop off the package at their pick-up locations. Call ahead for prices, weight and size limitations, and be prepared to pay the courier in advance if you don't have an account with the firm.

Don't overlook bus lines as a great way to get a package from here to there. Greyhound and Trailways have package service to virtually every city in the United States. Your package will be placed on the first available bus heading to its destination. For a higher cost, the bus lines will guarantee "next bus out" status for your gift. Bus lines sometimes offer an "all you can fit in at one price" packing box at their terminal locations. Come equipped with gifts and plenty of packing material. Bus delivery can be speedy and convenient if you and the recipient live or work near a terminal.

Railways provide a similar service. Packages will be sent out on the first available train to the specified destination. Trains usually have more space available and as with bus lines, they will transport the package from terminal to terminal.

Both rail and bus lines provide to-your-door delivery from the terminals at extra cost.

Comparison shopping by telephone is recommended for all package delivery options. Usually, early United States Parcel Post mailing is the most cost-effective way to send your Christmas gift. With any sort of mailing or delivery, remember: mail early, pack securely, and address accurately.

Returning a Gift

Invariably, with even the most arduous research and planning, there will be a gift or two each season that will need to be returned or exchanged, so keep those holiday receipts.

Return policies of most department stores and shops are similar—the return must be made within between ten to fourteen days from date of purchase. The item must be returned in purchased condition, unless it is a return involving a damaged item. The gift returned must be accompanied by a sales slip for most on-the-spot refunds or exchanges. The store will often accept a return without a sales slip but will usually send the refund through the mail. The choice of offering a refund, exchange, or store credit is the option of the retailer and must be indicated clearly at the time of purchase. If you plan to return a gift in person, your task will be simplified if you call the customer service department of the store before you go and clarify their policy on returns. Also, ask where the return department is in the store, if there is one. You may have to go directly to the department where the gift was purchased. Large department stores usually have a coded department number that appears before the item description on the sales slip. Refer to this for help. Also, seasonal items go on sale right after Christmas, so make the return as quickly as possible to meet the store's deadline and to find a good selection of merchandise.

The return policies of catalogue houses differ. You can return an item within thirty days at minimum, but some mail-order firms extend that time. Check the particular merchant for return deadlines. Your return must be securely packaged—in its original container, where applicable. If you're mailing the return item, send it insured, postage prepaid. (Some mail-order houses will return the cost of return postage.) You will need to include the packing/sales slip with your merchandise, a written explanation of the reason for exchange (wrong size, color, etc.), and a description of the sort of refund or exchange you expect. Many packing slips have return information on the back of the invoice.

The return time limitations of merchants merits serious consideration at the time you purchase a gift, especially for an out-of-town friend or relative. Your best bet is to use a catalogue to buy gifts of questionable size, color, or use that you plan to give to someone who lives far away. Purchase gifts locally for friends nearby.

If you receive a gift that *must* be returned, don't hesitate to call the giver of the gift and ask for the name of the merchant and for the sales slip. Insist they do the same! If you've sent a catalogue item, send your friend the packing slip, address, and encouragement to exchange the present for exactly what they want. Since being given a gift shouldn't be a chore, offer to help those friends and family that have difficulty making a return. The giving will continue after the gifts are opened.

STORIES, POEMS, AND SONGS OF CHRISTMAS PAST

EVERYWHERE, EVERYWHERE CHRISTMAS TO-NIGHT

CHRISTMAS in lands of the fir tree and pine,
   Christmas in lands of the palm tree and vine;
Christmas where snow peaks stand solemn and white,
Christmas where cornfields lie sunny and bright;
   Everywhere, everywhere Christmas to-night!

Christmas where children are hopeful and gay,
Christmas where old men are patient and gray;
Christmas where peace, like a dove in its flight;
Broods o'er brave men in the thick of the fight;
   Everywhere, everywhere Christmas to-night!

For the Christ child who comes is the Master of all;
No palace too great—no cottage too small.
The angels who welcome Him sing from the height,
"In the city of David, a King in His might."
   Everywhere, everywhere Christmas to-night!

Then let every heart keep its Christmas within,
Christ's pity for sorrow, Christ's hatred of sin,
Christ's care for the weakest, Christ's courage for right,
Christ's dread of the darkness, Christ's love of the light,
Everywhere, everywhere Christmas to-night!

So the stars of the midnight which compass us round,
Shall see a strange glory and hear a sweet sound,
And cry, "Look! the earth is aflame with delight.
O sons of the morning rejoice at the sight."
   Everywhere, everywhere Christmas to-night!

—PHILLIPS BROOKS

SPEAKIN' O' CHRISTMAS

BREEZES blowin' middlin' brisk,
Snow-flakes thro' the air a-whisk,
Fallin' kind o' soft an' light,
Not enough to make things white,
But jest sorter siftin' down
So 's to cover up the brown
Of the dark world's rugged ways
'N' make things look like holidays.
   Not smoothed over, but jest specked,
      Sorter strainin' fur effect,
         An' not quite a-gittin' through

What it started in to do.
Mercy sakes! it does seem queer
Christmas day is 'most nigh here.
Somehow it don't seem to me
Christmas like it used to be,—
Christmas with its ice an' snow,
Christmas of the long ago.
You could feel its stir an' hum
Weeks an' weeks before it come;
Somethin' in the atmosphere
Told you when the day was near,
Did n't need no almanacs;
That was one o' Nature's fac's.
Every cottage decked out gay—
Cedar wreaths an' holly spray—
An' the stores, how they were drest,
Tinsel tell you could n't rest;
Every winder fixed up pat,
Candy canes, an' things like that;
Noah's arks, an' guns, an' dolls,
An' all kinds o' fol-de-rols.
Then with frosty bells a-chime,
Slidin' down the hills o' time,
Right amidst the fun an' din
Christmas come a-bustlin' in,
Raised his cheery voice to call
Out a welcome to us all;
Hale and hearty, strong an' bluff,
That was Christmas, sure enough.
Snow knee-deep an' coastin' fine,
Frozen mill-ponds all ashine,
Seemin' jest to lay in wait,
Beggin' you to come an' skate.
An' you'd git your gal an' go
Stumpin' cheerily thro' the snow,
Feelin' pleased an' skeert an' warm
'Cause she had a-holt yore arm.
Why, when Christmas come in, we
Spent the whole glad day in glee,
Havin' fun an' feastin' high
An' some courtin' on the sly.
Bustin' in some neighbor's door
An' then suddenly, before
He could give his voice a lift,
Yellin' at him, "Christmas gift."
Now sich things are never heard,
"Merry Christmas" is the word.
But it's only change o' name,
An' means givin' jest the same.
There's too many new-styled ways
Now about the holidays.
I'd jest like once more to see
Christmas like it used to be!

—PAUL LAURENCE DUNBAR

HARK! THE HERALD ANGELS SING

F. MENDELSSOHN

CHAS. WESLEY

1. Hark! the her - ald an - gels sing, __ "Glo - ry to the new - born King!
2. Christ, by high - est heav'n a - dored;__ Christ the ev - er - last - ing Lord;
3. Hail! the heav'n-born Prince of peace!__ Hail! the Son of Right -eous - ness!

Peace on earth, and mer - cy mild, __ God and sin - ners re - con - ciled."
Late in time be - hold him come,__ Off - spring of the fa - vored one.
Light and life to all he brings,_ Risen with heal - ing in his wings.

Joy - ful, all ye na - tions, rise, __ Join the tri - umph of the skies;
Veil'd in flesh, the God - head see; __ Hail, th'in - car - nate De - i - ty:
Mild he lays his glo - ry by, __ Born that man no more may die:

With th'an - gel - ic host pro - claim, "Christ is __ born in Beth - le - hem."
Pleased, as man, with men to dwell, Je - sus,__ our Im - man - u - el!
Born to raise the sons of earth, Born to __ give them se - cond birth.

Hark! the her - ald an - gels sing, "Glo - ry__ to the new - born King!"

170

THE WASSAIL SONG

TRADITIONAL

1. Here we come a was-sail-ing A-mong the leaves so green, ___
2. We are not dai-ly beg-gars That beg from door to door, ___ But
3. Good Mas-ter and good Mis-tress, As you sit by the fire, ___ Pray

Here we come a wand-'ring, So fair ___ to be seen.
we are neigh-bor's chil-dren Whom you have seen be-fore.
think of us poor chil-dren As wand-'ring in the mire.

Chorus

Love and joy come to you, And to you your was-sail too, And God bless you and

send ___ you a hap-py new year, ___ And God send you a hap-py new ___ year.

4. We have a little purse
    Made of ratching leather skin;
    We want some of your small change
    To line it well within.   *Chorus*

5. Bring us out a table,
    And spread it with a cloth;
    Bring us out a moldy cheese,
    And some of your Christmas loaf.   *Chorus*

6. God bless the Master of this house,
    Likewise the Mistress too;
    And all the little children
    That round the table go.   *Chorus*

A Merry Christmas

LOUISA MAY ALCOTT

Jo was the first to wake in the gray dawn of Christmas morning. No stockings hung at the fireplace, and for a moment she felt as much disappointed as she did long ago, when her little sock fell down because it was so crammed with goodies. Then she remembered her mother's promise, and slipping her hand under her pillow, drew out a little crimson-covered book. She knew it very well, for it was that beautiful old story of the best life ever lived, and Jo felt that it was a true guide-book for any pilgrim going the long journey. She woke Meg with a "Merry Christmas," and bade her see what was under her pillow. A green-covered book appeared, with the same picture inside, and a few words written by their mother, which made their one present very precious in their eyes. Presently Beth and Amy woke, to rummage and find their little books also, —one dove-colored, the other blue; and all sat looking at and talking about them, while the east grew rosy with the coming day.

In spite of her small vanities, Margaret had a sweet and pious nature, which unconsciously influenced her sisters, especially Jo, who loved her very tenderly, and obeyed her because her advice was so gently given.

"Girls," said Meg seriously, looking from the tumbled head beside her to the two little night-capped ones in the room beyond, "mother wants us to read and love and mind these books, and we must begin at once. We used to be faithful about it; but since father went away, and all this war trouble unsettled us, we have neglected many things. You can do as you please; but *I* shall keep my book on the table here, and read a little every morning as soon as I wake, for I know it will do me good and help me through the day."

Then she opened her new book and began to read. Jo put her arm round her, and, leaning cheek to cheek, read also, with the quiet expression so seldom seen on her restless face.

"How good Meg is! Come, Amy, let's do as they do. I'll help you with the hard words, and they'll explain things if we don't understand," whispered Beth, very much impressed by the pretty books and her sisters' example.

"I'm glad mine is blue," said Amy; and then the rooms were very still while the pages were softly turned, and the winter sunshine crept in to touch the bright heads and serious faces with a Christmas greeting.

"Where is mother?" asked Meg, as she and Jo ran down to thank her for their gifts, half an hour later.

"Goodness only knows. Some poor creeter come a-beggin', and your ma went straight off to see what was needed. There never *was* such a woman for givin' away vittles and drink, clothes and firin'," replied Hannah, who had lived with the family since Meg was born, and was considered by them all more as a friend than a servant.

"She will be back soon, I think; so fry your cakes, and have everything ready," said Meg, looking over the presents which were collected in a basket and kept under the sofa, ready to be produced at the proper time. "Why, where is Amy's bottle of cologne?" she added, as the little flask did not appear.

"She took it out a minute ago, and went off with it to put a ribbon on it, or some such notion," replied Jo, dancing about the room to take the first stiffness off the new army-slippers.

"How nice my handkerchiefs look, don't they? Hannah washed and ironed them for me, and I marked them all my-self," said Beth, looking proudly at the somewhat uneven letters which had cost her such labor.

"Bless the child! she's gone and put 'Mother' on them instead of 'M. March.' How funny!" cried Jo, taking up one.

"Isn't it right? I thought it was better to do it so, because Meg's initials are 'M.M.,' and I don't want any one to use these but Marmee," said Beth, looking troubled.

"It's all right, dear, and a very pretty idea,—quite sensible, too, for no one can ever mistake now. It will please her very much, I know," said Meg, with a frown for Jo and a smile for Beth.

"There's mother. Hide the basket, quick!" cried Jo, as a door slammed, and steps sounded in the hall.

Amy came in hastily, and looked rather abashed when she saw her sisters all waiting for her.

"Where have you been, and what are you hiding behind you?" asked Meg, surprised to see, by her hood and cloak, that lazy Amy had been out so early.

"Don't laugh at me, Jo! I didn't mean any one should know till the time came. I only meant to change the little bottle for a big one, and I gave *all* my money to get it, and I'm truly trying not to be selfish any more."

As she spoke, Amy showed the handsome flask which replaced the cheap one; and looked so earnest and humble in her little effort to forget herself that Meg hugged her on the spot, and Jo pronounced her "a trump," while Beth ran to the window, and picked her finest rose to ornament the stately bottle.

"You see I felt ashamed of my present, after reading and talking about being good this morning, so I ran round the corner and changed it the minute I was up; and I'm *so* glad, for mine is the handsomest now."

Another bang of the street-door sent the basket under the sofa, and the girls to the table, eager for breakfast.

"Merry Christmas, Marmee! Many of them! Thank you for our books; we read some, and mean to every day," they cried, in chorus.

"Merry Christmas, little daughters! I'm glad you began at once, and hope you will keep on. But I want to say one word

before we sit down. Not far away from here lies a poor woman with a little new-born baby. Six children are huddled into one bed to keep from freezing, for they have no fire. There is nothing to eat over there; and the oldest boy came to tell me they were suffering hunger and cold. My girls, will you give them your breakfast as a Christmas present?"

They were all unusually hungry, having waited nearly an hour, and for a minute no one spoke; only a minute, for Jo exclaimed impetuously,—

"I'm so glad you came before we began!"

"May I go and help carry the things to the poor little chil-dren?" asked Beth eagerly.

"*I* shall take the cream and the muffins," added Amy, heroically giving up the articles she most liked.

Meg was already covering the buckwheats, and piling the bread into one big plate.

"I thought you'd do it," said Mrs. March, smiling as if satisfied. "You shall all go and help me, and when we come back we will have bread and milk for breakfast, and make it up at dinner-time."

They were soon ready, and the procession set out. Fortu-nately it was early, and they went through back streets, so few people saw them, and no one laughed at the queer party.

A poor, bare, miserable room it was, with broken win-dows, no fire, ragged bed-clothes, a sick mother, wailing baby, and a group of pale, hungry children cuddled under one old quilt, trying to keep warm.

How the big eyes stared and the blue lips smiled as the girls went in!

"Ach, mein Gott! it is good angels come to us!" said the poor woman, crying for joy.

"Funny angels in hoods and mittens," said Jo, and set them laughing.

In a few minutes it really did seem as if kind spirits had been at work there. Hannah, who had carried wood, made a fire, and stopped up the broken panes with old hats and her own cloak. Mrs. March gave the mother tea and gruel, and comforted her with promises of help, while she dressed the little baby as tenderly as if it had been her own. The girls, meantime, spread the table, set the children round the fire, and fed them like so many hungry birds, —laughing, talk-ing, and trying to understand the funny broken English.

"Das ist gut!" "Die Engel-kinder!" cried the poor things as they ate, and warmed their purple hands at the comfortable blaze.

The girls had never been called angel children before, and thought it very agreeable, especially Jo, who had been con-sidered a "Sancho" ever since she was born. That was a very happy breakfast, though they didn't get any of it; and when they went away, leaving comfort behind, I think there were not in all the city four merrier people than the hungry little girls who gave away their breakfasts and contented themselves with bread and milk on Christmas morning.

Mrs. March was both surprised and touched; and smiled with her eyes full as she examined her presents, and read the little notes which accompanied them. The slippers went on at once, a new handkerchief was slipped into her pocket, well scented with Amy's cologne, the rose was fastened in her bosom, and the nice gloves were pronounced a "perfect fit."

There was a good deal of laughing and kissing and explaining, in the simple, loving fashion which makes these home-festivals so pleasant at the time, so sweet to remember long afterward, and then all fell to work.

The morning charities and ceremonies took so much time that the rest of the day was devoted to preparations for the evening festivities. Being still too young to go often to the theatre, and not rich enough to afford any great outlay for private performances, the girls put their wits to work, and—necessity being the mother of invention—made whatever they needed. Very clever were some of their productions,—pasteboard guitars, antique lamps made of old-fashioned butterboats covered with silver paper, gorgeous robes of old cotton, glittering with tin spangles from a pickle factory, and armor covered with the same useful diamond-shaped bits, left in sheets when the lids of tin preserve-pots were cut out. The furniture was used to being turned topsy-turvy, and the big chamber was the scene of many innocent revels.

No gentlemen were admitted; so Jo played male parts to her heart's content, and took immense satisfaction in a pair of russet-leather boots given her by a friend, who knew a lady who knew an actor. These boots, and old foil, and a slashed doublet once used by an artist for some picture, were Jo's chief treasures, and appeared on all occasions. The smallness of the company made it necessary for the two principal actors to take several parts apiece; and they certainly deserved some credit for the hard work they did in learning three or four different parts, whisking in and out of various costumes, and managing the stage besides. It was excellent drill for their memories, a harmless amusement, and employed many hours which otherwise would have been idle, lonely, or spent in less profitable society.

On Christmas night, a dozen girls piled onto the bed which was the dress-circle, and sat before the blue and yellow chintz curtains in a most flattering state of expectancy. There was a good deal of rustling and whispering behind the curtain, a trifle of lamp-smoke, and an occasional giggle from Amy, who was apt to get hysterical in the excitement of the moment. Presently a bell sounded, the curtains flew apart, and the Operatic Tragedy began.

"A gloomy wood," according to the one play-bill, was represented by a few shrubs in pots, green baize on the floor, and a cave in the distance. This cave was made with a clothes-horse for a roof, bureaus for walls; and in it was a small furnace in full blast, with a black pot on it, and an old witch bending over it. The stage was dark, and the glow of the furnace had a fine effect, especially as real steam issued from the kettle when the witch took off the cover. A mo-

"That's loving our neighbor better than ourselves, and I like it," said Meg, as they set out their presents, while their mother was upstairs collecting clothes for the poor Hummels.

Not a very splendid show, but there was a great deal of love done up in the few little bundles; and the tall vase of red roses, white chrysanthemums, and trailing vines, which stood in the middle, gave quite an elegant air to the table.

"She's coming! Strike up, Beth! Open the door, Amy! Three cheers for Marmee!" cried Jo, prancing about, while Meg went to conduct mother to the seat of honor.

Beth played her gayest march, Amy threw open the door, and Meg enacted escort with great dignity.

ment was allowed for the first thrill to subside; then Hugo, the villain, stalked in with a clanking sword at his side, a slouched hat, black beard, mysterious cloak, and the boots. After pacing to and fro in much agitation, he struck his forehead, and burst out in a wild strain, singing of his hatred to Roderigo, his love for Zara, and his pleasing resolution to kill the one and win the other. The gruff tones of Hugo's voice, with an occasional shout when his feelings overcame him, were very impressive, and the audience applauded the moment he paused for breath. Bowing with the air of one accustomed to public praise, he stole to the cavern, and ordered Hagar to come forth with a commanding "What ho, minion! I need thee!"

Out came Meg, with gray horse-hair hanging about her face, a red and black robe, a staff, and cabalistic signs upon her cloak. Hugo demanded a potion to make Zara adore him, and one to destroy Roderigo. Hagar, in a fine dramatic melody, promised both, and proceeded to call up the spirit who would bring the love philter:

> Hither, hither, from thy home,
> Airy sprite, I bid thee come!
> Born of roses, fed on dew,
> Charms and potions canst thou brew?
> Bring me here, with elfin speed,
> The fragrant philter which I need;
> Make it sweet and swift and strong,
> Spirit, answer now my song!

A soft strain of music sounded, and then at the back of the cave appeared a little figure in cloudy white, with glittering wings, golden hair, and a garland of roses on its head. Waving a wand, it sang,—

> Hither I come
> From my airy home,
> Afar in the silver moon.
> Take the magic spell,
> And use it well,
> Or its power will vanish soon!

And, dropping a small, gilded bottle at the witch's feet, the spirit vanished. Another chant from Hagar produced another apparition,—not a lovely one; for, with a bang, an ugly black imp appeared, and having croaked a reply, tossed a dark bottle at Hugo, and disappeared with a mocking laugh. Having warbled his thanks and put the potions in his boots, Hugo departed; and Hagar informed the audience that, as he had killed a few of her friends in times past, she has cursed him, and intends to thwart his plans, and be revenged on him. Then the curtain fell, and the audience reposed and ate candy while discussing the merits of the play.

A good deal of hammering went on before the curtain rose again; but when it became evident what a masterpiece of stage carpentering had been got up, no one murmured at

the delay. It was truly superb! A tower rose to the ceiling; half-way up appeared a window, with a lamp burning at it, and behind the white curtain appeared Zara in a lovely blue and silver dress, waiting for Roderigo. He came in gorgeous array, with plumed cap, red cloak, chestnut love-locks, a guitar, and the boots, of course. Kneeling at the foot of the tower, he sang a serenade in melting tones. Zara replied, and, after a musical dialogue, consented to fly. Then came the grand effect of the play. Roderigo produced a rope-ladder, with five steps to it, threw up one end, and invited Zara to descend. Timidly she crept from her lattice, put her hand on Roderigo's shoulder, and was about to leap

she also defied her sire, and he ordered them both to the deepest dungeons of the castle. A stout little retainer came in with chains, and led them away, looking very much frightened, and evidently forgetting the speech he ought to have made.

Act third was the castle hall; and here Hagar appeared, having come to free the lovers and finish Hugo. She hears him coming, and hides; sees him put the potions into two cups of wine, and bid the timid little servant "Bear them to the captives in their cells, and tell them I shall come anon." The servant takes Hugo aside to tell him something, and Hagar changes the cups for two others which are harmless. Ferdinando, the "minion," carries them away, and Hagar puts back the cup which holds the poison meant for Roderigo. Hugo, getting thirsty after a long warble, drinks it, loses his wits, and, after a good deal of clutching and stamping, falls flat and dies; while Hagar informs him what she has done in a song of exquisite power and melody.

This was a truly thrilling scene, though some persons might have thought that the sudden tumbling down of a quantity of long hair rather marred the effect of the villain's death. He was called before the curtain, and with great propriety appeared, leading Hagar, whose singing was considered more wonderful than all the rest of the performance put together.

Act fourth displayed the despairing Roderigo on the point of stabbing himself, because he has been told that Zara has deserted him. Just as the dagger is at his heart, a lovely song is sung under his window, informing him that Zara is true, but in danger, and he can save her, if he will. A key is thrown in, which unlocks the door, and in a spasm of rapture he tears off his chains, and rushes away to find and rescue his lady-love.

Act fifth opened with a stormy scene between Zara and Don Pedro. He wishes her to go into a convent, but she won't hear of it; and, after a touching appeal, is about to faint, when Roderigo dashes in and demands her hand. Don Pedro refuses, because he is not rich. They shout and gesticulate tremendously, but cannot agree, and Roderigo is about to bear away the exhausted Zara, when the timid servant enters with a letter and a bag from Hagar, who has mysteriously disappeared. The latter informs the party that she bequeaths untold wealth to the young pair and an awful doom to Don Pedro, if he doesn't make them happy. The bag is opened, and several quarts of tin money shower down upon the stage, till it is quite glorified with the glitter. This entirely softens the "stern sire": he consents without a murmur, all join in a joyful chorus, and the curtain falls upon the lovers kneeling to receive Don Pedro's blessing in attitudes of the most romantic grace.

Tumultuous applause followed, but received an unexpected check; for the cot-bed, on which the "dress circle" was built, suddenly shut up, and extinguished the enthusiastic audience. Roderigo and Don Pedro flew to the rescue,

gracefully down, when, "Alas! alas for Zara!" she forgot her train,—it caught in the window; the tower tottered, leaned forward, fell with a crash, and buried the unhappy lovers in the ruins!

A universal shriek arose as the russet boots waved wildly from the wreck, and a golden head emerged, exclaiming, "I told you so! I told you so!" With wonderful presence of mind, Don Pedro, the cruel sire, rushed in, dragged out his daughter, with a hasty aside,—

"Don't laugh! Act as if it was all right!"—and, ordering Roderigo up, banished him from the kingdom with wrath and scorn. Though decidedly shaken by the fall of the tower upon him, Roderigo defied the old gentleman, and refused to stir. This dauntless example fired Zara:

and all were taken out unhurt, though many were speechless with laughter. The excitement had hardly subsided, when Hannah appeared, with "Mrs. March's compliments, and would the ladies walk down to supper."

This was a surprise, even to the actors; and, when they saw the table, they looked at one another in rapturous amazement. It was like Marmee to get up a little treat for them; but anything so fine as this was unheard-of since the departed days of plenty. There was ice-cream,—actually two dishes of it, pink and white,—and cake and fruit and distracting French bonbons, and, in the middle of the table, four great bouquets of hot-house flowers!

It quite took the breath away; and they stared first at the table and then at their mother, who looked as if she enjoyed it immensely.

"Is it fairies?" asked Amy.

"It's Santa Claus," said Beth.

"Mother did it;" and Meg smiled her sweetest, in spite of her gray beard and white eyebrows.

"Aunt March had a good fit, and sent the supper," cried Jo, with a sudden inspiration.

"All wrong. Old Mr. Laurence sent it," replied Mrs. March.

"The Laurence boy's grandfather! What in the world put such a thing into his head? We don't know him!" exclaimed Meg.

"Hannah told one of his servants about your breakfast party. He is an odd old gentleman, but that pleased him. He knew my father, years ago; and he sent me a polite note this afternoon, saying he hoped I would allow him to express his friendly feeling toward my children by sending them a few trifles in honor of the day. I could not refuse; and so you have a little feast at night to make up for the bread-and-milk breakfast."

"That boy put it into his head, I know he did! He's a capital fellow, and I wish we could get acquainted. He looks as if he'd like to know us; but he's bashful, and Meg is so prim she won't let me speak to him when we pass," said Jo, as the plates went round, and the ice began to melt out of sight, with "Ohs!" and "Ahs!" of satisfaction.

"You mean the people who live in the big house next door, don't you?" asked one of the girls. "My mother knows old Mr. Laurence; but says he's very proud, and doesn't like to mix with his neighbors. He keeps his grandson shut up, when he isn't riding or walking with his tutor, and makes him study very hard. We invited him to our party, but he didn't come. Mother says he's very nice, though he never speaks to us girls."

"Our cat ran away once, and he brought her back, and we talked over the fence, and were getting on capitally,—all about cricket, and so on,—when he saw Meg coming, and walked off. I mean to know him some day; for he needs fun, I'm sure he does," said Jo decidedly.

"I like his manners, and he looks like a little gentleman; so I've no objection to your knowing him, if a proper opportu-

nity comes. He brought the flowers himself; and I should have asked him in, if I had been sure what was going on upstairs. He looked so wistful as he went away, hearing the frolic, and evidently having none of his own."

"It's a mercy you didn't, mother!" laughed Jo, looking at her boots. "But we'll have another play, some time, that he *can* see. Perhaps he'll help act; wouldn't that be jolly?"

"I never had such a fine bouquet before! How pretty it is!" And Meg examined her flowers with great interest.

"They *are* lovely! But Beth's roses are sweeter to me," said Mrs. March, smelling the half-dead posy in her belt.

Beth nestled up to her, and whispered softly, "I wish I could send my bunch to father. I'm afraid he isn't having such a merry Christmas as we are."

THE HOLLY AND THE IVY

The holly and the ivy,
When they are both full grown,
Of all the trees that are in the wood,
The holly bears the crown.
The rising of the sun
And the running of the deer,
The playing of the merry organ,
Sweet singing in the choir.

The holly bears a blossom
As white as the lily flower,
And Mary bore sweet Jesus Christ
To be our sweet saviour.

The holly bears a berry
As red as any blood,
And Mary bore sweet Jesus Christ
To do poor sinners good.

The holly bears a prickle
As sharp as any thorn,
And Mary bore sweet Jesus Christ
On Christmas day in the morn.

The holly bears a bark
As bitter as any gall,
And Mary bore sweet Jesus Christ
For to redeem us all.

The holly and the ivy,
When they are both full grown,
Of all the trees that are in the wood
The holly bears the crown.

—OLD ENGLISH CAROL

CHRISTMAS CAROL

Villagers all, this frosty tide,
Let your doors swing open wide,
Though wind may follow and snow betide
Yet draw us in by your fire to bide:
Joy shall be yours in the morning.

Here we stand in the cold and the sleet,
Blowing fingers and stamping feet,
Come from far away, you to greet—
You by the fire and we in the street—
Bidding you joy in the morning.

For ere one half of the night was gone,
Sudden a star has led us on,
Raining bliss and benison—
Bliss tomorrow and more anon,
Joy for every morning.

Good man Joseph toiled through the snow—
Saw the star o'er the stable low;
Mary she might not further go—
Welcome thatch and litter below!
Joy was hers in the morning.

And then they heard the angels tell,
"Who were the first to cry Nowell?
Animals all as it befel,
In the stable where they did dwell!
Joy shall be theirs in the morning."

FROM WIND IN THE WILLOWS
—KENNETH GRAHAME

The Gift of the Magi

O. HENRY

ONE DOLLAR AND EIGHTY-SEVEN CENTS. That was all. And sixty cents of it was in pennies. Pennies saved one and two at a time by bulldozing the grocer and the vegetable man and the butcher until one's cheeks burned with the silent imputation of parsimony that such close dealing implied. Three times Della counted it. One dollar and eighty-seven cents. And the next day would be Christmas.

There was clearly nothing to do but flop down on the shabby little couch and howl. So Della did it. Which instigates the moral reflection that life is made up of sobs, sniffles, and smiles, with sniffles predominating.

While the mistress of the home is gradually subsiding from the first stage to the second, take a look at the home. A furnished flat at $8 per week. It did not exactly beggar description, but it certainly had that word on the lookout for the mendicancy squad.

In the vestibule below as a letter-box into which no letter would go, and an electric button from which no mortal finger could coax a ring. Also appertaining thereunto was a card bearing the name 'Mr. James Dillingham Young.'

The 'Dillingham' had been flung to the breeze during a former period of prosperity when its possessor was being paid $30 per week. Now, when the income was shrunk to $20, the letters of 'Dillingham' looked blurred, as though they were thinking seriously of contracting to a modest and unassuming D. But whenever Mr. James Dillingham Young came home and reached his flat above he was called 'Jim' and greatly hugged by Mrs. James Dillingham Young, already introduced to you as Della. Which is all very good.

Della finished her cry and attended to her cheeks with the powder rag. She stood by the window and looked out dully at a gray cat walking a gray fence in a gray backyard. Tomorrow would be Christmas Day, and she had only $1.87 with which to buy Jim a present. She had been saving every penny she could for months, with this result. Twenty dollars a week doesn't go far. Expenses had been greater than she had calculated. They always are. Only $1.87 to buy a present for Jim. Her Jim. Many a happy hour she had spent planning for something nice for him. Something fine and rare and sterling − something just a little bit near to being worthy of the honor of being owned by Jim.

There was a pier-glass between the windows of the room. Perhaps you have seen a pier-glass in an $8 flat. A very thin and very agile person may, by observing his reflection in a rapid sequence of longitudinal strips, obtain a fairly accurate conception of his looks. Della, being slender, had mastered the art.

Suddenly she whirled from the window and stood before the glass. Her eyes were shining brilliantly, but her face had lost its color within twenty seconds. Rapidly she pulled down her hair and let it fall to its full length.

Now, there were two possessions of the James Dillingham Youngs in which they both took a mighty pride. One was Jim's gold watch that had been his father's and his grandfather's. The other was Della's hair. Had the Queen of Sheba lived in the flat across the airshaft, Della would have let her hair hang out the window some day to dry just to depreciate Her Majesty's jewels and gifts. Had King Solomon been the janitor, with all his treasures piled up in the basement, Jim would have pulled out his watch every time he passed, just to see him pluck at his beard from envy.

So now Della's beautiful hair fell about her rippling and shining like a cascade of brown waters. It reached below her knee and made itself almost a garment for her. And then she did it up again nervously and quickly. Once she faltered for a minute and stood still while a tear or two splashed on the worn red carpet.

On went her old brown jacket; on went her old brown hat. With a whirl of skirts and with the brilliant sparkle still in her eyes, she fluttered out the door and down the stairs to the street.

Where she stopped the sign read: 'Mme. Sofronie. Hair Goods of All Kinds.' One flight up Della ran, and collected herself, panting. Madame, large, too white, chilly, hardly looked the 'Sofronie.'

'Will you buy my hair?' asked Della.

'I buy hair,' said Madame. 'Take yer hat off and let's have a sight at the looks of it.'

Down rippled the brown cascade.

'Twenty dollars,' said Madame, lifting the mass with a practiced hand.

'Give it to me quick,' said Della.

Oh, and the next two hours tripped by on rosy wings. Forget the hashed metaphor. She was ransacking the stores for Jim's present.

She found it at last. It surely had been made for Jim and no one else. There was no other like it in any of the stores, and she had turned all of them inside out. It was a platinum fob chain simple and chaste in design, properly proclaiming its value by substance alone and not by meretorious ornamentation – as all good things should do. It was even worthy of The Watch. As soon as she saw it she knew that it must be Jim's. It was like him. Quietness and value – the description applied to both. Twenty-one dollars they took from her for it, and she hurried home with the 87 cents. With that chain on his watch Jim might be properly anxious about the time in any company. Grand as the watch was, he sometimes looked at it on the sly on account of the old leather strap that he used in place of a chain.

When Della reached home her intoxication gave way a little to prudence and reason. She got out her curling irons and lighted the gas and went to work repairing the ravages made by generosity added to love. Which is always a tremendous task, dear friends – a mammoth task.

Within forty minutes her head was covered with tiny, close-lying curls that made her look wonderfully like a truant schoolboy. She looked at her reflection in the mirror long, carefully, and critically.

'If Jim doesn't kill me,' she said to herself, 'before he takes a second look at me, he'll say I look like a Coney Island chorus girl. But what could I do – oh! what could I do with a dollar and eighty-seven cents?'

At 7 o'clock the coffee was made and the frying-pan was on the back of the stove hot and ready to cook the chops.

Jim was never late. Della doubled the fob chain in her hand and sat on the corner of the table near the door that he always entered. Then she heard his step on the stairway down

on the first flight, and she turned white for just a moment. She had a habit of saying little silent prayers about the simplest everyday things, and now she whispered: 'Please God, make him think I am still pretty.'

The door opened and Jim stepped in and closed it. He looked thin and very serious. Poor fellow, he was only twenty-two – and to be burdened with a family! He needed a new overcoat and he was without gloves.

Jim stopped inside the door, as immovable as a setter at the scent of quail. His eyes were fixed upon Della, and there was an expression in them that she could not read, and it terrified her. It was not anger, nor surprise, nor disapproval, nor horror, nor any of the sentiments that she had been prepared for. He simply stared at her fixedly with that peculiar expression on his face.

Della wriggled off the table and went for him.

'Jim, darling,' she cried, 'don't look at me that way. I had my hair cut off and sold it because I couldn't have lived through Christmas without giving you a present. It'll grow out again – you won't mind, will you? I just had to do it. My hair grows awfully fast. "Merry Christmas!" Jim, and let's be happy. You don't know what a nice – what a beautiful, nice gift I've got for you.'

'You've cut off your hair?' asked Jim, laboriously, as if he had not arrived at that patent fact yet even after the hardest mental labor.

'Cut it off and sold it,' said Della. 'Don't you like me just as well, anyhow? I'm me without my hair, ain't I?'

Jim looked about the room curiously.

'You say your hair is gone?' he said, with an air almost of idiocy.

'You needn't look for it,' said Della. 'It's sold, I tell you – sold and gone, too. It's Christmas Eve, boy. Be good to me, for it went for you. Maybe the hairs on my head were numbered,' she went on with a sudden serious sweetness, 'but nobody could ever count my love for you. Shall I put the chops on, Jim?'

Out of his trance Jim seemed quickly to wake. He enfolded his Della. For ten seconds let us regard with discreet scrutiny some inconsequential object in the other direction. Eight dollars a week or a million a year – what is the difference? A mathematician or a wit would give you the wrong answer. The magi brought valuable gifts, but that was not among them. This dark assertion will be illuminated later on.

Jim drew a package from his overcoat pocket and threw it upon the table.

'Don't make any mistake, Dell,' he said, 'about me. I don't think there's anything in the way of a haircut or a shave or a shampoo that could make me like my girl any less. But if you'll unwrap that package you may see why you had me going a while at first.'

White fingers and nimble tore at the string and paper. And then an ecstatic scream of joy; and then, alas! a quick feminine charge to hysterical tears and wails,

necessitating the immediate employment of all the comforting powers of the lord of the flat.

For there lay The Combs – the set of combs, side and back, that Della had worshipped for so long in a Broadway window. Beautiful combs, pure tortoise shell, with jewelled rims – just the shade to wear in the beautiful vanished hair. They were expensive combs, she knew, and her heart had simply craved and yearned over them without the least hope of possession. And now, they were hers, but the tresses that should have adorned the coveted adornments were gone.

But she hugged them to her bosom, and at length she was able to look up with dim eyes and a smile and say: 'My hair grows so fast, Jim!'

And then Della leaped up like a little singed cat and cried, 'Oh, Oh!'

Jim had not yet seen his beautiful present. She held it out to him eagerly upon her open palm. The dull precious metal seemed to flash with a reflection of her bright and ardent spirit.

'Isn't it a dandy, Jim? I hunted all over town to find

it. You'll have to look at the time a hundred times a day now. Give me your watch. I want to see how it looks on it.'

Instead of obeying, Jim tumbled down on the couch and put his hands under the back of his head and smiled.

'Dell,' said he, 'let's put our Christmas presents away and keep 'em a while. They're too nice to use just at present. I sold the watch to get the money to buy your combs. And now suppose you put the chops on.'

The magi, as you know, were wise men – wonderfully wise men – who brought gifts to the Babe in the manger. They invented the art of giving Christmas presents. Being wise, their gifts were no doubt wise ones, possibly bearing the privilege of exchange in case of duplication. And here I have lamely related to you the uneventful chronicle of two foolish children in a flat who most unwisely sacrificed for each other the greatest treasures of their house. But in a last word to the wise of these days let it be said that of all who give gifts these two were the wisest. Of all who give and receive gifts, such as they are wisest. Everywhere they are wisest. They are the magi.

Good King Wenceslas

J. M. NEALE tr.

FROM THE LATIN

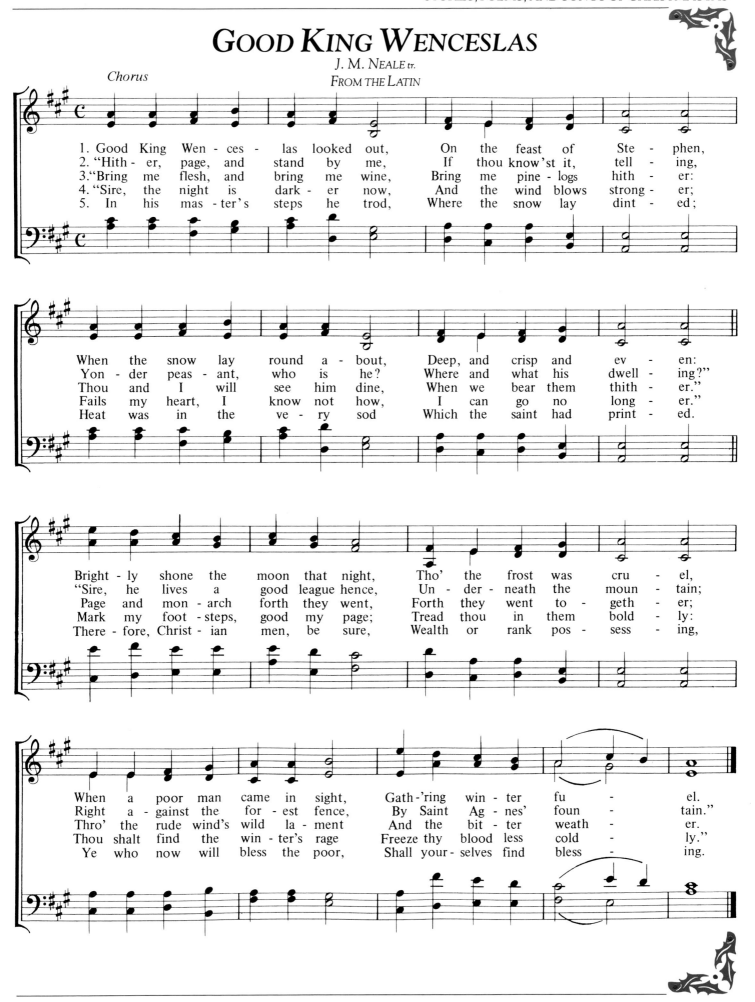

1. Good King Wen - ces - las looked out, On the feast of Ste - phen,
2. "Hith - er, page, and stand by me, If thou know'st it, tell - ing;
3. "Bring me flesh, and bring me wine, Bring me pine - logs hith - er:
4. "Sire, the night is dark - er now, And the wind blows strong - er;
5. In his mas - ter's steps he trod, Where the snow lay dint - ed;

When the snow lay round a - bout, Deep, and crisp and ev - en:
Yon - der peas - ant, who is he? Where and what his dwell - ing?"
Thou and I will see him dine, When we bear them thith - er."
Fails my heart, I know not how, I can go no long - er."
Heat was in the ve - ry sod Which the saint had print - ed.

Bright - ly shone the moon that night, Tho' the frost was cru - el,
"Sire, he lives a good league hence, Un - der - neath the moun - tain;
Page and mon - arch forth they went, Forth they went to - geth - er;
Mark my foot - steps, good my page; Tread thou in them bold - ly:
There - fore, Christ - ian men, be sure, Wealth or rank pos - sess - ing,

When a poor man came in sight, Gath - 'ring win - ter fu - el.
Right a - gainst the for - est fence, By Saint Ag - nes' foun - tain."
Thro' the rude wind's wild la - ment And the bit - ter weath - er.
Thou shalt find the win - ter's rage Freeze thy blood less cold - ly."
Ye who now will bless the poor, Shall your - selves find bless - ing.

THREE KINGS OF ORIENT

TRADITIONAL

1. We three kings of Or - i - ent are, Bear - ing gifts we tra - verse
2. Born a babe on Beth - le - hem's plain, Gold we bring to crown Him a -
3. Frank - in - cense to of - fer have I; In - cense owns a De - i - ty
4. Myrrh is mine; its bit - ter per - fume Breathes a life of gath - er - ing
5. Glo - rious now be - hold __ Him rise, King and God and Sac - ri -

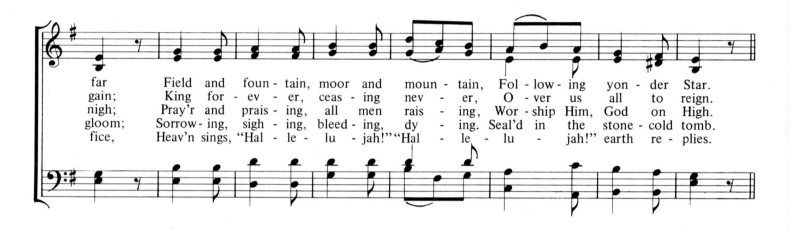

far   Field and foun - tain, moor and moun - tain, Fol - low - ing yon - der Star.
gain; King for - ev - er, ceas - ing nev - er, O - ver us all to reign.
nigh; Pray'r and prais - ing, all men rais - ing, Wor - ship Him, God on High.
gloom; Sor - row - ing, sigh - ing, bleed - ing, dy - ing. Seal'd in the stone - cold tomb.
fice, Heav'n sings, "Hal - le - lu - jah!" "Hal - le - lu - jah!" earth re - plies.

Chorus

Oh, __ star of won - der, star of might, Star with roy - al beau - ty bright,

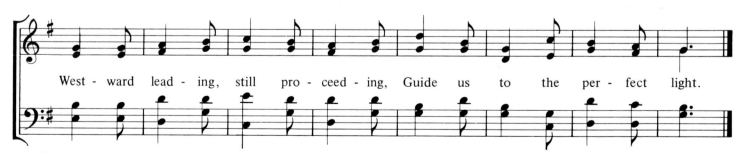

West - ward lead - ing, still pro - ceed - ing, Guide us to the per - fect light.

THE THREE KINGS

THREE Kings came riding from far away,
Melchior and Gaspar and Baltasar;
Three Wise Men out of the East were they,
And they travelled by night and they slept by day,
For their guide was a beautiful, wonderful star.

The star was so beautiful, large, and clear,
That all the other stars of the sky
Became a white mist in the atmosphere,
And by this they knew that the coming was near
Of the Prince foretold in the prophecy.

Three caskets they bore on their saddlebows,
Three caskets of gold with golden keys;
Their robes were of crimson silk with rows
Of bells and pomegranates and furbelows,
Their turbans like blossoming almond-trees.

And so the Three Kings rode into the West,
Through the dusk of night, over hill and dell,
And sometimes they nodded with beard on breast,
And sometimes talked, as they paused to rest,
With the people they met at some wayside well.

"Of the child that is born," said Baltasar,
"Good people, I pray you, tell us the news;
For we in the East have seen his star,
And have ridden fast, and have ridden far,
To find and worship the King of the Jews."

And the people answered, "You ask in vain;
We know of no king but Herod the Great!"
They thought the Wise Men were men insane,
As they spurred their horses across the plain,
Like riders in haste, and who cannot wait.

And when they came to Jerusalem,
Herod the Great, who had heard this thing,
Sent for the Wise Men and questioned them;
And said, "Go down unto Bethlehem,
And bring me tidings of this new king."

So they rode away; and the star stood still,
The only one in the gray of morn;
Yes, it stopped,—it stood still of its own free will,
Right over Bethlehem on the hill,
The city of David, where Christ was born.

And the Three Kings rode through the gate and the guard,
Through the silent street, till their horses turned
And neighed as they entered the great inn-yard;
But the windows were closed, and the doors were barred,
And only a light in the stable burned.

And cradled there in the scented hay,
In the air made sweet by the breath of kine,
The little child in the manger lay,
The child, that would be king one day
Of a kingdom not human but divine.

His mother Mary of Nazareth
Sat watching beside his place of rest,
Watching the even flow of his breath,
For the joy of life and the terror of death
Were mingled together in her breast.

They laid their offerings at his feet:
The gold was their tribute to a King,
The frankincense, with its odor sweet,
Was for the Priest, the Paraclete,
The myrrh for the body's burying.

And the mother wondered and bowed her head,
And sat as still as a statue of stone;
Her heart was troubled yet comforted,
Remembering what the Angel had said
Of an endless reign and of David's throne.

Then the Kings rode out of the city gate,
With a clatter of hoofs in proud array;
But they went not back to Herod the Great,
For they knew his malice and feared his hate,
And returned to their homes by another way.

—HENRY WADSWORTH LONGFELLOW

185

A CHILD'S CHRISTMAS SONG

LORD, I'm just a little boy
Born one day like You,
And I've got a mother dear
And a birthday, too.
But my birthday comes in spring,
When the days are long,
And the robin in the tree
Wakens me with song.
Since the birds are all away,
Lord, when You are born,
Let Your angels waken me
On Your birthday morn.
Lord, I'm just a little boy,
Hidden in the night;
Let Your angels spy me out
Long before it's light.
I would be the first to wake
And the first to raise
In this quiet house of ours
Songs of love and praise.
You shall hear me first, dear Lord,
Blow my Christmas horn;
Let Your angels waken me
On Your birthday morn.

—T. A. DALEY

Jeannette

LOUIS FRECHETTE

JEANNETTE, a chubby little maid, roly-poly and plump, with inviting dimples and wary black eyes, had, at first—oh! immediately! almost from birth—shown an instinctive antipathy for her father.

When he leaned over her cradle with a kiss on his lips, she would outline a grimace of dislike at him, and if he opened his arms for an embrace, she would turn to her mother, with outstretched hands, as if to implore help.

A painful circumstance, which changed the face of things, came to console him.

Jeannette fell ill.

During several days, a devouring fever hollowed her cheeks, dulled her eyes, and, so to speak, gnawed her thin and shivering little limbs.

The father did his best to encourage his wife in despair. When the poor mother took a little rest, he in his turn sat at the bed-side of the little one, and bending over her with tear-dimmed eyes, heavy-hearted and dejected, he almost imprecated his powerlessness to relieve the dear child for whose health he would so willingly have given his own, a thousand times.

One morning Jeannette opened her eyes at the very moment when a heavy tear splashed on her poor, pale, helpless little hand.

She had the strength to turn her head toward her father; and then, these two beings so different in age and in nature, exchanged one of those looks that are never forgotten, and by which is sometimes effected that transfusion of souls, that only those who are made to love passionately can understand.

The father had conquered the heart of his child; the child had guessed and sounded that of her father.

Convalescence is rapid with the little ones. The dear invalid took a new lease on life; her cheeks bloomed anew, her large, velvety eyes recovered their pristine brightness, her pretty dimples appeared once more as the lurking-place of sweet kisses, her lips, long mute and livid, found again their smile, their color and their silvery notes.

The house became once more as ringing as a spring day, and as cheerful as a sunbeam.

A revolution had taken place in Jeannette's character; she adored her father.

She was never happier than, when sitting on his knees, she pulled his beard, tickled his neck, or teased him with a thousand coaxing caresses, while she prattled as uninterruptedly as a finch on a marauding expedition.

On his side, never was the father more beaming with joy than when he rocked the arch little lass in his arms, relating to her the adventures of Hop-o'-my-Thumb, or singing to her some ballad of the times of yore.

Do not ask me if they were happy.

But all this is digression.

Jeannette had grown; she was now turned four years, and the affection she had vowed to her father had not diminished.

On the contrary, the little one had become his inseparable companion; and, as long as he was at home, she deafened, or rather charmed him by her chatter, told him a myriad of adorable nothings, and asked him a thousand questions which the good papa answered with imperturbable complacency.

At the coming of Christmas, a holiday so impatiently awaited by the little folks, the conversation between the parents and babies runs, naturally enough, on the presents to which this time of the year almost always gives rise in well-to-do families.

This was Jeannette's great preoccupation. The day before Christmas Eve, as the family dinner was drawing to a close, all at once she became pensive, and after a moment's reflection, during which the graceful curve of her eye-brows had become somewhat marred in the struggle of a confused thought, she said brusquely:

"Tell me, papa, is it the Infant-Jesus or Santa Claus who comes down in the chimney to put presents in the shoes of the little children who have been good?"

"Why do you ask me that?"

"Well, there are some people who say that it is Santa Claus, and others who say it is the Infant-Jesus."

"They both come, my love; each one in turn, each one his year."

"And this year it is the turn of..."

"Of the Infant-Jesus."

And as the child clapped her hands with a joyous exclamation, the father added:

"You are glad?"

"Oh! yes."

"You love the Infant-Jesus better than Santa Claus?"

"Yes, indeed."

"But why?"

"Because...!"

And Jeannette put her finger in her mouth with a deliciously provoking expression of face.

"Tell me why," insisted the father; "Santa Claus brought you handsome toys last year."

"Are you sure that Santa Claus gives nothing to the poor children?"

"I am; Rosina told me so."

"Who is Rosina?"

"The washerwoman's little girl. I asked her if she was going to put her shoes in the chimney to-morrow night. She said she had put them last year, but that she had found nothing in them, although she had been ever so good. Her mother says that Santa Claus only goes to rich people. But since it is the Infant-Jesus who comes this year, I will tell Rosina to try again. Little Jesus must love poor people as much as others, since he was poor himself."

"But are you sure that he will go?"

Jeannette remained a few moments non-plussed; but after a moment's reflection:

"Yes," she said. "He will go. I shall pray him hard, hard, and surely he won't refuse me."

An hour after; softly enveloped in her fresh white night dress, her chin propped upon her primly folded hands, and her knees sunk in the long silky hairs of a llama skin rug, Jeannette prayed like a little angel that she was; then while the mother gave her the good night kiss, and tucked in warmly the covering of the little bed, the name of Rosina passed like a sigh on the lips of the sleeping child.

When the morning sun stained with pink the window of the room where she slept, Jeannette rose absorbed in thought. Her father's last words "Are you sure that he will go?" returned to her memory, and the child began not to be so sure of the efficacy of her prayer.

"After all, perhaps he will not go," she said to herself. And this supposition saddened her almost to tears.

"What is the matter with you this morning, my Jeannette," said the father; "you are not so gay as usual. Don't you know that tonight is Christmas Eve, and that, since you have been very good, to-morrow morning your little shoes, and even your little stockings perhaps, will be crammed with pretty things?"

Jeannette smiled, but remained pensive.

"Papa," she said as though she had suddenly come to a decision, "if I knew how to write...but I can only sign my name."

"What would you do if you could write?"

"I would write a letter."

"To whom?"

"To little Jesus."

"Well, my love, tell me what you want to tell the Infant-Jesus; I will write to him, and you will sign."

"Truly?"

"At once, if you want."

"And it will be the same thing?"

"Exactly the same."

"Oh! dear good papa!"

And the little one threw herself into the arms of the "dear good papa," who, a few minutes after, was sitting

"Yes."

"With a beautiful big doll."

"Yes."

"Then why don't you love him?"

"Because...he is not good to everybody."

"He is not good to everybody?"

"No; he does not love the little children who are poor; he does not give them anything."

at his desk writing the following letter dictated word for word by his spoilt pet:

DEAR LITTLE JESUS,
   To-morrow is your feast of Christmas, and as I have been very good, I put my shoes on the hearthstone, just like the other children. But give me only your picture, and take the presents to Rosina who is very good also, but whose mother is a poor widow. You know her house, don't you? It's on Sanguinet street. There is a big tree, right in front—

Here Jeannette jumped.

A big tear, similar to the one that had wakened her one day by falling on her sick little hand, had just wet the paper, where the father's nervous fingers had some difficulty in following the lines.

"Why do you cry?" she asked, passing a pudgy little arm around his neck and looking tenderly into his eyes.

Too much moved to answer, the good father took his child in his arms, pressed her closely to his heart, enveloping her in a lasting passionate embrace; and for a long, long time, he jealously contemplated his treasure through the tears of happiness and love that filled his eyes.

When the little one had scribbled her name at the foot of her touching letter to the Infant-Jesus, her father stood up and walked up and down for a few minutes to recover himself. Then, with his back turned, he stood for some time before the window of his study, his gaze lost in the brilliant azure of the December sky; and when entering the room, the mother—tenderly loved also—heard him murmur in a half-sob:

"Provided God does not take her away from us...."

At night the naive missive, carefully directed, lay in the little shoe slid behind the fire dogs; and, after having said her prayers as the night before, Jeannette softly fell asleep amid her white laces, to dream of Child Jesus, of the good Angels and of Paradise.

Not far from there, in a humble and lowly home, at the first glimmer of dawn, a poor little girl—who sometimes accompanied her mother when the latter brought newly-washed clothes to the house of Jeannette's parents—the little Rosina so warmly recommended in the letter to the Infant-Jesus, had a great surprise and a great joy.

Beaming with happiness, she carried to her mother's bedside a pink-cheeked, yellow-haired doll in elaborate costume.

Her old shoes had disappeared, yielding the place in the corner of the chimney to warm and elegant boots in both of which shone a gold coin.

Of course it is unnecessary to add that on the special recommendation of her mother, the child's first visit was to Jeannette.

"Me," said the latter, "I have not a doll, nor new shoes, nor gold pieces, but I have more than all that. The little Jesus gave me his picture. Here it is."

And she ran to get a pretty chromo-lithograph, very brilliantly festooned with gold arabesques, showing the divine Infant in his manger. On the back of the picture was inscribed in a superb round hand:

To Jeannette, from the Little Jesus.

"It comes from Him?"

"Yes, I found it in my shoe."

"Oh! how beautiful He is!" cried Rosina enthusiastically.

"Is He not charming?" approved Jeannette.

"And how well He writes!"

"Yes, He writes just like Marius."

By the way, Marius was a valet, whose graphical talent was generally put into requisition when there was some careful writing to be done.

No, Jeannette had no other presents for Christmas that year, but she lost no time by waiting, for papa and mamma took their revenge royally on the New Year.

Jeannette is now nineteen.

She is a tall, handsome brunette, who has made her début at the last St. Catherine ball, and who cherishes her father as much as ever.

Recently she happened to unlock an elegant casket in the presence of one of her friends.

"Here," she said, "this is a picture I have kept since I was a four years old little bit of a thing."

"Really? Oh! the pretty Christ Child."

"Is it not nice?"

"Why don't you put this little jewel among your other knick-knacks?"

"Ah! well, do you see," answered the young girl hesitatingly, "I don't know why, but every time that papa looks at it, it never fails to bring a tear to his eyes."

THE SHEPHERDS HAD AN ANGEL

The shepherds had an angel,
    The wise men had a star;
But what have I, a little child,
    To guide me home from far,
Where glad stars sing together,
    And singing angels are?

Lord Jesus is my Guardian,
    So I can nothing lack;
The lambs lie in His bosom
    Along life's dangerous track:
The wilful lambs that go astray
    He, bleeding, brings them back.

Those shepherds thro' the lonely night
    Sat watching by their sheep,
Until they saw the heav'nly host
    Who neither tire nor sleep,
All singing Glory, glory,
    In festival they keep.

Christ watches me, His little lamb,
    Cares for me day and night,
That I may be His own in heav'n;
    So angels clad in white
Shall sing their Glory, glory,
    For my sake in the height.

Lord, bring me nearer day by day,
    Till I my voice unite,
And sing my Glory, glory,
    With angels clad in white.
All Glory, glory, giv'n to Thee,
    Thro' all the heav'nly height.
                    —CHRISTINA G. ROSSETTI

THE LAMB

Little Lamb, who made thee?
Dost thou know who made thee?
Gave thee life, and bid thee feed,
By the stream and o'er the mead;
Gave thee clothing of delight,
Softest clothing, woolly, bright;
Gave thee such a tender voice,
Making all the vales rejoice?

Little Lamb, who made thee?
Dost thou know who made thee?

Little Lamb, I'll tell thee,
Little Lamb, I'll tell thee:

He is called by thy name,
For He calls Himself a Lamb.
He is meek, and He is mild;
He became a little child.
I a child, and thou a lamb,
We are calléd by His Name.

Little Lamb God Bless Thee!
Little Lamb God Bless Thee!
                    —WILLIAM BLAKE

Come, All Ye Faithful

J. Reading

THE WORCESTERSHIRE CAROL

How grand and how bright
That wonderful night
When angels to Bethlehem came.
They burst forth like fires
They struck their gold lyres
And mingled their sound with the flame.

The shepherds were amazed
The pretty lambs gazed
At darkness thus turned into light.
No voice was there heard
From man, beast or bird
So sudden and solemn the sight.

And then when the sound
Re-echoed around
The hills and the dales all awoke.
The moon and the stars
Stopt their fiery ears
And listened while Gabriel spoke.

"I bring you," said he,
"From the glorious tree,
A message both gladsome and good.
The Saviour is come
To the world as His home
But he lies in a manger of wood."

At the mention of this
The source of all bliss
The angels sang loudly and long.
They soared to the sky
Beyond mortal eye
But left us the words of their song:

"All glory to God
Who laid by his rod
To smile on the world through his Son.
And peace be on earth
For this holy birth
Most wonderful conquests has won."
　　　　　　—17TH-CENTURY ENGLISH CAROL

THE CHRISTMAS DINNER

WASHINGTON IRVING

Lo! now is come our joyful'st feast!
  Let every man be jolly;
Eache roome with yvie leaves is drest,
  And every post with holly,
Now all our neighbours' chimneys smoke,
  And Christmas blocks are burning;
Their ovens they with bak't meats choke,
  And all their spits are turning.
      Without the door let sorrow lie,
      And if, for cold, it hap to die,
      We'll bury't in a Christmas pye,
      And evermore be merry.
            —WITHERS' JUVENILLA

I HAD finished my toilet, and was loitering with Frank Brace-bridge in the library, when we heard a distinct thwacking sound, which he informed me was a signal for the serving up of the dinner. The squire kept up old customs in kitchen as well as hall; and the rolling-pin, struck upon the dresser by the cook, summoned the servants to carry in the meats.

Just in this nick the cook knock'd thrice,
And all the waiters in a trice
  His summons did obey;
Each serving man, with dish in hand,
March'd boldly up, like our train band,
  Presented and away.

The dinner was served up in the great hall, where the squire always held his Christmas banquet. A blazing crackling fire of logs had been heaped on to warm the spacious apartment, and the flame went sparkling and wreathing up the wide-mouthed chimney. The great picture of the crusader and his white horse had been profusely decorated with greens for the occasion; and holly and ivy had likewise been wreathed round the helmet and weapons on the opposite wall, which I understood were the arms of the same warrior. I must own, by the by, I had strong doubts about the authenticity of the painting and armour as having belonged to the crusader, they certainly having the stamp of more recent days; but I was told that the painting had been so considered time out of mind; and that, as to the armour, it had been found in a lumber-room, and elevated to its present situation by the squire, who at once determined it to be the armour of the family hero; and as he was absolute authority on all such subjects in his own household, the matter had passed into current acceptation. A sideboard was set out just under this chivalric trophy, on which was a display of plate that might have vied (at least in variety) with Belshazzar's parade of the vessels of the temple: "flagons, cans, cups, beakers, goblets, basins, and ewers;" the

gorgeous utensils of good companionship that had gradually accumulated through many generations of jovial housekeepers. Before these stood the two Yule candles, beaming like two stars of the first magnitude; other lights were distributed in branches, and the whole array glittered like a firmament of silver.

We were ushered into this banqueting scene with the sound of minstrelsy, the old harper being seated on a stool beside the fireplace, and twanging his instrument with a vast deal more power than melody. Never did Christmas

side with a large wax-light, and bore a silver dish, on which was an enormous pig's head, decorated with rosemary, with a lemon in its mouth, which was placed with great formality at the head of the table. The moment this pageant made its appearance, the harper struck up a flourish; at the conclusion of which the young Oxonian, on receiving a hint from the squire, gave, with an air of the most comic gravity, an old carol, the first verse of which was as follows:

> Caput apri defero
> Reddens laudes Domino.
> The boar's head in hand bring I,
> With garlands gay and rosemary,
> I pray you all synge merily
> Qui estis in convivio.

Though prepared to witness many of these little eccentricities, from being apprised of the peculiar hobby of mine host; yet, I confess, the parade with which so odd a dish was introduced somewhat perplexed me, until I gathered from the conversation of the squire and the parson, that it was meant to represent the bringing in of the boar's head; a dish formerly served up with much ceremony and the sound of minstrelsy and song, at great tables, on Christmas day. "I like the old custom," said the squire, "not merely because it is stately and pleasing in itself, but because it was observed at the college of Oxford at which I was educated. When I hear the old song chanted, it brings to mind the time when I was young and gamesome—and the noble old college hall—and my fellow-students loitering about in their black gowns; many of whom, poor lads, are now in their graves!"

The table was literally loaded with good cheer, and presented an epitome of country abundance, in this season of overflowing larders. A distinguished post was allotted to "ancient sirloin," as mine host termed it; being, as he added, "the standard of old English hospitality, and a joint of goodly presence, and full of expectation." There were several dishes quaintly decorated, and which had evidently something traditional in their embellishments; but about which, as I did not like to appear over-curious, I asked no questions.

I could not, however, but notice a pie, magnificently decorated with peacock's feathers, in imitation of the tail of that bird, which overshadowed a considerable tract of the table. This, the squire confessed, with some little hesitation, was a pheasant pie, though a peacock pie was certainly the most authentical; but there had been such a mortality among the peacocks this season, that he could not prevail upon himself to have one killed.[1]

It would be tedious, perhaps, to my wiser readers, who may not have that foolish fondness for odd and obsolete things, to which I am a little given, were I to mention the other makeshifts of this worthy old humorist, by which he was endeavouring to follow up, though at humble distance, the quaint customs of antiquity. I was pleased, however, to see the respect shown to his whims by his children and relatives;

board display a more goodly and gracious assemblage of countenances; those who were not handsome were, at least, happy; and happiness is a rare improver of your hard-favoured visage.

The parson said grace, which was not a short familiar one, such as is commonly addressed to the Deity in these uncere-monious days; but a long, courtly, well-worded one of the ancient school. There was now a pause, as if something was expected; when suddenly the butler entered the hall with some degree of bustle: he was attended by a servant on each who, indeed, entered readily into the full spirit of them, and seemed all well versed in their parts; having doubtless been present at many a rehearsal. I was amused, too, at the air of profound gravity with which the butler and other servants executed the duties assigned them, however eccentric. They had an old-fashioned look; having, for the most part, been brought up in the household, and grown into keeping with the antiquated mansion, and the humours of its lord; and most probably looked upon all his whimsical regulations as the established laws of honourable housekeeping.

When the cloth was removed, the butler brought in a huge silver vessel of rare and curious workmanship, which he placed before the squire. Its appearance was hailed with acclamation; being the Wassail Bowl, so renowned in Christmas festivity. The contents had been prepared by the squire himself; for its was a beverage in the skilful mixture of which he particularly prided himself; alleging that it was too abstruse and complex for the comprehension of an ordinary servant. It was a potation, indeed, that might well make the heart of a toper leap within him; being composed of the richest and raciest wines, highly spiced and sweetened, with roasted apples bobbing about the surface.[2]

The old gentleman's whole countenance beamed with a serene look of indwelling delight, as he stirred this mighty bowl. Having raised it to his lips, with a hearty wish of a merry Christmas to all present, he sent it brimming round the board, for every one to follow his example, according to the primitive style; pronouncing it "the ancient fountain of good-feeling, where all hearts met together."[3]

There was much laughing and rallying as the honest emblem of Christmas joviality circulated, and was kissed rather coyly by the ladies. When it reached Master Simon, he raised it in both hands, and with the air of a boon companion struck up an old Wassail chanson:—

The brown bowle,
The merry brown bowle,
As it goes round-about-a,
    Fill
    Still,
Let the world say what it will,
And drink your fill all out-a.
The deep canne,
The merry deep canne,
As thou dost freely quaff-a
    Sing
    Fling,
Be as merry as a king,
And sound a lusty laugh-a.

The dinner-time passed away in this flow of innocent hilarity; and, though the old hall may have resounded in its time with many a scene of broader rout and revel, yet I doubt whether it ever witnessed more honest and genuine enjoyment. How easy it is for one benevolent being to diffuse pleasure around him; and how truly is a kind heart a fountain of gladness, making everything in its vicinity

to freshen into smiles; the joyous disposition of the worthy squire was perfectly contagious; he was happy himself, and disposed to make all the world happy; and the little eccentricities of his humour did but season, in a manner, the sweetness of his philanthropy.

When the ladies had retired, the conversation, as usual, became still more animated; many good things were broached which had been thought of during dinner, but which would not exactly do for a lady's ear; and though I cannot positvely affirm that there was much wit uttered, yet I have certainly heard many contests of rare wit produce much less laughter. Wit, after all, is a mighty, tart, pungent, ingredient, and much too acid for some stomachs; but honest good humour is the oil and wine of a merry meeting, and there is no jovial companionship equal to that where the jokes are rather small, and the laughter abundant.

I found the tide of wine and wassail fast gaining on the dry land of sober judgment. The company grew meerrier and louder as their jokes grew duller. Master simon was in as

the mock fairies about Falstaff; pinching him, plucking at the skirts of his coat, and tickling him with straws.

When I returned to the drawing-room, I found the company seated round the fire listening to the parson, who was deeply ensconced in a high-backed oaken chair, the work of some cunning artificer of yore, which had been brought from the library for his particular accommodation. From this venerable piece of furniture, with which his shadowy figure and dark weazen face so admirably accorded, he was dealing out strange accounts of the popular superstitions and legends of the surrounding country, with which he had become acquainted in the course of his antiquarian researches. I am half inclined to think that the old gentleman was himself somewhat tinctured with superstition, as men are very apt to be who live a recluse and studious life in a sequestered part of the country, and pore over black-letter tracts, so often filled with the marvellous and supernatural. He gave us several anecdotes of the fancies of the neighbouring peasantry, concerning the effigy of the crusader, which lay on the tomb by the church altar. As it was the only monument of the kind in that part of the country, it had always been regarded with feelings of superstition by the good wives of the village. It was said to get up from the tomb and walk the rounds of the churchyard in stormy nights, particularly when it thundered; and one old woman, whose cottage bordered on the churchyard, had seen it through the windows of the church, when the moon shone, slowly pacing up and down the aisles. It was the belief that some wrong had been left unredressed by the deceased, or some treasure hidden, which kept the spirit in a state of trouble and restlessness. Some talked of gold and jewels buried in the tomb, over which the spectre kept watch; and there was a story current of a sexton in old times who endeavoured to break his way to the coffin at night, but, just as he reached it, received a violent blow from the marble hand of the effigy, which stretched him senseless on the pavement. These tales were often laughed at by some of the sturdier among the rustics, yet when night came on, there were many of the stoutest unbelievers that were shy of venturing alone in the footpath that led across the churchyard.

From these and other anecdotes that followed, the crusader appeared to be the favourite hero of ghost stories throughout the vicinity. His picture which hung up in the hall, was thought by the servants to have something supernatural about it; for they remarked that, in whatever part of the hall you went, the eyes of the warrior were still fixed on you. The old porter's wife too, at the lodge, who had been born and brought up in the family, and was a great gossip among the maid-servants, affirmed, that in her young days she had often heard say, that on Mid-summer eve, when it was well known all kinds of ghosts, goblins, and fairies become visible and walk abroad, the crusader used to mount his horse, come down from his picture, ride about the house, down the avenue, and so to the church to visit the tomb; on which occasion the church door most civilly swung open

chirping a humour as a grasshopper filled with dew. The parson, too, began to show the effects of good cheer, having gradually settled down into a doze, and his wig sitting most suspiciously on one side. Just at this juncture we were summoned to the drawing-room, and I suspect, at the private instigation of mine host, whose joviality seemed always tempered with a proper love of decorum.

After the dinner-table was removed, the hall was given up to the younger members of the family, who, prompted to all kind of noisy mirth by the Oxonian and Master Simon, made its old walls ring with their merriment, as they played at romping games. I delight in witnessing the gambols of children, and particularly at this happy holiday season, and could not help stealing out of the drawing-room on hearing one of their peals of laughter. I found them at the game of blind-man's-bluff. Master Simon, who was the leader of their revels, and seemed on all occasions to fulfil the office of that ancient potentate, the Lord of Misrule,[4] was blinded in the midst of the hall. The little beings were as busy about him as of itself; not that he needed it; for he rode through closed gates and even stone walls, and had been seen by one of the dairymaids to pass between two bars of the great park gate, making himself as thin as a sheet of paper.

All these superstitions I found had been very much countenanced by the squire, who, though not superstitious himself, was very fond of seeing others so. He listened to every goblin tale of the neighbouring gossips with infinite gravity, and held the porter's wife in high favour on account of her talent for the marvellous. He was himself a great reader of old legends and romances, and often lamented that he could not believe in them; for a superstitious person, he thought, must live in a kind of fairyland.

Whilst we were all attention to the parson's stories, our ears were suddenly assailed by a burst of heterogeneous sounds from the hall, in which were mingled something like the clang of rude minstrelsy, with the uproar of many small voices and girlish laughter. The door suddenly flew open, and a train came trooping into the room, that might almost have been mistaken for the breaking-up of the court of Fairy. That indefatigable spirit, Master Simon, in the faithful discharge of his duties as Lord of Misrule, had conceived the idea of a Christmas mummery or masking; and having called in to his assistance the Oxonian and the young officer, who were equally ripe for anything that should occasion romping and merriment, they had carried it into instant effect. The old housekeeper had been consulted; the antique clothes-presses and wardrobes rummaged, and made to yield up the relics of finery that had not seen the light for several generations; the younger part of the company had been privately convened from the parlour and hall, and the whole had been bedizened out, into a burlesque imitation of an antique mask.[5]

Master Simon led the van, as "Ancient Christmas," quaintly apparelled in a ruff, a short cloak, which had very much the aspect of one of the old housekeeper's petticoats, and a hat that might have served for a village steeple, and mus indubitably have figured in the days of the Covenanters. From under this his nose curved boldly forth, flushed with a frost-bitten bloom, that seemed the very trophy of a December blast. He was accompanied by a blue-eyed romp, dished up as "Dame Mince Pie," in the venerable magnificence of a faded brocade, long stomacher, peaked hat, and high-heeled shoes. The young officer appeared as Robin Hood, in a sporting dress of Kendal green, and a foraging cap with a gold tassel.

The costume, to be sure, did not bear testimony to deep research, and there was an evident eye to the picturesque, natural to a young gallant in the presence of his mistress. The fair Julia hung on his arm in a pretty rustic dress, as "Maid Marian." The rest of the train had been metamorphosed in various ways; the girls trussed up in the finery of the ancient belles of the Bracebridge line, and the striplings bewhiskered with burnt cork, and gravely clad in broad skirts, hanging sleeves, and full-bottomed wigs, to represent the character of Roast Beef, Plum Pudding, and other worthies celebrated in ancient maskings. The whole was under the control of the Oxonian, in the appropriate character of Misrule; and I observed that he exercised rather a mischievous sway with his wand over the smaller personages of the pageant.

The irruption of this motley crew, with beat of drum, according to ancient custom, was the consummation of uproar and merriment. Master Simon covered himself with glory by the stateliness with which, as Ancient Christmas, he walked a minuet with the peerless, though giggling, Dame Mince Pie. It was followed by a dance of all the characters, which, from its medley of costumes, seemed as though the old family portraits had skipped down from their frames to join in the sport. Different centuries were figuring at cross hands and right and left; the dark ages were cutting pirouettes and rigadoons; and the days of Queen Bess jiggling merrily down the middle, through a line of succeeding generations.

to pause in this garrulity. Methinks I hear the questions asked by my graver readers, "To what purpose is all this—how is the world to be made wiser by this talk?" Alas! is there not wisdom enough extant for the instruction of the world? And if not, are there not thousands of abler pens labouring for its improvement!—It is so much pleasanter to please than to instruct—to play the companion rather than the preceptor.

What, after all, is the mite of wisdom that I could throw into the mass of knowledge; or how am I sure that my sagest deductions may be safe guides for the opinion of others? But in writing to amuse, if I fail, the only evil is in my own disappointment. If, however, I can by any lucky chance, in these days of evil, rub out one wrinkle from the brow of care, or beguile the heavy heart of one moment of sorrow; if I can now and then penetrate through the gathering film of misanthropy, prompt a benevolent view of human nature, and make my reader more in good humour with his fellow-beings and himself, surely, surely, I shall not then have written entirely in vain.

[1]The peacock was anciently in great demand for stately entertainments. Sometimes it was made into a pie, at one end of which the head appeared above the crust, in all its plumage, with the beak richly gilt; at the other end the tail was displayed. Such pies were served up at the solemn banquets of chivalry, when knights-errant pledged themselves to undertake any perilous enterprise; whence came the ancient oath, used by Justice Shallow, "by cock and pie."

The peacock was also an important dish for the Christmas feast; and Massinger, in his *City Madam*, gives some idea of the extravagance with which this, as well as other dishes, was prepared for the gorgeous revels of the olden times:—

"Men may talk of country Christmasses:
    Their thirty pound butter'd eggs—their pies of carps' tongues:
    Their pheasants drench'd with ambergris; *the carcases of three fat wethers bruised for gravy to make sauce for a single peacock!*"

[2]The Wassail Bowl was sometimes composed of ale instead of wine; with nutmeg, sugar, toast, ginger, and roasted crabs; in this way the nut-brown beverage is still prepared in some old families, and round the hearths of substantial farmers at Christmas. It is also called Lamb's Wool, and is celebrated by Herrick in his *Twelfth Night*.

"Next crowne the bowle full
    With gentle Lamb's Wool;
Add sugar, nutmeg, and ginger,
    With store of ale too;
    And thus ye must doe
To make the Wassaile a swinger."

[3]The custom of drinking out of the same cup gave place to each having his cup. When the steward came to the doore with the Wassel, he was to cry three times, *Wassel, Wassel, Wassel,* and then the chappell (chaplein) was to answer with a song.—ARCHAEOLOGIA.

[4]At Christmasse there was in the Kinge's house, wheresoever hee was lodged, a lorde of misrule, or mayster of merie disportes, and the like had ye in the house of every nobleman of honor, or good worshippe, were he spirituall or temporall.—STOWE.

[5]Maskings or mummeries were favourite sports at Christmas in old times: and the wardrobes at halls and manor-houses were often laid under contribution to furnish dresses and fantastic disguisings. I strongly suspect Master Simon to have taken the idea of his from Ben Jonson's *Masque of Christmas*.

The worthy squire contemplated these fantastic sports, and this resurrection of his old wardrobe, with the simple relish of childish delight. For my part I was in a continual excitement, from the varied scenes of whim and innocent gaiety passing before me. It was inspiring to me to see wild-eyed frolic and warm-hearted hospitality breaking out from among the chills and glooms of winter, and old age throwing off his apathy, and catching once more the freshness of youthful enjoyment. I felt also an interest in the scene, from the consideration that these fleeting customs were posting fast into oblivion, and that this was, perhaps, the only family in England in which the whole of them were still punctiliously observed. There was a quaintness, too, mingled with all this revelry, that gave it a peculiar zest: it was suited to the time and place; and as the old manorhouse almost reeled with mirth and wassail, it seemed echoing back the joviality of long-departed years.

But enough of Christmas and its gambols; it is time for me

RING OUT, WILD BELLS

F. Paolo Tosti
Alfred Tennyson

Moderato

1. Ring out, wild bells, ___ to the wild sky, ___ The fly - ing cloud, ___ the fros - ty
2. Ring out false pride ___ in place and blood, ___ The civ - ic slan - der and the

light, The year is dy - ing in the night, For-ev - er and for-ev - er; Ring out the
spite, Ring in the love __ of truth and right, For-ev - er and for-ev - er; Ring out old

più animato   *crescendo*   *a tempo*

old, ___ ring in the new, ___ Ring, hap - py bells, ___ a - cross the snow, ___ The year is
shapes ___ of foul dis - ease, ___ Ring out the har - row-ing lust of gold, ___ Ring out the

rit.   *a tempo*

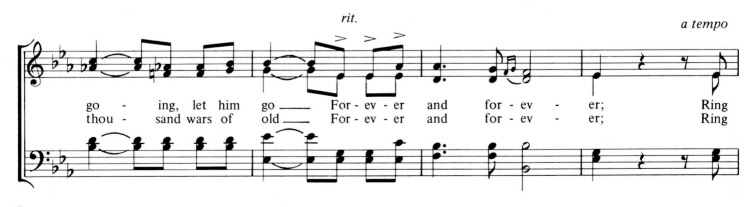

go - ing, let him go ___ For - ev - er and for - ev - er; Ring
thou - sand wars of old ___ For - ev - er and for - ev - er; Ring

Christmas at Sutter's Fort in 1847

John Bonner

Perhaps the most remarkable Christmas in the history of California was the one kept with revel at Capt. Sutter's settlement of New Helvetia in 1847, nearly half a century ago. The great California Baron was in high spirits, as might have been expected. Things had come about as he had anticipated. The country has passed into American hands, and for a long time he has been a better American than Swiss, German or Frenchman. He was as undisputably monarch of all he surveyed as Robinson Crusoe on his island. He had an estate larger than a German principality or an English shire. His cattle were past counting.

His fort had been completed in 1845. It was a quadrangular stockade, fifteen feet high and 500 feet long by 150 feet wide. To an assailant without artillery it was impregnable. On two of the corners rose stout blockhouses which mounted a cannon each; other pieces of artillery were placed en barbette on the top of the wall so as to command the approach from the river. Within the quadrangle adobe houses furnished shelter for 500 men. There was a storehouse full of supplies, furs and ammunition, likewise a dwellinghouse in which Sutter had lived before he built his rancheria on the Feather and where he still kept his office.

His fort was the first resting place which Eastern immigrants struck after crossing the mountains. Here they found food and shelter. Sutter turned no man away on the petty pretense that he was penniless. Careless of paying his own debts, he was indulgent to his debtors. Nor did he too closely scrutinize the reasons which immigrants gave for moving to California. His broad, generous soul forgave everything but horsestealing.

When his family joined him—he had a wife, daughter and two sons, all of whom have passed away—he built him a rancheria on the Feather River, which he called Rancheria de Hoch, and in which he spent most of his time. The building consisted of three or four gables, whose ends fronted the river. Here he sat on his balcony, watched his men catch salmon in the sparkling waters of the Feather and speculated on what would become of his baronial estate when he was gone. He had tasted adversity, he had courted danger; was the present halcyon era of prosperity and eminence going to last? Thoughts passed through that far-reaching mind which he told no man. In the dim vista of the future he discerned many things.

On the Christmas day of 1847 he resolved that he and his should be merry. His man James W. Marshall had selected a site for a sawmill in a valley which the Indians called Culuma, which meant in their tongue "pleasant valley." It was in the heart of a forest of big trees. When their trunks were sawn into boards he could substitute frame houses for the adobes in which his people lived. His orchards and his vineyards were thriving; his herds had multiplied amazingly; he had horses which could cover the distance to Sonoma in a day and the distance to the Bay in a day and a half. People were growing to understand him, and the better they knew

him the more they liked him. Even Vallejo, who had once called him a pestilent intruder, had been won over by his kindness at the time the Lord of Sonoma was im prisoned by the Bear flag insurgents and was his good friend.

He resolved that his retainers should keep Christmas royally. A feast should be given within the fort, which they would remember to the end of their days. The fattest cattle in his herd were slaughtered and the flesh cleaned from the ribs to make frezadas. The Indians cared little for meat or pork; their chief delicacy was fried jackass meat, and the captain sacrificed several burros to gratify them, though a donkey was worth four times as much as a horse. There were hecatombs of frijoles and tortillas, and salmon was served in many shapes, boiled, baked and fried. From the storeroom fruits of all kinds, the products of the New Helvetia orchards, were taken with a lavish hand and set down on the long board table. Barrels of wine were set out and their contents drawn off in panikins and pitchers. When Sutter founded this fort he found the valleys covered with the wild grape, from which he made a wine which was agreeable to the taste of trappers, hunters and Indians. This was supplied in profusion, and in deference to the occasion the Baron pretended not to notice the ravages the fluid wrought on the wits and muscles of his guests. To his European proteges he served aguardiente in bottles. The banquet began at noon; before the Christmas sunset the interior of the fort was strewed with inert revelers, who lay where they originally fell.

The Baron entertained his personal friends at his Rancheria de Hoch. To that hospitable resort the neighbors had been invited from far and wide. Guests had come from such distant points as San Francisco and Sonoma. From the ranche-

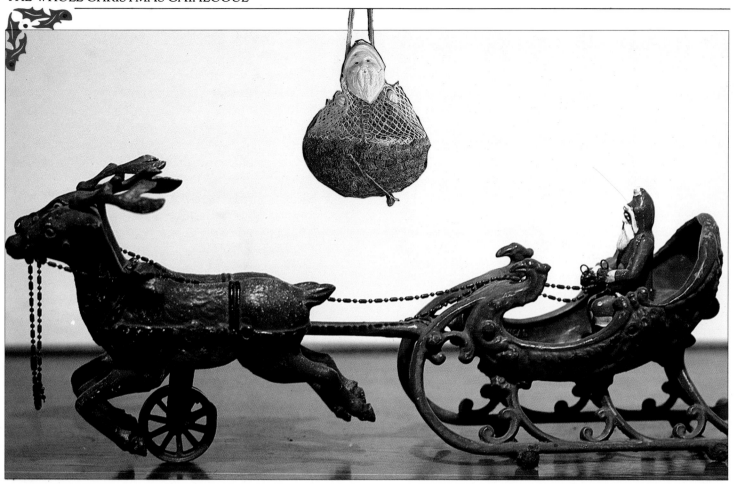

ros along the river whole families had ridden, the ladies in saddle, their courtiers sitting behind to hold them straight on their horses. An army of Indian hostlers took charge of their beasts when the riders dismounted. For those who arrived early and who wished to stimulate an appetite for dinner, lunches had been provided on the river; the young men fished and shot ducks and geese; while for the ladies, Sutter's new stern-wheel steamer offered a new and exciting form of promenade.

Dinner was at five. Sutter had lived in Geneva and Paris, and knew what a good dinner should be. He had one or two cooks whom he had trained on sound gastronomical principles. They made him a soup of many ingredients; it could not have been surpassed in New York. Besides the salmon which he caught at his own door, the fish we now call the Sacramento perch, the brook trout, and the barracuda from the coast, were served with suitable sauces. After these came several entrees—pozoles or pig's feet, and peppers, frijoles and the delicate parts of the beef, with chile and tomatoes, an olia podrida, containing all manner of meats and vegetables stewed together, and various fricasses of chicken and turkey. The roti was veal, though a tender sirloin occupied one corner of the board; and the dinner closed with an assortment of feathered game—quail, grouse, ducks, geese and pigeons—fit to bring the water to the mouth of a gourmand. In his own house he did not drink the wine from the native grape; he had planted the mission grape and had a cellar

full of the wine; nor was champagne wanting, brought up the river from San Francisco.

The guests were all in full dress; the men in silk jackets, embroidered waist-coats, velveteen breeches with gilt lacings and open below the knee and a sash round the waist; the ladies in bare arms, without corsets, in silk or crape gowns, sashes of bright colors, satin shoes and scarlet or flesh-colored stockings. Both sexes wore jewelry; jewels flashed from the ears and necks of the pretty girls.

After the feast was over and the wines drunk, the party adjourned to the long room which Captain Sutter had built expressly for balls and assemblies. There had been some impromptu dancing on the grass in true California fashion, but at the close of December the days are short and as night falls the air is nipping; the captain's guests were not sorry to take refuge indoors.

A guitar and a violin were tuned, and the piano, which Sutter had imported from France, soon began to give voice. The fun commenced as usual with a jota, in which every lady in turn was taken out by the master of ceremonies and danced a few steps, singing at the same time a little verse which she was supposed to improvise. Then followed the bamba, the zorrita, the fandango, the jarabe, and the ball wound up with the contra danza. Dancing was kept up till the tops of the sierras began to be tipped with gold, and the senoras and senoritas and their cavaliers reluctantly retired to the rooms provided for them.

CHRISTMAS IN OLDEN TIME

Heap on more wood!—the wind is chill;
But let it whistle as it will,
We'll keep our Christmas merry still.
Each age has deem'd the new-born year
The fittest time for festal cheer:
Even, heathen yet, the savage Dane
At Iol more deep the mead did drain;
High on the beach his galleys drew,
And feasted all his pirate crew;
Then in his low and pine-built hall,
Where shields and axes deck'd the wall,
They gorged upon the half dress'd steer;
Caroused in seas of sable beer;
While round, in brutal jest, were thrown
The half-gnaw'd rib, and marrow-bone:
Or listen'd all, in grim delight,
While Scalds yell'd out the joys of fight.
Then forth, in frenzy, would they hie,
While wildly loose their red locks fly,
And dancing round the blazing pile,
They make such barbarous mirth the while,
As best might to the mind recall
The boisterous joys of Odin's hall.

And well our Christian sires of old
Loved when the year its course had roll'd,
And brought blithe Christmas back again,
With all his hospitable train.
Domestic and religious rite
Gave honour to the holy night;
On Christmas eve the bells were rung;
On Christmas eve the mass was sung:
That only night in all the year,
Saw the stoled priest the chalice rear.
The damsel donn'd her kirtle sheen;
The hall was dress'd with holly green,
Forth to the wood did merry-men go,
To gather in the mistletoe.
Then open'd wide the Baron's hall
To vassal, tenant, serf, and all;
Power laid his rod of rule aside,
And Ceremony doff'd his pride.
The heir, with roses in his shoes,
That night might village partner choose;

The Lord, underogating, share
The vulgar game of 'post and pair.'
All hail'd, with uncontroll'd delight,
And general voice, the happy night,
That to the cottage, as the crown,
Brought tidings of salvation down.

The fire, with well-dried logs supplied,
Went roaring up the chimney wide;
The huge hall-table's oaken face,
Scrubb'd till it shone, the day to grace,
Bore then upon its massive board
No mark to part the squire and lord.
Then was brought in the lusty brawn,
By old blue-coated serving-man;
Then the grim boar's head frown'd on high,
Crested with bays and rosemary.
Well can the green-garb'd ranger tell,
How, when, and where, the monster fell;
What dogs before his death he tore,
And all the baiting of the boar.
The wassel round, in good brown bowls,
Garnish'd with ribbons, blithely trowls.
There the huge sirloin reek'd; hard by
Plum-porridge stood, and Christmas pie;
Nor fail'd old Scotland to produce,
At such high tide, her savoury goose.
Then came the merry maskers in,
And carols roar'd with blithesome din;
If unmelodious was the song,
It was a hearty note, and strong.
Who lists may in their mumming see
Traces of ancient mystery;
White shirts supplied the masquerade,
And smutted cheeks the visors made;
But, O! what maskers, richly dight,
Can boast of bosoms half so light!
England was merry England, when
Old Christmas brought his sports again.
'Twas Christmas broach'd the mightiest ale;
'Twas Christmas told the merriest tale;
A Christmas gambol oft could cheer
The poor man's heart through half the year.
—SIR WALTER SCOTT

CHRISTMAS HYMN

HENRY DIFLMAN
REV. JOHN MCCAFFREY

Maestoso ma con spirito

1. With glory lit the midnight air Revealed bright angels
2. Then sweetly spoke th'angelic voice: "Fear not; let Heav'n and
3. The choirs of Heav'n still bless the morn, When God through love for

ho-ver-ing there, In fear, beheld the rap-tured swains When
earth re-joice; The Child, in Beth-le-hem's crib that lies, Is
man was born, That God we hum-bly bow be-fore, And

Chorus

rose the Heav-en in-spired strains.
God, de-scend-ed from the skies."
praise with an-gels and a-dore.
Glo-ry, glo-ry,

dolce *mf*

glo-ry to God, and peace to earth, and peace to

O TANNENBAUM

Traditional

A VISIT FROM ST. NICHOLAS

Twas the night before Christmas, when all through the house
Not a creature was stirring, not even a mouse;
The stockings were hung by the chimney with care,
In hopes that St. Nicholas soon would be there;
The children were nestled all snug in their beds,
While visions of sugar-plums danced through their heads;
And mamma in her kerchief, and I in my cap,
Had just settled our brains for a long winter's nap,—
When out on the lawn there arose such a clatter,
I sprang from my bed to see what was the matter.
Away to the window I flew like a flash,
Tore open the shutters and threw up the sash.
The moon, on the breast of the new-fallen snow,
Gave a lustre of midday to objects below;
When what to my wondering eyes should appear,
But a miniature sleigh and eight tiny reindeer,
With a little old driver, so lively and quick
I knew in a moment it must be St. Nick.
More rapid than eagles his coursers they came,
And he whistled and shouted and called them by name:
"Now, Dasher! now, Dancer! now, Prancer and Vixen!
On, Comet! on, Cupid! on, Donder and Blitzen!

To the top of the porch, to the top of the wall!
Now, dash away, dash away, dash away all!"
As dry leaves that before the wild hurricane fly,
When they meet with an obstacle, mount to the sky,
So, up to the house-top the coursers they flew,
With a sleigh full of toys,—and St. Nicholas too.

And then in a twinkling I heard on the roof
The prancing and pawing of each little hoof.
As I drew in my head and was turning around,
Down the chimney St. Nicholas came with a bound.
He was dressed all in fur from his head to his foot,
And his clothes were all tarnished with ashes and soot;
A bundle of toys he had flung on his back,
And he looked like a peddler just opening his pack.
His eyes how they twinkled! his dimples how merry!
His cheeks were like roses, his nose like a cherry;
His droll little mouth was drawn up like a bow,
And the beard on his chin was as white as the snow.
The stump of a pipe he held tight in his teeth,
And the smoke it encircled his head like a wreath.
He had a broad face, and a little round belly
That shook, when he laughed, like a bowl full of jelly.
He was chubby and plump,—a right jolly old elf—
And I laughed when I saw him, in spite of myself.
A wink of his eye and a twist of his head
Soon gave me to know I had nothing to dread.
He spoke not a word, but went straight to his work,
And filled all the stockings; then turned with a jerk,
And laying his finger aside of his nose,
And giving a nod, up the chimney he rose.
He sprang to his sleigh, to his team gave a whistle,
And away they all flew like the down of a thistle;
But I heard him exclaim, ere he drove out of sight:
"Happy Christmas to all, and to all a good-night!"
                                    —CLEMENT CLARKE MOORE

CHRISTMAS
PHOTOGRAPHS

Getting the Most from

At Christmastime homes are decorated, presents are exchanged, and families are reunited. Good spirits are in the air everywhere. The excitement offers material for great holiday photos, but many people are disappointed when they see their pictures—they fall short of capturing the essence of the times just past.

A really good photo doesn't happen all by itself. However, with only a little thought and planning an average snapshot can become an exceptional photo—a memento that you'll want to keep and enjoy for years to come. It doesn't take a great deal of work, but you have to be patient and take the time to think about what's being recorded on film. Just as the painter only puts exactly what he or she wants on the easel, so must a photographer try to control what's appearing on his or her canvas, the viewfinder.

There are two main aspects to improving your photography: technique and personal style. Both are equally important. Without good technique, personal style can get lost, and having good technique with no personality leads to well-composed boring photos. Having neither results in those stacks of dark, blurry pictures that rarely make it out of the desk drawer. The following section suggests ways to improve both so that when you pull out your camera this Christmas, you can be confident that your holiday pictures will be your best yet.

Most people own one of three basic types of cameras: Instamatic-type automatic ones like the disc or other pocket cameras, Polaroid-type instant cameras, and single-lens-reflex or rangefinder 35mm cameras. Essentially, the more exposure options that are available to you, the more creative control you have, but even with a fully automatic camera, you can obtain very nice results. Although the fully automatic cameras are sometimes a little less versatile in difficult lighting situations, if you make the effort, you can almost always find a way to take a good photo. Many of the helpful hints that follow are applicable to all cameras; where they're not, I've added information for each type of camera.

Observation

Observation is one of the key elements to good picture taking. Once you decide that you're going to take a certain shot, take a moment to look around before you pick up your camera. What is there for you to shoot? If you are photographing people, what is the nicest background available? At Christmastime decorated trees, stacks of presents, swags and roping, and mantels with stockings provide that extra holiday touch for your pictures, even if they're not the main element of your shot. If you're shooting outside, look around for the best light as well as a good background (more about lighting later). People will generally be pretty amenable to moving wherever you want them for a posed shot.

If you're doing candids, the background is more difficult to control, but nothing stops you from moving around to find the best spot and waiting for your unsuspecting subjects to move into range of your viewfinder. It's only after you've decided what you want in your photo, and guessed at the place you should be to get it, that you should bring the camera to your face. You may be surprised at how often the picture is already set to take, with little or no adjustments needed. The more often you preplan your pictures like this, the better your previsualization will become. This concept works with all cameras.

Personal Style

Having a personal style in your photos is something that takes some time to develop. You must look at your photos as

Your Holiday Pictures

well as those of others and form opinions about what you see. Once you know what you like and don't like, it will be easier to take pictures that please you. Unfortunately, there are no step-by-step instructions for developing a personal style—it's a very individual process. Many professional photographers change their style from time to time, but they *always* think about it. A professional is responsible for the images he or she produces, whether to satisfy a client or to please his or her sensibility. For your holiday snapshots the stakes aren't so high, but your standards should be.

For some people a pleasing photograph consists of a picture of friends and family relaxing together. For others individual portraits are more interesting. Some people really like close-ups. Others prefer outdoor action shots. Kids and animals can also make great subjects. It doesn't really matter what

you like to shoot, as long as you are taking pictures that you will want to look at again and again.

Composition

In addition to developing your own style, you can produce better photos by improving your technique. A few simple precautions can greatly enhance a photograph. You can improve the composition of your pictures. Composition simply means the way things are placed in the frame. One common mistake is to center a person's face in the picture. This kind of photo usually has a lot of unused space at the top, and the subjects are often cropped at the knees. Pointing the camera slightly downward, to move the heads nearer to the top of the frame, can substantially improve the picture's composition. Also, by moving in a step or two, you can get more of a close-up and crop at the waist or higher. Or you can move a step or two back to get a full figure. Space is a limited commodity in your photo—it's best not to waste it.

Another way to control composition is to control the background. Most photos consist of a foreground, generally the subject(s), and the background. To avoid problems like trees growing out of people's heads, often a step or two to the right or left is all that's necessary. In general, if the subject is reasonably far from the background, moving from side to side can effectively control the composition.

Composition can also be manipulated by changing your subject's distance from the background. You and the subject must move around until you establish the right relationship between the two. For example, if you want to shoot children opening presents and you want to show the tree as well, try putting the kids directly under or a few feet away from the tree. This gives the tree prominence in the photo, and the relationship between the background and foreground is clear. If you place the tree far away from the children, it may still be in the background, but it may become too small a feature for the connection to be clear. In other cases, if the background is confusing or not particularly interesting, you can move your subjects away from it, either putting it out of focus or simply diminishing its importance. This type of composition control should be used no matter what camera is used.

Exposure

When it comes to exposure control, camera differences become more noticeable, and 35mm cameras generally have the most versatility. Most 35s on the market have an automatic exposure system, and many have a manual override as well, allowing you to control the exposure independently of the automatic system. In most cases, the automatic exposure system will provide you with good exposures, allowing you the freedom to better compose the photo and get more involved with the subject. This is especially true when you are using negative (print) film, which has a greater latitude than slide film. Whichever medium you use—print or slide film—camera metering systems have become so sophisticated that most shots taken in the automatic mode will be perfectly exposed.

Backlighting

There are some situations, however, in which it's wiser to take the camera off the automatic setting, or if your camera doesn't have that option, to fool the camera into taking a better-exposed photo. Backlighting, the most common of these instances, occurs when the sun or source of light is behind the subject (but not in the picture), lighting the background but not the subject. Camera light meters have a tendency to expose for the overall picture, so when the meter sees the light in the background, which is much brighter than the light on the subject, the meter will expose primarily for the background. The result will be a well-exposed background and a dark subject.

The best way to rectify a backlit condition is to add some light to the subject so that both the subject and the back-

A great action shot. In this case, the snow fooled the meter and caused underexposure.

Sometimes, in order to capture the moment, you have to make technical compromises. This photo suffers from overcompensation (about ½-stop overexposed); it has a nice feeling, nonetheless.

ground have the same amount of light on them. To do this requires a flash; the technique is referred to as a fill-in flash. To do a fill-in flash, first set the shutter speed on the camera to the flash setting (generally 1/60 or 1/90). Then turn the meter on, read the amount of light on the background (without the subject in the frame), and set the camera aperture to this reading. Then set the flash to put out the same amount of light as the background is reading (either manually or automatically, depending on the type of flash you have). Finally, put the subject back in the scene and take the picture. The result will be that the flash will light the subject to the same degree that the other light source is illuminating the background; the resulting picture will be evenly exposed. This technique may sound complicated, but it is really quite simple and logical.

The next best way to deal with a backlighting situation, and essentially the only way if you don't have a flash with you, is to compensate in the exposure setting. Some cameras have a built-in backlight compensation button that automatically opens the aperture 1½ stops when depressed. This gives the entire picture 1½ stops more light than the meter would dictate in that situation. The background will become somewhat washed out or overexposed, but the subject will be closer to the correct exposure for good skin tones. Unlike the fill-in flash, this solution is imbalanced, but it is an adequate compromise. If you don't have the backlight button (most cameras don't), the principle remains the same. All you have to do is take the camera off automatic, meter the scene, and open the aperture 1½ stops beyond what the meter says is correct.

If your camera is completely automatic with no manual override, you can fool it by changing the ASA setting on the camera to 1⅓ stops less (slower) than the film really is. For example, if you are using 100 ASA film, change the ASA setting to 40. The camera will then think the film is 1⅓ stops slower than it really is and will give the picture 1⅓ stops more light, achieving the desired result. *Remember to change the setting back to the correct ASA* after the shot, or the rest of the roll will come out incorrectly exposed.

If you have a Polaroid-type or an Instamatic-type camera and you are confronted with a backlighting situation, use the fill-in flash method or try to avoid the shot altogether. For both types of cameras the exposure adjustment with fill-in flash is pretty much automatic. If you don't have a flash and

Christmas lights, taken with a macro lens, are good mood shots that can be useful for separating sections in your photo album.

These out-of-focus Christmas lights are just for fun. You can use pictures like these in Christmas crafts or decor for years to come.

have a Polaroid-type camera, there is generally a lighter/darker control instead of an f-stop control, and by experience you will be able to judge how far you have to move the knob toward the lighter end to get the correct compensation.

Another situation that requires compensation and occurs frequently during the holiday season is taking pictures in the snow. Snow, white and reflective, has a tendency to fool camera meters. Meters are designed to read and correctly expose for average scenes, which contain a certain amount of whites, grays, and blacks. When there is a disproportionate amount of white in the scene, the meter, which is going for the average, exposes the white snow as gray, making the people in the picture proportionately too dark or underexposed. To correct the lighting, the film needs to be overexposed by about 1½ stops beyond what the meter reads. A fill-in flash isn't necessary unless the subject is also being backlit.

Flash Photography

The majority of holiday pictures are taken indoors. Unless you are in a very bright house and are using a fast film, you will need to use a flash. Taking a flash shot is generally simple, but there are a few tricks that can make them better.

your subject is wearing white clothes and the background is a white wall, you may want to move the subject some feet away from the background in order to darken it and thereby provide a better separation between the subject and the background.

Another nice effect that can be utilized with flash photos (and cameras that have variable shutter speeds) is to play around with different shutter speeds in order to bring up the exposure of the existing room lights. Very often flash photos have a sterile floodlit look to them because the only light that is exposing the picture is the flash, which is invariably right above the camera. Allowing room lights to also come into play can add a little subtlety to flash pictures. To do this, take the shutter speed off the flash synch speed (normally 1/60 or 1/90), and instead set the speed to 1/8, 1/15, or 1/30. The aperture setting remains the same, since the flash is still doing the main exposure, and the decreased shutter speed allows lamps and room lights to look as if they are actually on (assuming they are). You don't need to worry about the picture being blurry, because the flash is doing the main exposure

A well-lit nighttime flash photo of a Christmas tree shot at f8 and 1/30 to bring up the Christmas lights. The exposure could have been 1/15 or 1/8 even—to make the lights brighter.

One problem to avoid when you are using a flash is reflective glare. If you are facing a shiny surface such as a paneled wall or a mirror, the surface will reflect your flash when it goes off and the photo will have a large bright spot in the background. This is not only unattractive but it can also foul up the automatic exposure on your flash, darkening the rest of the picture. A simple way to correct this situation is to shoot these backgrounds at an angle rather than facing them directly. The angle doesn't need to be great, just enough so the light bouncing off the surface will bounce past you instead of at you.

Another control to be aware of is the subject's distance from the background. Flash lighting has a tendency to fall off very rapidly. If your subject is very close to a wall, for example, the wall will be well lit. If the subject is 10 feet away from the wall, the same wall will be quite dark. Being aware of this can help you take photos that have a pleasing relationship between subject and background. If, for example,

This shot could have used a fill-in flash to clean it up. The camera meter was fooled by the light outside and the overall photo is too dark.

This snapshot is a good example of well-developed style; it is well lit, natural, and unobtrusive.

and will stop the action, though it is a good idea to hold pretty still so the lamps won't blur. The exact shutter speed ultimately has to be determined by experience, because it's affected by the ASA of the film, the intensity and amount of room lights, and the amount of light the flash is putting out. At ASA 100 with the flash putting out f8, a good starting point for room lights is about 1/15.

A problem some people have, especially with Instamatic-type cameras, is red-eye, which is caused by the flash lighting the back of the subject's retina. Similar to glare, this problem arises because of the relationship between the angle of the light in respect to the background (in this case the eyes) and the camera lens. You can avoid red-eye by putting the flash a little farther away from the lens, thus increasing the angle. Most good camera stores carry brackets for all types of cameras. These brackets hold the flash a couple of inches away and are even available for flash cubes. They should eliminate

red-eye completely. If red-eye still persists, see a doctor!

When you are taking flash pictures, especially when there is more than one person in the shot, it's a good idea to take at least two or three frames for every shot. Not only will it improve your chances of getting good facial expressions, but invariably someone will have blinked in one or two of the photos. In the long run the film cost is less important than making sure you get attractive shots that can be enlarged later on.

The Christmas season is one of the nicest times of the year—people are in good spirits and families are gathered together. The opportunities for memorable photos are every-where, and the difference in effort between taking average photos and taking special ones isn't that great. Some of the suggestions may seem a little complicated at first, but don't be put off. It's all very logical, and with a little practice and patience your holiday photos will soon be looking great.

Christmas Books

A Book of Christmas
By William Sansom
New York: McGraw-Hill, 1968
A thorough history of Christmas, including excerpts from Christmas literature and folktales.

Carols for Christmas
Compiled and arranged by David Willcocks
New York: The Metropolitan Museum of Art and Holt, Rinehart and Winston, 1983
A book of favorite Christmas carols, with beautiful color illustrations for each song.

Christmas Gif' : An anthology of Christmas poems, songs and stories written by and about Negroes*
Compiled by Charlemae Rollins
Chicago: Follett Publishing Company, 1963
A collection of works by both famous and anonymous Black authors.

The Christmas Piñata*
By Jack Kent
New York: Parents Magazine Press, 1975
An illustrated story for children about a little pot that is turned into a piñata for a Mexican Christmas celebration.

Merry Christmas: A History of the Holiday
By Patricia Bunning Stevens
New York: Macmillan Publishing Co., Inc., 1979
A complete history of Christmas from ancient times to today.

Nutcracker*
By E. T. A. Hoffman
New York: Crown, 1984
The nutcracker story, with one hundred color illustrations by Maurice Sendak.

Told Under the Christmas Tree*
Compiled by The Association for Childhood Education International
New York: Macmillan Publishing Co., Inc., 1948
Christmas stories and poems from around the world.

(A Brief Selection)

The Angel Trees: The Loretta Hines Collection of 18th Century Neapolitan Crèche Figures at the Metropolitan Museum of Art
By Linn Howard and Mary Jane Pool
New York: Alfred A. Knopf, 1984
Contains a brief history of the crèche and pages of beautiful four-color plates.

Christmas Cookbook*
By Susan Purdy Gold
New York: Watts, 1976
Includes recipes from around the world, with easy instructions for young cooks.

Christmas Crafts for Everyone
By Roy Wallace
Photos by Sid Dorris
Nashville: Abingdon Press, 1976
A collection of Christmas crafts and recipes from Europe.

The Christmas Tree Book: The History of the Christmas Tree and Antique Christmas Tree Ornaments
By Phillip V. Snyder
New York: Viking Press, 1976
A detailed history of the Christmas tree and its ornaments.

The Decorated Tree: Recreating Traditional Christmas Ornaments
By Carol E. Sternberg and Nancy Johnson
New York: Harry N. Abrams, Inc., 1982

An Old-Fashioned Christmas: American Holiday Traditions
By Karen Cure, Neely Bruce, and Lois Brown
New York: Harry N. Abrams, Inc., 1984
A collection of traditional American decorations, menus, recipes, and music.

*Recommended for children

INDEX

PHOTOGRAPHY CREDITS
KEY TO CODES
r: right; l: left; b: bottom; t: top; c: center; tl: top left; tc: top center; tr: top right; bl: bottom left; bc: bottom center; br: bottom right

David Arky: 123(all), 124(all), 125(all), 126(t), 127(b), 128(all)

Bettmann Archive: 16, 185

© Christopher Bain: 119, 126(b), 131

Tony Cenicola: 81(b), 85, 108, 153, 157(bl), 182

Jack Deutsch: 212-213, 214(all), 215(all), 216(all), 217

© Manuel Dos Passos: 129(t), 198-199

© Sandra Dos Passos: 129

Susan Duane: 188-189

© Derek Fell: 28, 29, 140-141, 194-195

Keith Glasgow: 61(tl,tr), 64, 65, 66(all), 67, 68(t), 74, 75, 76, 82, 91(t), 92, 93(all), 96, 98, 99, 100, 101, 102, 104, 106, 107(tl,r), 114(b), 115(all), 116-117, 127(t), 134(all), 135, 137, 140, 141, 143, 144, 145

Boyce Graham: 60

Robert Gray: 12, 13, 19, 20, 22(all), 24(all), 25(all), 26(tr,bl,br), 27(tr), 32(bl,br), 33(all), 34(tl,bl), 35, 36(l), 38(all), 39(all), 40(all), 41(all), 43(bl), 45, 46(all), 47(all), 48, 49, 50, 51, 57(r), 59, 69(c), 78, 105, 114(t), 129(c), 133, 138(all), 139(all), 142, 147, 149, 164, 174, 175, 176, 177, 186, 191, 196-197, 202, 204, 211

Eileen Hohmuth: 23

© Everett C. Johnson/Stockfile: 156(t)

© John Lei/Omni-Photo Communications, Inc.: 54

© Lynn Karlin: 80(r), 86(b) reprinted by permission from House Beautiful/April 1981, 87, 129(b), 130

© Matthew Klein: 84(t)

Keith Scott Morton: 11, 17, 18, 21, 27(tl,bl), 32(tl), 34(tr,br), 36(r), 37(1), 63(br), 69(1), 77, 89, 90(all), 91(b), 97, 107(bl), 129(b), 167, 172, 178, 193, 203, 209

© Jeffrey W. Myers/FPG International: 118

© E. Nagele/FPG International: 55

Illustration by Thomas Nast, Dover Publications, Inc., © 1985: 180

© Mark Niederman: 81(t), 84(b), 111, 113(t), 121, 155, 157(r)

North Wind Picture Archives: 42, 43(tr)

Bo Parker: 86(t)

Randy O'Rourke: 27(br), 30, 37(r), 68(b), 70, 73

© P.A. Enterprises/FPG International: 57(1)

© Peter Paige: 31

© Robert Perron: 26(tl), 79

© Jonathan E. Pite: 165

© Rod Planck/Tom Stack & Associates: 179

Public Domain: 14, 15

Courtesy Tea Council USA: 80(1)

© Joe Viesti/Viesti Associates, Inc.. 52, 56(all)

Richard E. Waldmann: 53

ACKNOWLEDGMENTS

For permission to print certain stories and poems in *The Whole Christmas Catalogue 1985*, grateful appreciation is expressed to the following:

"A Merry Christmas" by Louisa May Alcott. Reprinted from *Little Women*, by permission of Little, Brown and Company.

"Christmas at Sutter's Fort in 1847" by John Bonner from *Christmas in California*. Printed by Lawton Kennedy. Courtesy of The California Historical Society.

"Everywhere, Everywhere Christmas To-night" by Phillips Brooks. Reprinted from *The Golden Treasury of Poetry*, by permission of Golden Press.

"A Child's Christmas Song" by T. A. Daley. Reprinted from *Christmas Verse*, by permission of Oxford University Press.

"Speakin' o' Christmas" by Paul Laurence Dunbar. Reprinted from *The Complete Poems of Paul Laurence Dunbar*, by permission of Dodd, Mead and Company.

"Jeannette" by Louis Frechette. Reprinted from *Christmas in French Canada*, by permission of George N. Morang and Company, Limited.

"Christmas Dinner" by Washington Irving. Reprinted from *The Keeping of Christmas at Bracebridge Hall*, by permission of E. P. Dutton Inc.

"Christmas in Olden Time" by Sir Walter Scott. Reprinted from *The Poems of Sir Walter Scott*, by permission of Oxford University Press.

"The Worcestershire Carol" reprinted from *A Garland of Christmas Carols*, edited by Joshua Sylvester.

In addition, thanks are due to the Alberta Government Tourist Office, Dolores Bean of Qantas Airlines, Mr. Brown of the Gotham Book Mart and Gallery, The Canadian Consulate Library, Tom Carney of Mendik Realty, The Children's Library of the U.S. Committee for Unicef, Judy Cohn of Macy's, Shirley Dutton of the Seaman's Bank for Savings, The French Embassy, The German National Tourist Office, The Italian Cultural Institute, The Italian Government Travel Office, Rabiya Kelly of the Brooklyn Botanic Garden, Jean Madsen of the Manhattan Savings Bank, Mr. Takao Matsuda of The Bank of Tokyo, Hussain Mirza of The Roosevelt Hotel, The New York Historical Society Library, The Norwegian Information Service, The Philippine Center Library, Ruth Sarfaty and the New York State Theater, The Swedish Information Service, and Eileen Trawinski of Emigrant Savings Bank—all in New York City. Also, Buttercup & Friends and Early Spring Farm Antiques in Piermont, New York; Lisa Brownell of Mystic Seaport in Mystic, Connecticut; Arthur Leibundguth of the Antiquarian and Landmarks Society of Hartford, Connecticut; Mrs. Alice Nemeth of Willistead Manor in Windsor, Ontario; The California Historical Society of San Francisco; and The Winterthur Museum in Winterthur, Delaware.

Special thanks are also due to Wendy Baker, John Bralower, Chris Cancelli, Mary Forsell, Judy Habegger, Jamie Harrison, Bob Hein, the Hynes Family, Rod Johnson, Katherine Maier, Jean Mills, Frances Pellegrini, Louise Quayle, Bee Radcliffe, Lura and Julie Rogers, Christina Zwart—and to Robert Gray, principal photographer.